Essays and Studies 2023

Series Editor: Ceri Sullivan

The English Association

The English Association is a membership body for individuals and organisations passionate about the English language and its literatures. Our membership includes teachers, students, authors, and readers, and is made up of people and institutions from around the world.

Our aim is to further the knowledge, understanding and enjoyment of English studies, and to foster good practice in their teaching and learning at all levels, by

- encouraging the study of English language and literature in the community at large
- working toward a fuller recognition of English as core to education
- fostering discussion about methods of teaching English at all levels
- supporting conferences, lectures, and publications
- responding to national consultations and policy decisions about the subject

More information about the Association is on our website: http://bit.ly/join-the-EA

Publications

The Year's Work in English Studies – published annually, *The Year's Work in English Studies* is a qualitative narrative bibliographical review of scholarly work that year about the English language or literatures in English, from Old English to contemporary criticism.

The Year's Work in Critical and Cultural Theory – a companion volume in the field of critical and cultural theory, recording significant debates in a broad field of research in the humanities and social sciences.

Essays and Studies – published since 1910, *Essays and Studies* is an annual collection of essays on topical issues in English, edited by a different distinguished academic each year. The volumes cover a range of subjects and authors, from medieval to modern.

English – published quarterly, *English* is a forum for people who think hard and passionately about literature and who want to communicate those thoughts to a wide audience. It includes scholarly essays and reviews on all periods of literary history, and new work by contemporary poets.

English 4 to 11 – published three times a year, this magazine contains material produced by, and for, the classroom leader. It is a reader-friendly magazine, backed by sound pedagogy, offering ideas for developing classroom practice.

The Use of English – published three times per year, this journal's articles and reviews are designed to encourage teachers to further their own interest and expertise in the subject.

Newsletter – produced three times per year, the *Newsletter* contains topical articles, news items, and interviews about English studies, and updates about The English Association's activities.

Benefits of Membership

Unity and voice – members join others with a wealth of experience, knowledge, and passion for English, to foster the discussion of teaching methods and respond to national issues.

Resources – members can access high quality resources on the Association's website, and in its volumes, journals, magazines, and newsletters.

Networking – members can network with colleagues and leading practitioners, including joining national special interest groups and their local Regional Group. Members also are given reduced rates for the Association's conferences and other events.

Essays and Studies 2023

The Literature and Politics of the Environment

Edited by
John Parham

for the English Association

D. S. BREWER

ESSAYS AND STUDIES
IS VOLUME SEVENTY-SIX IN THE NEW SERIES
OF ESSAYS AND STUDIES COLLECTED ON BEHALF OF
THE ENGLISH ASSOCIATION
ISSN 0071-1357

First published 2023
D. S. Brewer, Cambridge

D. S. Brewer is an imprint of Boydell & Brewer Ltd
PO Box 9, Woodbridge, Suffolk IP12 3DF, UK
and of Boydell & Brewer Inc.
668 Mt Hope Avenue, Rochester, NY 14620-2731, USA
website: www.boydellandbrewer.com

ISBN 978-1-84384-697-0

A CIP catalogue record for this book is available
from the British Library

Contents

Notes on Contributors

Nora Castle is an Early Career Fellow at the Institute of Advanced Study of the University of Warwick. Her research is situated at the interstices of science fiction studies, food studies, and the environmental humanities. She recently passed her viva for her PhD thesis, 'Food Futures: Food, Foodways, and Environmental Crisis in Contemporary Science Fiction'.

Mark Frost is Principal Lecturer in English at the University of Portsmouth. His research specialisms in literature and environment are predominately nineteenth century. He has published books and articles on John Ruskin, Richard Jefferies, Charles Dickens, and Wilkie Collins, and his next monograph will be on pastoral and modernity in early Victorian fiction.

Dominic Head is Emeritus Professor of English Literature at the University of Nottingham, where he served as Head of the School of English 2007–10. His most recent books are *Modernity and the English Rural Novel* (Cambridge University Press, 2017) and *Nature Prose: Writing in Ecological Crisis* (Oxford University Press, 2022).

Karín Lesnik-Oberstein is Professor of Critical Theory at the University of Reading. Her earliest work on ecocriticism appeared in the edited volume *Writing the Environment: Ecocriticism and Literature* (Zed Books, 1998). As a transdisciplinary critical theorist, she publishes across the disciplines from children's literature to literary and queer theory, mathematics, (neuro) science, and philosophy.

Pippa Marland is a Lecturer in Humanities at the University of Bristol. She is co-author of *Modern British Nature Writing, 1789–2020* (Cambridge University Press, 2022) and author of *Ecocriticism and the Island* (Rowman and Littlefield, 2022). She is currently completing *The Pen and the Plough*, an account of the literary representation of farming.

John Parham is Professor of Environmental Humanities at the University of Worcester. He has written six books, most recently the *Cambridge Companion to Literature and the Anthropocene*. He co-edited *Green Letters: Studies in Ecocriticism* for twenty years and writes mainly on Victorian literature and ecology, ecomedia, and contemporary environmental fiction.

Sam Solnick is Senior Lecturer in English at the University of Liverpool, where he co-directs the Literature and Science Hub. He has published widely in the environmental humanities, including the monograph *Poetry and the Anthropocene* (Routledge, 2017). He is currently working on a project on horror and ecology.

Amanda Thomson is a visual artist and writer, and Lecturer at the Glasgow School of Art. Published works include *A Scots Dictionary of Nature* (Saraband Books, 2018), *microbursts* (hybrid, lyric essays, with Elizabeth Reeder, Prototype Press, 2021) and *Belonging: Natural Histories of Place, Identity and Home* (Canongate Books, 2022)

Aidan Tynan is Senior Lecturer in English literature at Cardiff University. He is the author of two monographs, the most recent being *The Desert in Modern Literature and Philosophy: Wasteland Aesthetics* (Edinburgh University Press, 2020). He is currently working on a book entitled *Ecofascist Cultures: the Far Right and the Environmental Imagination.*

Caitlin Vandertop is Assistant Professor at the University of Warwick. Her current research interests include postcolonial studies, ecocriticism, island literatures, the oceanic humanities, and resource regimes in the Pacific. She is the author of *Modernism in the Metrocolony: Urban Cultures of Empire in Twentieth Century Literature* (Cambridge University Press, 2021).

Acknowledgements

The editor would like to thank the contributors for contributing their expertise and time to thinking about what literature can do to address one of the most pressing issues facing humanity. He is grateful to the staff of Boydell and Brewer and The English Association for their cheerful efficiency in setting up and producing the volume. Finally, he appreciates the help given by the General Editor of the series in finalising the volume.

The index was prepared by James Helling.

Introduction

JOHN PARHAM

Much as the complexities of climate change and the Anthropocene have queried the limits and exclusions of literary representation, so, too, have the challenges recently presented by climate activism and intersectional environmentalism, animal rights, and even the 'thing-power' (as Jane Bennett puts it) of material forms like oil, plastic, and heavy metals.[1] Social and protest movements have revived the question of whether there can be such a thing as an activist ecocriticism. These movements resurrect a still-unanswered question first posed by Jonathan Bate in 1991: can ecocriticism only concern itself with consciousness, or might it politicise literary criticism in a new way?[2]

Attempting to respond, this volume coalesces around three interrelated strands: material ecologies, past and present British politics, and the act of writing itself. Contributors consider the ways in which literary form has foregrounded the complexities of both matter (in essays on water, sugar, and land) and political economics (from empire and nationalism to environmental justice movements and local and regional communities). The volume asks how life writing, nature writing, creative nonfiction, and autobiography, although genres entrenched in capitalist political realities, can also confront these by reinserting personal experience. Through such personal narratives, the volume addresses the extent to which literary ecocriticism might support Extinction Rebellion's fifth principle, of establishing a cycle of 'action, reflection and learning, and planning for more action', to help repair a near fatally damaged world. Can we bring a more sustainable planet into being by focusing on those literary forms which can imagine the conditions and systems needed to do so?

The first three essays focus on place. Mark Frost looks at Victorian reworkings of the pastoral in novels by Harriet Martineau, George Eliot, Benjamin Disraeli, and Charlotte Brontë, whose innovations in genre help to reveal the operation and impact of political economy. Set in the industrialised coun-

---

[1]   Jane Bennett, 'The Force of Things: Steps Toward an Ecology of Matter', *Political Theory* 32.3 (2004), pp. 347–72 (p. 348).
[2]   Jonathan Bate, *Romantic Ecology: Wordsworth and the Environmental Tradition* (London, 1991).

tryside of the Midlands or North, the novels strip away pastoral's idyllic idealisation of country life to reveal the 'accelerating intersections of town and country', and the imposition of environmental exploitation, air pollution, and economic globalisation. More broadly, they expose a mechanism of environmental sovereignty, an assumed 'unquestioned right to do as we will with everything we describe as nonhuman and label as resource', says Frost, a label which encompasses both industry and farming. Hence, these novels expose what Elizabeth Miller has called extractivist ecologies, a way of life that proceeds by depleting the future.[3] Like Frost, Caitlin Vandertop's essay discusses how past political-economic transformations (in this case, by the British Empire) shape the environmental vulnerabilities of the present. She considers two texts from a place little discussed in ecocriticism but significant in Britain's colonial past: Hong Kong. Vandertop uses concepts from the blue humanities and queer ecology to argue that Timothy Mo's *An Insular Possession* and Xi Xi's 'Strange Tales from a Floating City' exemplify the way in which postcolonial literature experiments with form to unpick the complex relationship of material ecology and political economy. Hong Kong's 'hydrocolonial' nature allows images of water to encapsulate the vast circulatory systems of money and power which enable large-scale land reclamation, the racialised nature of such flows, and the fact that, in their reliance on material resources, empire and globalisation are ultimately fragile. Typhoons, rain, water-borne disease, and the movement of water disturbs colonial, capitalist expansion, and water deities or dragons, invoked in Mo and Xi Xi's narratives, suggesting local knowledge and alternative ways of living in the world. The latter perspective is picked up by Sam Solnick's essay, which starts with Elizabeth DeLoughrey's argument that, to make them meaningful, it is necessary to 'provincialize' the ecological transformations of the Anthropocene.[4] Solnick adds a corresponding temporal dimension: Merseyside's long relationship with sugar plantations, the oil industry, and slavery, and its role in the subsequent growth of hydrocarbon capitalism. Place can be haunted by the social and ecological disruptions caused by the slow violence of capitalism. Using Jennifer Wenzel's notion of reading literature under the 'duress' of the Anthropocene, Solnick argues that visual and verbal arts which are rooted in place reveal the separation of nature and society as a mode of resistance and resilience.[5] Touching upon teaching methods which can encourage

[3] Elizabeth Miller, *Extraction Ecologies and the Literature of the Long Exhaustion* (Princeton, 2021), pp. 1–19.
[4] Elizabeth M. DeLoughrey, *Allegories of the Anthropocene* (Durham NC, 2019), p. 10.
[5] Jennifer Wenzel, 'Stratigraphy and Empire: Waiting for the Barbarians, Reading

students to study literature in relation to place, he explores the legacy of sugar in Liverpool, in forms as varied as eighteenth-century eclogues, public art and gardens, and the EcoGothic of Clive Barker's 'Candyman' story.

The second three essays examine the political ecocriticism evident in some contemporary literature. Nora Castle's essay examines a recent 'nonhuman turn' in science fiction by looking at two novels by Adam Roberts. In *Bête*, an implanted chip enables animals to use human speech; in *By Light Alone*, a technology, 'New Hair', allows humans to photosynthesise through their hair. However, in *Bête* the technology, rather than eliminating the hierarchy between humans and nonhuman animals, actually sparks conflict, whereas in *By Light Alone* the radical possibilities of 'becoming-plant' are foreclosed by class. The rich shave their heads because they can afford 'real' food. They continue exploiting the poor (the 'leafheads'), now seen as closer to nature, and, like the environment, a passive and unruly resource, unworthy of ethical consideration. Castle demonstrates that utopian posthuman futures of inter-species harmony will be impossible unless humanity first moves beyond the ethical and social frameworks of capitalist world ecology: the technological fix needs to be accompanied by sociopolitical change. Aidan Tyan's essay starts with one of Timothy Morton's key ideas, 'dark ecology', which under-mines the naturalness of stories about how humanity is involved in nature and the eco-technologies often embraced by liberal/leftist environmental-ism.[6] In response to the difficult question of what sort of politics dark ecology leaves readers with, Tynan turns to Paul Kingsnorth's novel *The Wake*, coun-terposing its fleeting vision of 'benevolent green nationalism' and 'ecological Englishness' against the variants of right-wing environmentalism (such as eco- or fossil fascism), which accompany any philosophy of place or dwell-ing. Tynan concludes that, while ecocritics should return to place, they must realise this concept is entangled in a political world ecology. Finally, the essay by Karín Lesnik-Oberstein addresses a paradox: the much-repeated faith in ecocriticism in representation, affect, effect, narrative, and story shares an emphasis on agency and impact with neoliberal discourse. The essay detects several dangers: of adopting a communal but proprietary 'we' (a critic who speaks for everyone), of disregarding how stories about agency rarely consider the historical production of people's lives, and of a focus on human excep-tionalism. Through a close analysis of a canonical British environmental text, Henry Williamson's *Tarka the Otter*, and critical responses to this, Lesnik-

---

under Duress', Tobias Menely and Jesse Oak Taylor, eds, *Anthropocene Reading: Literary History in Geologic Times* (University Park PA, 2017), pp. 167–83 (p. 168).
[6] Timothy Morton, *Dark Ecology: For a Logic of Future Coexistence* (New York, 2016), p. 5.

Oberstein attributes the 'twists and turns' by which critical animal studies' anti-anthropocentrism fails to understand other animals because it is trapped in a markedly human form of language. Lesnik-Oberstein argues that literary pedagogy and activism need to read differently, with less emphasis on accumulating knowledge, and more on reading as immersive critical thinking without a specific aim in mind.

The final group of essays explores the mixture of local politics and identity politics in writing about walking, nature writing, and writing by and about farmers and land workers. Given a tradition of nature writing where the pastoral has dominated the georgic, Pippa Marland's essay asks how the social and cultural hostility towards farming and farmers, which arose after the impacts of post-war industrialised farming were realised, began to filter into environmentalist discourse, and hence into public consciousness. The essay is based on her own involvement in collaborative research which has included 'slow conversations' between conservationists, academics, and farmers and land workers, and creative writing workshops for the latter group. In vivid and touching examples of 'new Georgic' writing, which picture the precarity, joy, and rewards of agricultural work, Marland demonstrates that giving a voice to farmers (hitherto marginalised by class, geography, and the urban–rural divide) can increase public knowledge about how nature-friendly practices, like regenerative farming, may have an impact on material circumstances. For Dominic Head, a 'problem of privilege and exclusion' continues to hinder 'the ethical credentials (and range) of new nature writing'. His essay identifies three themes in books about walking in nature which tackle this problem: the healing properties of walking, vagrancy and homelessness, and ethnicity and the unequal access to the outdoors. Head juxtaposes authentic experiences documented in such writing against privileged examples of 'project' walking and (echoing Tynan) the sentiment 'that you can only really belong in a place if you have deep roots there'. Walking literature, Head argues, is forging new literary devices in order to speak for positions on the margins of society: Neil Ansell reinvents the literature of the solitary wanderer in nature to write about homelessness, Testament reinvents the dramatic chorus, and Jini Reddy dismantles the mysticism surrounding heritage to confront the racial exclusions of place. Written in new voices, shaped by new literary form, these writers show us what new nature writing *could* and *does* do. The volume closes with Amanda Thomson's short piece of creative writing. Describing the Scots pinewoods of Abernethy, Thomson underlines the importance of attention, whether through walking, scientific surveys, or writing, to reveal beautiful realities, such as a series of curved tree trunks denoting heavy snow last winter. 'Three tiny pearls of brown eggs', nested in the square spaces of a scientific survey, prompt questions about how humanity infringes upon space. Attentiveness, then, should encompass historical and political ecologies: starting with the 'I' in a place, but reaching out into how this is entangled in family histories, and then again into forms of slow violence, such as racism and colonialism. Thomson cites Louisa Gairn's argument that 'contemporary poetry, and lyricism more generally, constitute an ecological "line of defence" ... a space in which reader and author can examine their relationship to the world around them'.[7] As water, rocks, trees, and birds intersect with human experience and creative writing, the web of life, Thomson writes, will 'resonate out and out and out'.

The Association for the Study of Literature and Environment speaks of how the slow thinking of scholarly and creative research and writing must meet swift action, since 'we cannot truly be environmental humanists unless we are willing to become environmental activists'.[8] *The Literature and Politics of the Environment* has been put together because its contributors care about the effects of environmental degradation on humans and non-humans alike. They offer ways to imagine alternative futures in partnership with the natural world.

[7] Louisa Gairn, *Ecology and Modern Scottish Literature* (Edinburgh, 2008), p. 156.
[8] Association for the Study of Literature and Environment, 'Vision and History' (2022), https://www.asle.org/discover-asle/vision-history.

1

Industry and Environmental Violence in the Early Victorian Novel: Pastoral Re-visions

MARK FROST

This chapter contends that early Victorian authors often reformulated pastoral modes in ways that disclosed anxieties about unprecedented environmental, sociopolitical, demographic, and technological change. Employing what I would like to call pastoral ecocriticism, I argue for pastoral's enduring power, not as an archaic poetic mode centred on idyllic imaginings, but as the principal form through which western authors and artists have addressed the problematical relationship between definitions of culture and nature. I turn to four early Victorian novels which are keenly aware of industry and other 'urban' phenomena in 'rural' areas: Harriet Martineau's *Deerbrook* (1839), Benjamin Disraeli's *Sybil* (1845), Charlotte Brontë's *Shirley* (1849), and George Eliot's *Adam Bede* (1859). They demonstrate the position of the British countryside within an international network of capitalist economic and environmental exploitation, substantiating John Miller's claim that 'the Victorian period is a pivotal stage in the nexus of ecological and political violence'.[1] Under economic, social, and environmental pressure, traditional pastoral contrasts between rural (good) and urban (bad) break down in revealing ways. The novels undermine impulses towards simplistic pastoral idylls (representations of harmonious rural communities clearly distinct from their world-weary urban counterparts), instead finding in rural societies conflict and inequality, but also opportunity, diversity, and change. They reveal complex intersections between villages, towns, and cities (such as the presence of industries and crafts, the influence of city culture, and traffic between urban and rural) which traditional pastoral is incapable of representing.

Divisions between urban and rural were pressurised, and often rendered meaningless, by intensified capitalist networks of environmental violence and technological control that were clearly evident in the countryside. While small-scale industrial activity has long characterised rural economies, the

---

[1]   John Miller, 'Postcolonial Ecocriticism and Victorian Studies', *Literature Compass* 9.7 (2012), pp. 476–88 (p. 476).

tendency of conservative forms of pastoral to idealise agricultural life often obscures the farm labour that sustains both countryside and city, while also pushing other rural economic activities to the representational peripheries. Although strongly focused on the social life of agricultural communities, these novels, set in periods from 1799 to 1839, focus on the expanding rural industries, industrial workers, and labour migrations, and are sometimes aware of the environmental impacts of mining, quarrying, metalworking, and milling. Reflecting the changing Victorian and pre-Victorian country-side, and the varied state of its economic activities, they undercut the long-standing and illusory myth that the countryside rests on cultivation of land alone. I begin by discussing pastoral complexities, before turning to textual analyses, first of the complex representations of country life in *Deerbrook* and *Adam Bede*, and then, in *Shirley* and *Sybil*, of the latter novels' keener focus on the socio-environmental impacts of rural industries.

Pastoral Ecocriticism

There is no critical consensus about what pastoral is, except that it involves representations of peopled environments (thus distinguishing it from representations of wilderness landscapes, allegedly empty of all but the solitary observer). Born in ancient European and Middle Eastern cultures, pastoral has always been multifaceted, mercurial and complex, dividing critics since pastoral theory began in the sixteenth century. One camp, exemplified by René Rapin, Bernard de Fontenelle, and Alexander Pope, regarded pastoral as a purely poetic form, involving idealised, artificial representations of rural shepherd societies, and designed to delight, in Pope's words, by 'exposing the best side only of a shepherd's life, and in concealing its miseries'.[2] A suspicion that pastoral merely involves saccharine representations of nymphs and shepherds often hounds the genre, but a counter-critical tradition has long seen pastoral not as a narrow poetic genre but as a broader cultural mode, a set of conceptual tools and attitudes articulated in many forms, and neither narrowly associated with idylls nor inevitably conservative and escapist. Endorsing W. W. Greg's argument that as 'a distinct and distinctive part in the history of human thought', pastoral is 'the expression of instincts and impulses deep-rooted in the nature of humanity', pastoral criticism – not least

---

[2]   Alexander Pope, 'A Discourse on Pastoral Poetry' (1717), Brian Loughrey, ed., *The Pastoral Mode* (London, 1984), pp. 53–63 (p. 51). See also René Rapin, *Dissertatio de carmine pastorali* (1659); Bernard le Bouvier de Fontenelle, *Digression sur les Anciens et les Modernes* (1688).

in ecocriticism – now recognises its broader reach.[3] As Greg Garrard argues, while 'classical pastoral precedes the perception of a general crisis in human ecology by thousands of years [...] it provides the pre-existing set of literary conventions and cultural assumptions that have been crucially transformed to provide a way for Europeans and Euro-Americans to construct their landscapes'.[4] The pastoral impulse, unconfined by period or genre, provides opportunities to reflect on socio-environmental relations. Examining pastoral's historical manifestations with an ecocritical lens provides a means to understand the roots of our Anthropocene predicaments.

From early on, in *The Epic of Gilgamesh*, Hesiod's Golden Age myths, the story of Eden, and Theocritus's *Idylls* (the latter often described as the starting point of pastoral), tales of harmonious human-environmental relations (the pastoral idyll) go hand-in-hand with pastoral elegy (tales of their loss, as a result of human sin, folly, or failed stewardship). The idyll reaches for a state of harmony precisely because humanity routinely fails to achieve it. The elegy more directly acknowledges the socio-environmental impacts of the agricultural and urbanising impulses. Even idyllic pastoral, though, owes its being to the fact of city life: as Garrard shows, 'the emergence of the bucolic idyll correlates closely with large-scale urbanisation in the Hellenic period'.[5] Pastoral writers since classical times often position their societies as bearing unprecedented burdens of change, seeking imaginary escape from urban modernity by constructing salutary rural values. Rather than arising from shepherd experiences, as Rapin, Fontanelle, and Pope argue, urban pastoralists construct idealised alternatives to city life. A specific form of the idyll involves the pastoral retreat, in which world-weary urban travellers discover wisdom and fulfilment in the simple lives and attitudes of rustics existing in harmony with a nature that gives forth its riches, with no apparent effort from either party.

There is some cross-over in the anti-pastoral tradition with georgic social critiques. Virgil's *Georgics* depicts Roman agricultural life, and shows itself keenly aware of its tensions and inequalities. As Raymond Williams points out, in Virgil's early *Eclogues* too, though the text is routinely regarded as idyllic pastoral, 'the rural disturbance of his own Italy often breaks through into the poetically distant Arcadia', including 'the threat of loss and eviction'.[6]

[3] W. W. Greg, 'Pastoral Poetry and Pastoral Drama: A Literary Inquiry with Special Reference to the Pre-Restoration Stage in England' (1906), Loughrey, ed., *Pastoral Mode*, pp. 77–81 (p. 78).

[4] Greg Garrard, *Ecocriticism*, 2nd edn (Abingdon, 2012), p. 38.

[5] *Ibid.*, p. 39.

[6] Raymond Williams, *The Countryside and the City* (London, 1985), pp. 16, 17.

Because the boundaries between georgic and pastoral are unclear, one might see the former as part of the larger pastoral tradition, and related to an anti-pastoral line developed before the mid-nineteenth century novels studied here (exemplified, for instance, in George Crabbe's *The Village* (1783), William Wordsworth's 'Michael' (1800), and many works by John Clare).

Critics are at least agreed that pastoral is defined by two contrasts: between rural and urban, and past and present, the former in each pair being valorised in conservative pastoral.[7] Experiencing intense urbanisation, Victorian writers reformulate traditional pastoral expectations, through georgic or anti-pastoral complications of the idyllic impulse. This article is particularly focused on their awareness that the clear-cut boundaries between rural and urban on which traditional pastoral rests are inadequate to describe the complexities of British country life. A pastoral ecocritical approach to these texts therefore seeks nuanced accounts of the accelerating intersections of town and country within environmentally exploitative capitalist economies.

Pastoral (Re)visions: *Deerbrook* and *Adam Bede*

Considering those debates over whether pastoral obscures or highlights 'real conditions' in the countryside, Martineau's *Deerbrook* and Eliot's *Adam Bede* are rewarding and revealing novels. The opening of the former and the second chapter of the latter illustrate how Victorians engage with older pastoral tropes in relatively radical ways, while also responding to the related picturesque mode in painting, which sought pleasure in representation of tumbledown rural ruins. For many Victorians, conventional pastoral and picturesque effaced rural misery while idealising landscapes. As Williams suggests, the conservative idyll's contrast between 'natural' countryside and 'worldly' city depends on 'the suppression of work in the countryside, and of the property relations through which this work is organised'. Many Victorian authors resist this representation of the countryside by focusing precisely on those socio-economic features occluded from conservative pastorals.[8]

As John Rignall argues, Eliot participates in 'an interest in landscape [that] was in part a product of the growing urbanisation of nineteenth-century society', but was suspicious of 'the merely picturesque' because it

---

[7]   I see William Empson's attempt to define pastoral alternatively (as the act of 'putting the complex into the simple') as a blind alley that leads readers away from the more essential focus on boundary constructions: see *Some Versions of Pastoral* (1935), ed. Lisa A. Rodensky (London, 1995), p. 25.

[8]   Williams, *Countryside and the City*, p. 46.

'ignores the extent to which landscape is a construction, a product of human labour and a place of often arduous work'.[9] Eliot was alive to the limitations and urban roots of traditional pastoral and picturesque in an essay on 'The Natural History of German Life' (1856), which decries 'the notion that peasants are joyous, that the typical moment to represent a man in a smock-frock is when he is cracking a joke and showing a row of sound teeth, that cottage matrons are usually buxom, and village children necessarily rosy and merry'.[10] Because such 'prejudices [are] difficult to dislodge from the artistic mind, which looks for its subjects into literature instead of life', and because painters are 'still under the influence of idyllic literature, which has always expressed the imagination of the cultivated and town-bred, rather than the truth of rustic life', Eliot advises that readers should be 'taught to feel, not for the heroic artisan or the sentimental peasant, but for the peasant in all his coarse apathy'.[11] In sympathy with broader mid-century novelistic and documentary investigations of the socio-economic 'condition of England', this entailed detailed representations of rural lives and work. In *Deerbrook* and *Adam Bede*, novels that differ in historical settings but share much in their approaches, an understanding of rural life was developed by self-aware deployments of the modes of the pastoral and the picturesque. Set in 1799, Eliot's novel resists the valorisation of past over present (that is, pastoral elegy) and complicates idyllic constructions of country life. *Deerbrook* (seemingly set in its Victorian present) shares this suspicion of the idyll.

The early chapters of these novels offer strikingly comparable visions of travel into villages in ways that foreground increased mobility, urban perspectives, and the aesthetic gaze. Both dangle an image of the idyll, before revealing far more complex worlds enmeshed in capitalist production and modern demographics. The brilliance of Martineau's opening lies in a self-conscious desire to undermine pastoral expectations. It begins by conjuring a definitively urban perspective:

> Every town-bred person who travels in a rich country region knows what it is to see a neat white house planted in a pretty situation, – in a shrubbery, or commanding a sunny common, or nestling between two hills, – and to say to

---

[9] John Rignall, 'Landscape', Margaret Harris, ed., *George Eliot in Context*, (Cambridge, 2013), pp. 168–75 (pp. 168, 169).

[10] George Eliot, 'The Natural History of German Life' (*Westminster Review*, 19 July 1856), Nathan Shep.pard, ed., *The Essays of 'George Eliot', Complete* (New York, 1883), pp. 141–77 (p. 143).

[11] *Ibid.*, pp. 143, 145.

himself, as the carriage sweeps past its gate, 'I should like to live there,' – 'I could be very happy in that pretty place'.[12]

The passage promises pastoral retreat to a plentiful country secluded between hills, but Martineau also archly demonstrates that the urge for pastoral retreat rests on idealisation of the countryside by urbanites who do not understand it:

> Transient visions pass before his mind's eye of dewy summer mornings, when the shadows are long on the grass, and of bright autumn afternoons, when it would be luxury to saunter in the neighbouring lanes; and of frosty winter days, when the sun shines in over the laurustinus at the window, while the fire burns with a different light from that which it gives in the dull parlours of a city (p. 1).

The essential rural-urban conflict of pastoral is there in the familiar invocation of city weariness and rural, floral comforts, but the continuing passage upsets confidence in the countryside's assured superiority. The second paragraph shows how the status of Mr Grey's house and garden as an idyll that had 'been the object of this kind of speculation to one or more persons' is enabled by modern technological infrastructure, exemplified by 'the stage-coach [that] had begun to pass through Deerbrook' (p. 1) thrice weekly. For urban travellers thus enabled to travel, the 'rather pretty village' offers picturesque delights that are linked to aesthetic control: 'the woods of a fine park [...] formed the background to its best points of view', while the prominence of 'Mr Grey's [...] prettiest house' is due to its location, 'standing in a field, round which the road swept' (p. 1). More significant, however, is what is *not* revealed to the stage-coach traveller's urban gaze: 'the timber and coal yards, and granaries, which stretched down to the river side, were hidden by a nice management of the garden walls, and training of the shrubbery' (p. 1). The novel's opening thus discloses Deerbrook's position within expanding economic networks, while the idyllic shrubberies and walls screen the roots of local economic power, which rest not solely on agricultural production, but on exploitation of natural resources in the coal, grain, and timber business co-owned by Mr Grey. Martineau's idyll thus playfully enacts the obfuscation described by Williams by foregrounding the carefully-constructed bounties of 'nature' while drawing attention to the occlusion of environmental exploitation on which the village economy relies.

---

[12]   Harriet Martineau, *Deerbrook* (London, 1983), p. 1. Subsequent references to this work give page numbers in parentheses in the main text.

As the third paragraph proceeds, we learn more of the village's economic foundation, and of the importance of viewpoint in controlling and limiting gaze. The Greys prefer their dining room/parlour because its views 'commanded the house of Mr Rowland, Mr Grey's partner in the corn, coal, and timber business', whereas the drawing room 'looked merely into the garden' and 'was so dull, that it was kept for company [...] about three times a-year' when 'the ground-windows, which opened upon the lawn, [were] thrown wide, to afford to the rare guests of the family a welcome from birds and flowers' (p. 2). Preferring the parlour/dining room views of scenes of human action, the Greys are not the simple rustics of traditional pastoral, but urbane figures bored by nature and immersed in essentially urban economic cultures. Just as the stage-coach traveller is led *not* to see the timber yards, the drawing-room is deployed in a knowing pastoral manoeuvre to beguile visitors with 'natural' charms. Later descriptions of the Greys' garden, zoo, and view reinforce the carefully stage-managed construction of a bourgeois 'pastoral' space that includes an artfully 'overturned wheelbarrow', a turf full of crocuses, 'a wilderness of daffodils on either side', periwinkles that 'overran the borders, and 'the field where the Greys' pet animals were wont to range' (p. 291). What is absent, as 'the gazers' from this vantage point 'overlooked a wide extent of country', are many signs of village labour. 'A few white cottages [...] peeped out from the lanes, and seemed to sit down to rest in the meadows, so profound was the repose which they seemed to express', but while the river winds and 'nature seemed asleep', 'nothing was seen to move but the broad sail of a wherry, and a diminished figure of a man beside his horse, bush-harrowing in a distant green field' (p. 291). Given the environmentally exploitative nature of the Grey's economic power, it is unsurprising that nature here is a pacified psychological resource; nor that economic activities on land and water (the commercial boat and agricultural labourer) are 'diminished' in order to satisfy the bourgeois visual appetites of those who can afford to reside in a world of pet lambs, ponies, carefully-maintained hedges, and precisely-choreographed displays of floral abundance. The wherry and the ploughman are simultaneously present and marginal. Martineau's knowing account of the ways in which economic realities are overlaid by pastoral idealisations is, therefore, a reminder that the English countryside has long been formed by structures of concerted environmental exploitation that exemplify what Timothy Morton describes as 'agrilogistics', 'a highly addictive logic of agriculture that began in the Fertile Crescent', 'whose logical structure is never examined, though it underpins the [...] Agricultural and then Industrial Revolutions', and that rests on 'the control of lifeforms' and claims to sovereignty over the nonhuman.[13] However much conservative pastoral seeks to stage-manage the countryside, to construct the myth of a 'green and pleasant England' that persists even in our times of droughts, wildfires, rampant pasturage, and dying rivers, other, more troubling truths are available to those who resist pastoral idealisation.

Chapter 2 of *Adam Bede* presents another self-conscious, urban, aesthetic gaze, another subtle critique of picturesque and pastoral modes, and another attempt to depict a far more complex countryside than that of traditional pastoral. While Rignall's claim that this chapter is typical of a 'predominately pastoral' representation in the novel could be more nuanced, his suggestion that 'the narrative that follows is committed to a realism that knows the limitations of the idyllic setting' is astute.[14] As Stephen Gill notes, Eliot reflected upon pictorial conventions in a series of 1850s *Westminster Review* articles (including 'The Natural History of German Life'), which guided her fictional attempts to create forensic yet sympathetic portraits of rural communities.[15]

In Chapter 2, an urban traveller pauses at a viewpoint overlooking Hayslope village in rural Loamshire. Like the stagecoach gazers in *Deerbrook*, he seeks pastoral delights. While much of the lengthy description that follows focuses on 'the beauty of the view' across traditional agricultural countryside, the picture is 'divided' when he is struck by 'the singular contrast presented by the groups of villagers with the knot of Methodists', which include a 'young female preacher' (p. 19) on the nearby green. Why the presence of this religious sect is disruptive is not immediately apparent, because the traveller's eye is initially absorbed by the rural 'view of gently swelling meadow, and wooded valley, and dark masses of distant hill', but it becomes clearer as the narrator observes that the 'rich undulating district of Loamshire to which Hayslope belonged lies close to a grim outskirt of Stonyshire', a more urban county overlooking Loamshire. While Stonyshire is 'a bleak treeless region, intersected by lines of cold grey stone', Loamshire offers 'swelling hills, muffled with hedgerows and long meadow-grass and thick corn', a world dominated, socially and economically, by 'some fine old country-seat nestled in the valley or crowning the slope, some homestead with

---

[13]   Timothy Morton, 'The Biosphere Which Is Not One: Towards Weird Essentialism', *The Journal of the British Society for Phenomenology* 46 (2015), pp. 141–55 (p. 141). The Fertile Crescent is a term used to denote a crescent-shaped region of the Middle East (stretching from Palestine up to Iraq and Turkey and down to western Iran) where agriculture is thought to have first begun.

[14]   Rignall, 'Landscape', p. 174.

[15]   George Eliot, *Adam Bede*, ed. Stephen Gill (Harmondsworth, 1980), pp. xv–xix Subsequent references to this work give page numbers in parentheses in the main text.

its long length of barn and its cluster of golden ricks' (p. 19). Highlighting the aesthetic quality of his experience, the narrator notes that 'it was just such a picture as this last that Hayslope Church had made to the traveller as he began to mount the gentle slope leading to its pleasant uplands. Now from his station near the Green he had before him in one view nearly all the other typical features of this pleasant land', this intensely pastoral 'region of corn and grass', 'specked with sheep', dominated by woods, valleys, and 'a large sweep of park' (pp. 19–20) owned by the local gentry family, the Donnithornes. Emphasising a rural economy seemingly rooted in traditional agriculture, Hayslope is glimpsed at 'that moment in summer when the sound of the scythe being whetted makes us cast more lingering looks at the flower-sprinkled tresses of the meadows' (pp. 19–20). Acutely attentive to aesthetic expectations, the chapter gradually disrupts the pastoral and picturesque, firstly by those references to the troubling proximity of Stonyshire, conjoined to Loamshire in a description of them 'as a pretty blooming sister [...] linked in the arm of a rugged, tall, swarthy brother' (pp. 19–20). The kinship metaphor begins to undermine the traditional separation of urban and rural, while the traveller's conversation with Mr Casson, landlord of the Donnithorne Arms, reveals a complex rural society in which the poor speak a local 'dileck' that is 'hard work to hunderstand' for those like Casson, who ape gentry speech and seek middle-class status. In such moments Eliot is emphatically not, as George Willis Cooke argued, the novelist of 'the pleasant country, the common people, the quiet villages'.[16] More perceptively, Anne Mozley's contemporary review praised the novel as providing 'a closely true picture of purely rural life', in which 'every class that makes up a village community has its representative'.[17] Because the class system was alive and well in the traditional countryside, pastoral idylls depicting harmony, unity, and universal accord cannot provide the representational tools Eliot requires.

The traveller expresses surprise at a Methodist gathering in what he terms 'this agricultural spot', but Casson points out that 'there's a pretty lot o' workmen round about' (p. 18). The village has both agricultural labourers directly dependent on land and artisanal 'workmen' who occupy a more complex position in the capitalist rural economy, with greater access to, and appetite for, urban education, training, and culture (as exemplified by the presence of Bartle Massey's evening school). Located within the spatial world of the squirearchy, the workmen are nonetheless mobile, and exposed

16   George Willis Cooke, *George Eliot: A Critical Study* (London, 1883), p. 2.
17   David Carroll, *George Eliot: The Critical Heritage* (London, 1971), p. 97.

to city ideas. Casson notes that the local market town of Treddleston has 'a fine batch o' Methodisses' (p. 18), while those from Snowfield in Stonyshire regularly wander into the countryside to hold meetings, including the gathering on the Green that the traveller has observed. While the landlord reports limited conversions to nonconformism in this Anglican stronghold, the urban threat of Methodism is strongly embodied in Dinah Morris, a staunch Methodist preacher, rooted in Snowfield but troublingly (from the point of view of traditional pastoral visions) able to slide between urban and rural locations:

> She comes out o' Stonyshire, pretty nigh thirty mile off. But she's a-visitin' hereabout at Mester Poyser's at the Hall Farm [...]. She's own niece to Poyser's wife, [...] I've heared as there's no holding these Methodisses when the maggit's once got i' their head (p. 18).[18]

While Casson is anxiously alert to the intersections of urban Snowfield and rural Hayslope, represented by Dinah's mobility and her kinship to a family rooted in the land, the novel disrupts attempts to police boundaries between these realms. Just as *Deerbrook*'s views are divided between a constructed pastoral rurality and glimpses of an agrilogistic economy, so the urban traveller's 'divided' gaze reveals Hayslope does not conform to a simple agricultural model, but is stratified and complex. As Carol A. Martin notes, Eliot's Midlands roots made her 'keenly aware of how the urban-rural dynamic had changed over the first half of the century'.[19] Intrusions of urban ideas into the Hayslope countryside are therefore common. At a gathering to celebrate Arthur Donnithorne's birthday, tenants and labourers are joined by local quarrymen, the distinctive subculture of 'the band of the Benefit Club' who 'mustered in all its glory [...] carrying its banner with the motto "Let brotherly love continue," encircling a picture of a stone-pit' (p. 254). Set against the conservativism of the gentry estate, the radical politics of brotherly love are centred on an image of industrial work which is as much a part of the local rural economy as the Donnithorne's agricultural lands. In the five chapters detailing the celebrations, however, this band of workers remains in the

---

[18] That Eliot associates Nonconformism with urban working-class centres is also evident from *Silas Marner* (1861), in which the weaver moves from a Calvinist community in a northern slum to the countryside of Raveloe, bringing a distinctive set of values with him.
[19] Carol A. Martin, 'Rural Life', in Margaret Harris, ed., *George Eliot in Context* (Cambridge, 2013), pp. 256–63 (p. 256).

margins, and there is no mention of what role it plays in the festivities; while part of Hayslope, it is not fully integrated in it.

A broader comparison of the ways in which both novels break down conservative pastoral visions is revealing. *Deerbrook* thwarts a key pastoral contrast, setting the rural but conniving and worldly Greys against their visiting Birmingham cousins, the virtuous Misses Ibbotson, who exemplify loyalty, fortitude, simple values, and courage. Rural society (from the aristocratic Sir William Hunter to most of the rural poor) is represented as a venal site of ignorance and crime, which only urban ideas can reform. Hester Ibbotson marries the local apothecary, Mr Hope, and they set up house with her sister. As urban figures inserted into the rural countryside, they bring relatively progressive ideas (social and medical) that are distasteful to Hunter and Mrs Grey, who pursue a campaign of disinformation, exclusion, and harassment. One result of this victimisation is that an epidemic outbreak at the same time as harvest failure is exacerbated because Hope's medical expertise is rejected. The result is death, starvation, and disorder. Instead of finding the succour, harmony, and wisdom of pastoral retreat within a simple rural community, the urban trio face worldly intrigue and a violent assault on their house as the apparent idyll of the opening chapter collapses. Their ultimate vindication at the novel's close is a victory of city values, another inversion of traditional pastoral binaries and of pastoral's preference for rural over urban.

In *Adam Bede*, the resistance of the Poysers, an upright farming family who fight attempts by their landlords, the financially grasping Donnithornes, to take some of their land, reveals that both are enmeshed in wider economic networks and laissez-faire ideas, undercutting the notion that the gentry preside over a harmonious community. Those most closely associated with traditional village life and values (the Donnithornes, Reverend Irwine, and Hetty Sorrel, especially) are immoral, ineffective, or morally weak. Some of the most sympathetic rural characters (Adam and Seth Bede, and Bartle Massey) are, meanwhile, strongly influenced by urban ideas, education, and aspirations.

While the novel does not definitively favour urban over rural, its attitude to the city and city dwellers is intensely sympathetic, and its characterisation of Hayslope often disenchanted. In chapter 8, the nonconformist Dinah gently challenges the Anglican stalwart Mr Irwine, when he describes Snowfield, a mill town, as 'a dreary bleak place'. Accepting that it is 'very different from this country' (p. 89), she points out that she and other millworkers 'have reason to be grateful' for the employment. A transgressive hybrid, Dinah represents the accelerating interpenetration of rural and urban in the period. Her first memory of preaching, she tells Irwine, involved the industrial countryside. Travelling to Hetton-Deeps, 'a village where the people get their living by working in the lead-mines', she found a place 'where there's no church nor preacher, but they live like sheep without a shepherd' (p. 91). Obliquely rebuking Anglican failures to provide pastoral care, her celebration of complex, faintly Romantic landscapes is a rejection of traditional pastoral countryside: in the hills, 'where there's no trees [...], as there is here, to make the sky look smaller, but you see the heavens stretched out like a tent, and you feel the everlasting arms around you', she feels 'a wonderful sense of the Divine love' (p. 91). This also permits her to move transgressively across a range of rural locations which ambiguously undermine distinctions between rural and urban. At Hetton-Deeps, feeling 'a great movement in my soul' as she encountered 'the hard looks of the men, who seemed to have their eyes no more filled with the sight of the Sabbath morning than if they had been dumb oxen that never looked up to the sky', Dinah was inspired to preach to 'the little flock' (p. 92). Such pastoral/bucolic allusions radically revise traditions, for Dinah admires the urban-rural hybrids of Hetton-Deeps, 'rough ignorant people' and 'men that looked very hard and wild' (p. 92), but who are courteous and grateful for her guidance. By contrast, she finds that in villages like Hayslope, 'where the people lead a quiet life among the green pastures and the still waters, tilling the ground and tending the cattle, there's a strange deadness to the Word, as different as can be from the great towns' (p. 93). Mr Irwine accedes that 'farm labourers are not easily roused' and 'take life almost as slowly as the sheep and cows' (p. 93). The locus of traditional pastoral, the village rooted in rural activities, shifts here to Hetton Deeps and Snowfield. While the men of Hetton Deeps are not the 'dumb oxen' they first seem, Hayslope's inhabitants are not the shepherds/cowherds of traditional pastoral/bucolic, but 'almost' sheep and cattle.

'Not like the lasses o' this country-side' (in Lisbeth Bede's words), Dinah is rooted simultaneously in country and city, collapsing urban-rural distinctions. Gazing across the Poysers' land, 'her heart was very full' at the sight of 'pasture', 'milch cows', and 'meadow', but 'to her, bleak Snowfield had just as many charms' (p. 156). She repeatedly commits to 'the brethren and sisters at Snowfield, who are favoured with very little of this world's good; where the trees are few [...] and there's very hard living for the poor in the winter' (pp. 113, 37).

For Adam Bede, Snowfield too has a hybrid identity: while 'it looked like a town' amidst 'a hungry land', it was 'fellow to the country', because 'the stream through the valley where the great mill stood gave a pleasant greenness to the lower fields' (pp. 394–5). Both town and country are blurred in this sophisticated novel, their previously defined and separate identities complicated, their relationships foregrounded, and their economic intersections revealed. Josephine McDonagh's argument that Eliot's *Middlemarch* 'maintains the village intact, as a separate and independent social unit that becomes newly connected to the town' is also partly true of *Adam Bede,* as is her observation that her villages are 'a point of connection in a network of fiscal relations, alongside, but not necessarily subordinate to, the town'.[20]

The Pastoral and Environmental Violence: *Shirley* and *Sybil*

While *Adam Bede* and *Deerbrook* complicate traditional pastoral assumptions in various ways, they pay less attention to industrial labour or its impacts on environment than *Shirley* and *Sybil*. The former historical novel portrays the 1810s, while the latter is set in the recent past, centring on 'the calling of the Chartist National Convention and the delivery of the great petition to the House of Commons' in 1839, and drawing on Disraeli's 'recent encounters with artisans and workers in the north'.[21] Again we find resistance to pastoral idealisation of the countryside. While both elegise the past, crucially these novels also provide insight into the conjunctions of socio-environmental exploitation, under a globalising capitalist system increasingly underscored by fossil fuel extraction and other forms of environmental exploitation.

Both depict a socio-economically complex countryside enmeshed in wider economic networks. As Judith Hook and Andrew Hook argue, *Shirley* describes 'political, economic, and religious forces' which create the 'bitterness and hatred which is on the point of tearing the whole fabric of English society violently apart', and which are 'no less powerful in society in 1848–9'. In depicting an earlier era, Brontë also points to her own. Amid Napoleonic conflict and poor harvests, the Hooks point out, 'the government's Orders in Council had produced an economic backlash crippling English merchants and exporters', leading to 'economic stagnation' and high unemployment, particularly in northern textiles districts like those in *Shirley*.[22] Amidst fears of revolution, as Luddism oversaw attacks on mills and millowners, the State mobilised 12,000 troops to ensure the virtual suppression of the movement by 1813.[23] Brontë's discussion of those 'Orders in Council' underlines local-global intersections under capitalism: seeking

[20] Josephine McDonagh, 'Imagining Locality and Affiliation: George Eliot's Villages', Amanda Anderson and Harry E. Shaw, ed., *A Companion to George Eliot* (London, 2013), pp. 353–69 (p. 364).
[21] David Cesarani, *Disraeli: The Novel Politician* (New Haven, 2016), pp. 103–4.
[22] Charlotte Brontë, *Shirley: A Tale*, ed. Andrew Hook and Judith Hook (Harmondsworth, 1985), p. 25. Subsequent references to this work give page numbers in parentheses in the main text.
[23] See also Frank Peel, *The Risings of the Luddites: Chartists and Plug-drawers*, 4th edn (Abingdon, 2018).

to restrict trade between France and neutral nations, the legislation 'had, by offending America, cut off the principal market of the Yorkshire woollen trade, and brought it consequently to the verge of ruin' (p. 62). Connections between glutted 'foreign markets', domestic harvest failures, and new mill machinery, mean the northern poor face a 'hopeless struggle against what their fears or their interests taught them to regard as an invincible power' (pp. 62, 183). *Shirley* depicts a complex rural district plagued by conflict and inequality, enmeshed in wider economic networks and military-diplomatic intrigues. Mill owner, Gérard Moore, lacking roots in Yorkshire, is trans-planted there only because of the failure of his Flemish family's investments in earlier global financial networks.

The globalisation of markets which Brontë identifies is yet more marked in Disraeli's Victorian world, where aristocratic wealth is as much mercantile as agricultural. 'In a commercial country like England', Disraeli notes, 'some new and vast source of public wealth' regularly 'brings into national notice a new and powerful class'.[24] The 'Turkey merchant', 'West Indian Planter', and Indian 'Nabob' had each 'in their zenith in turn merged in the land, and became English aristocrats', an example followed by 'the Manufacturer, who in turn aspires to be "large-acred"' (p. 77). What is revealed is the located-ness of the English countryside within what Laura Dassow Walls, in another context, describes as an 'industrial, consumer capitalism [that] was reshaping the globe through expanding circuits of capital and commerce, and reshaping the planet too, felling forests, draining marshes, and levelling mountains'.[25]

These countrysides are a far cry from pastoral visions of traditional rural life rooted in the land, withdrawn from urban centres, and promis-ing retreat, harmony, and wisdom. Brontë's acuity and Disraeli's cynicism show that the rural does not exist as a pure, separate realm, untouched by wider economic forces. They also depict the countryside as riven by dissent, disunity, and disharmony as a result. Early in *Sybil*, we learn of rick-burning on one of Lord Marney's tenant farms. While Marney's brother, Charles Egremont, tells one of the tenant's labourers that incendiarism 'will not make the times easier', there is tacit support for arson in the reply, 'I think 'tis hard times for the poor, sir' (p. 58). Lord Marney's response to incendi-arism is remorselessly Malthusian, blaming it on 'a surplus population in the kingdom' (pp. 69, 112), and advocating a globalised solution via mass emi-

---

[24]   Benjamin Disraeli, *Sybil: Or, the Two Nations*, ed. Sheila M. Smith (Oxford, 1981), p. 77. Subsequent references to this work give page numbers in parentheses in the main text.
[25]   Laura Dassow Walls, 'Foreword', Dewey W. Hall, ed., *Victorian Ecocriticism: The Politics of Place and Early Environmental Justice* (Lanham, 2011), pp. xiii–xvii (p. xv).

gration. The novel also turns on its depiction of Chartist agitation, which brings urban political activism to rural locations. As this conflict builds, a pastoral figure, 'a herdsman following some kine', is confronted one evening by 'a vast crowd with some assumption of an ill-disciplined order' coming from the town of Mowbray, many 'armed with bludgeons and other rude weapons' (p. 402). Scenes of mob violence abound in Disraeli's countryside: the model mill at Trafford is threatened, Mowbray Castle is burned down, and Lord Mowbray is stoned to death. In *Shirley*, the countryside witnesses poverty and conflict: Gérard Moore thwarts an attack on his mill, while elsewhere there is fever in 'the poor cottages of the district' and 'families starving to death in Briarfield' (pp. 450, 268). Brontë's preferred solution to this, Shirley Keeldar's charitable exertions, 'served for the present greatly to alleviate the distress of the unemployed poor', but, for Moore, 'eleemosynary relief never yet tranquillized the working-classes', who 'receive orders from their chiefs' (pp. 288, 289) in Nottingham, Manchester, and Birmingham. Likewise, Disraeli's Young England Toryism, seeking to unite the 'two nations' of rich and poor under enlightened landowner leadership, does not address the underlying economic imperatives that have transformed the countryside and created inequality and dissent. Riven by conflict, and interwoven with urban centres of power, education, and political unrest, the countryside in both novels is deeply unpastoral.

While Moore's textile mill transplants industry and political strife to the Yorkshire countryside, *Sybil* offers a wide-ranging account of the blurring of boundaries between rural and urban which accompanies industrial development. Mowbray and district together form a rural area undergoing considerable industrial and demographic expansion, something that has financially benefited the Earl of Mowbray but affected the pastoral nature of his landholdings. Describing the Mowbray estate as 'very grand [...] but like all places in the manufacturing districts, very disagreeable', Lady Marney notes the environmental impacts of skies darkened by coal smoke: 'your toilette table is covered with blacks; the deer in the park seem as if they had bathed in a lake of Indian ink; and as for the sheep, you expect to see chimney-sweeps for the shepherds' (p. 75). The displacement of pastoral shepherds by urban sweeps symbolises the processes through which Mowbray village has become a town. Its main thoroughfare is 'called Castle Street after the ruins of the old baronial stronghold in its neighbourhood', but this emblem of traditional landed power is surrounded by 'blazing gas-lights', 'huge warehouses', 'magnificent shops', and 'some ancient factory built among the fields in the infancy of Mowbray' that together 'indicated its modern order and prosperity' (p. 88). Mowbray's rapid transformation from rural to urban occurred within the single lifetime of Chaffing Jack, who has 'lived in Mowbray man and boy for fifty years; seen it a village, and now a great town full of first-rate institutions' (p. 95).

In a curious inversion of the pastoral retreat and traditional pastoral values, the mills now attract rural migrants whom the locals regard as simple and uneducated:

> 'I pity them poor devils in the country,' said Mick; 'we got some of them at Collinson's – come from Suffolk they say; what they call hagricultural labourers, a very queer lot, indeed'.
>
> 'Ah! them's the himmigrants', said Caroline; 'they're sold out of slavery, and sent down by Pickford's van into the labour market to bring down our wages' (p. 98).

Pastoral's urban journey to the countryside is reversed, while a traditional pastoral trope, in which the unlearned simplicity of rural figures represented a reservoir of deeper knowledge which could be salutary for urban travellers to access, is no longer available. Meanwhile, Suffolk labourers and Mowbray millers are at the mercy of the same economic system. Something similar is evident in *Shirley*, in a conversation between Moore and his servant, Joe, where traditional pastoral divisions strain under Joe's preference for urban over rural: 'I reckon 'at us manufacturing lads i' th' north is a deal more intelligent, and knaws a deal more nor th' farming folk i' th' south. Trade sharpens wer wits; and them that's mechanics like me is forced to think' (p. 88).[26]

In *Sybil*, there is a yet more transgressive and liminal space than Mowbray, an urban centre (but not exactly a city) emerging within the countryside (but decidedly not rural):

> Wodgate was a sort of squatting district of the great mining region to which it was contiguous, a place where adventurers in the industry which was rapidly developing, settled themselves; for though [it was] deficient in those mineral and metallic treasures which had enriched its neighbourhood [it had] advantages [...] of a kind which touch the fancy of the lawless (p. 164).

Wodgate is 'land without an owner', where 'no one claimed any manorial right', and 'a district recognized by no parish; so there were no tithes, and no meddlesome supervision' (p. 164). Ben Moore persuasively argues that 'Wodgate reveals the lawlessness that results from a lack of structure, whether architectural, legal, or symbolic', but this transgressive space can also

[26] This inversion is also strongly evident in Elizabeth Gaskell's *North and South* (1854).

be read ecocritically.[27] Rich 'in fuel which cost nothing', an extractive land-scape attracts highly skilled metalworkers to a countryside 'to which neither Nature nor art had contributed a single charm; where a tree could not be seen, a flower was unknown, where there was neither belfry nor steeple, nor a single sight or sound that could soften the heart' (p. 164). Lacking either natural or Christian pastoral support, Wodgate is an ambiguous rural-urban monster, more marked than Snowfield as a point of breakdown of pastoral boundaries brought under strain by capitalist modes of production. It 'soon assumed the form of a large village, and then in turn soon expanded into a town of swarming thousands, lodged in the most miserable tenements in the most hideous burgh in the ugliest country in the world' (p. 165). While Hayslope and Deerbrook are still dominated by traditional landed power and the established church, here 'there are no landlords', 'no church', and 'no municipality, no magistrate, no local acts, no vestries, no schools of any kind' (p. 165). Apparently drawing on Disraeli's investigations of parliamen-tary blue-books on Willenhall in the West Midlands, he shows Wodgate as encapsulating the results of rapid, unplanned growth, and, through the impacts of industrial capitalism, effectively erases pastoral boundaries between rural and urban.[28]

Sybil is also striking in its representation of the socio-environmental impacts of industrial activities in the countryside. If attempts in the early chapters of *Adam Bede* and *Deerbrook* to achieve a pastoral vision subtly mis-carry, the descriptions here of Mowbray's mining district involve a starker defamiliarisation of the countryside:

> The last rays of the sun, contending with clouds of smoke that drifted across the country, partially illumined a peculiar landscape [...] A wilderness of cot-tages or tenements that were hardly entitled to a higher name, were scattered for many miles over the land; some detached, some connected in little rows, some clustering in groups [...] but interspersed with blazing furnaces, heaps of burning coal, and piles of smouldering ironstone; while forges and engine chimneys roared and puffed in all directions, and indicated the frequent pres-ence of the mouth of the mine and the bank of the coal-pit (p. 141).

This 'vast rabbit warren' is scarred by extraction capitalism, 'with canals crossing each other at various levels', 'heaps of mineral refuse or of metal-

---

[27]   Ben Moore, 'Disraeli and the Archi-Textual: Constructions of Authority in *Sybil*', *Modern Language Review* 110.1 (2015), pp. 47–68 (p. 56).
[28]   See Sheila Smith, 'Willenhall and Wodgate: Disraeli's Use of Blue-Book Evidence', *Review of English Studies* 13 (1962), pp. 368–84.

lic dross', 'whole rows of houses awry, from the shifting and hollow nature of the land', and occasional patches of 'grass and corn' appearing 'as if in mockery' (p. 141) of pastoral dreams. While Disraeli is most interested in the human toll on the miners, the novel provides some insight into the environmental impacts of what became a leading source of wealth in the Victorian countryside.

What we have seen of Victorian quarrying and mining in the countryside exemplifies what Naomi Klein terms 'extractivism', a 'resource-depleting model' founded in a 'nonreciprocal, dominance-based relationship with the earth' which, as Elizabeth Carolyn Miller observes, also involves a 'lack of regenerative capacity' of fossil-fuel resources, an exhaustion narrative that 'previews the mode of living that we all experience today, a way of life that proceeds by depleting the future'.[29] Although works like *Sybil* offer a primarily anthropocentric critique of mining districts, they are also like the proverbial canary in the coal mine in offering an early warning of environmental disaster.

In response to disruption and conflict, *Shirley* advocates restoration of the idyll through philanthropy and sympathy, but the efficacy of this approach is ultimately moot. While Shirley represents an idealised, old-fashioned landowner who (in bucolic fashion) keeps a herd of 'deep-dew-lapped, Craven cows, reared on the sweet herbage and clear waters of bonny Airedale' (p. 345) to provide free milk for her tenants, she is elegised as a type now passed away. Meanwhile Moore's economic visions have created a 'new industrial society'; as Hook and Hook suggest, 'present, past and future collapse into each other' in the final chapter in ways that indicate the price of Moore's success.[30]

Moore's plans for 'doing good' involve doubling 'the value of their mill property' by lining 'yonder barren Hollow with lines of cottages and rows of cottage-gardens' (p. 597). When his wife, Caroline, exclaims, 'And root up the copse?', Moore responds, 'the copse shall be firewood ere five years elapse', and predicts that 'the beautiful wild ravine' and 'the lonely slopes' will be covered in cottages, while 'the rough pebbled track shall be an even, firm, broad, black, sooty road, bedded with the cinders from my mill' (p. 597). Horrified by these presentiments of urbanisation, Caroline's fear that 'you will change our blue hill-country air into the Stilbro' smoke atmos-

[29]   Naomi Klein, *This Changes Everything: Capitalism vs the Climate* (New York, 2014), p. 169; Elizabeth Miller, *Extraction Ecologies and the Literature of the Long Exhaustion* (Princeton, 2021), p. 9.
[30]   Brontë, *Shirley*, pp. 31–2.

phere' (p. 598) is confirmed by the narrator's closing reflections, written elegiacally from the Victorian 'present':

> Robert Moore's prophecies were, partially at least, fulfilled. The other day I passed up the Hollow, which tradition says was once green, and lone, and wild; and there I saw the manufacturer's day-dreams embodied in substantial stone and brick and ashes – the cinder-black highway, the cottages, and the cottage gardens; there I saw a mighty mill, and a chimney ambitious as the tower of Babel (p. 599).

The collapse of pastoral boundaries is complete, the idyll lost to industrial modernity. Looking yet further back to a semi-mythic past that deepens the elegiac note while heightening the account of environmental loss, the narrator's housekeeper recalls the building of the first mill:

> One summer evening, fifty years syne, my mother coming running in just at the edge of dark, almost fleyed out of her wits, saying she had seen a fairish (fairy) in Fieldhead Hollow; and that was the last fairish that ever was seen on this countryside (though they've been heard within these forty years). A lonesome spot it was, and a bonny spot, full of oak trees and nut trees. It is altered now (p. 599).

As the Hooks point out, 'the natural beauty of the Hollow has been swept away by the stone, brick and ashes of the new industrialism', while 'the fading folk-memory of the "fairish" [...] further back in the pre-industrial past, hints at the imagination's inability to survive in the context of such a brave new world'.[31] It is not simply human imagination, however, that is threatened by the accelerating expansion of Victorian industry. The costs are environmental, the coterminous loss of fairies, oaks, and nut trees resulting from the remorseless impetus of a capitalism claiming absolute sovereignty over environment.

The presence of industry in the countryside in these novels speaks of a particular form of that violence, but it must not be forgotten that farming itself belongs within this category, and that all celebrations of the pastoral are attempts to obscure this vital truth. Giorgio Agamben's account of political sovereignty and Michel Foucault's concept of 'biopower' (both pointing to the self-assumed right of the sovereign in a state of exception to decide whether those subjected to its power live or die) can be adapted to what we may term environmental sovereignty: our assumption of an unquestioned

---

[31]   Brontë, *Shirley*, p. 32.

right to do as we will with everything we describe as nonhuman and label as resource.[32] It is this assumption of sovereignty that we see starkly outlined in Moore's lofty transformation of the Hollow, and in the state of Disraeli's mining districts.

Conclusion

All four novels reveal ways in which the Victorian countryside was rapidly changing through intensified industrial activity, through urban-rural traffic (physical, demographic, intellectual, religious, and cultural), and by the immersion of rural economic power (old and new money) in international exchange networks. Attuned to these changes, Victorian writers found older pastoral visions of a purely agricultural countryside inadequate, but rather than eschewing pastoral, they pursued inventive, self-conscious forms that blurred established conceptual boundaries between country and city, inverting or querying the traditional valorisation of the former.

The chief driver of the environmental sovereignty that we glimpse, however imperfectly, in these novels is our conceptual separation of the human and nonhuman (culture and nature) and the policing of these boundaries to justify the exploitation of that which is othered. Critics from diverse disciplines have sought to interrogate this fundamental binary construction, all in different ways sharing Michael Mack's desire to produce accounts that recognise 'the simultaneous interdependence of what has previously been conceived of as separate or opposed'.[33] Pastoral, meanwhile, is also rooted in these conceptual boundaries, constructing human and environmental realms that in the idyll are in harmony, and in the elegy in conflict. Pastoral, therefore, has always reflected the uneasy results of our dual impulse: to divide ourselves from the earth or to belong. Victorian uses of pastoral are particularly significant precisely because they resist its more

[32]   See Giorgio Agamben, *Homo sacer: Sovereign Power and Bare Life*, trans. Daniel Heller-Rozen (Stanford, 1998); Michel Foucault, 'Lecture 11', '*Society Must Be Defended': Lectures at the College de France, 1975–76*, ed. Mauro Bertani and Alessandro Fontana, trans. David Macey (London, 2004), pp. 239–64.

[33]   Michael Mack, *Contaminations: Beyond Dialectics in Modern Literature, Science and Film* (Edinburgh, 2016), p. 1. For a range of such commentary, see Jane Bennett, *Vibrant Matter: A Political Ecology of Things* (Durham NC, 2010); Dipesh Chakrabaty, 'The Climate of History: Four Theses', *Critical Inquiry* 35.2 (2009), pp. 197–222; Jesse Oak Taylor, *The Sky of Our Manufacture: The London Fog in British Fiction from Dickens to Woolf* (Charlottesville, 2016); Donna Haraway, *When Species Meet* (Minneapolis, 2008); Karen Barad, *Meeting the Universe Half Way: Quantum Physics and the Entanglement of Matter and Meaning* (Durham NC, 2007).

conservative elements, undermine its conceptual boundaries, and reveal a more troubled relationship between that which is constructed as nature or culture. Appearing long before the conceptualisation of the Anthropocene, but when the results of environmental damage were viscerally evident in skies, lands, and waters, Victorian pastoral fiction conjures a world of unease and anxiety that is curiously anticipatory of our own, and, indeed, borne from precisely the same phenomena.

2

Floating Cities, Imperial Bodies: Reading Water in Timothy Mo's An Insular Possession (1986) and Xi Xi's 'Strange Tales from a Floating City' (1986)

CAITLIN VANDERTOP

In reflecting on the fragile material ecologies of the former British Empire, postcolonial writers have shown how the transformations of the colonial era continue to shape the environmental vulnerabilities of the present.[1] This overlap between colonial pasts and ecological futures is especially visible, as this essay will suggest, in literary imaginaries of the 'floating city'. While floating cities and islands have featured in imaginative literature from Homer to Verne, they also surface at different moments in the specific history of Hong Kong. Dung Kai-cheung, in his 'fictional archaeology' published in the year of the handover from Britain, describes Hong Kong as a 'marvellous invention' and as a 'mirage' – an island 'born from the waves of the sea' whose towers extend into the air.[2] Writing in the same year, Ackbar Abbas remarks on the city's '"floating" identity' as a space of flows in which 'everything floats – currencies, values, human relations'.[3] More recently, Leonard Kwok-kou Chan has emphasised Hong Kong's status as 'a floating city' due to the uniqueness of its literary culture.[4] Across these accounts, metaphors of floating capture the distinctiveness of Hong Kong's identity, whether as a colonial entrepôt turned 'cosmopolitan' financial centre, or as an archipelago comprising over 250 islands and one of the most vertical cities in the world.

---

[1]   See, for example, Amitav Ghosh, *The Great Derangement: Climate Change and the Unthinkable* (Chicago, 2016).

[2]   Dung Kai-cheung, *Atlas: The Archaeology of an Imaginary City*, trans. Dung Kai-cheung, Anders Hansson, and Bonnie S. McDougall (New York, 2012), pp. xi, 45.

[3]   Ackbar Abbas, *Hong Kong: Culture and the Politics of Disappearance* (Minneapolis, 1997), p. 4.

[4]   Leonard Kwok-kou Chan, quoted in Sylvia Chang, 'Hong Kong: A "Floating City in Literature"', *China Daily* (13 September 2018), https://www.chinadailyhk.com/articles/150/198/29/1536806382699.html.

These floating metaphors also appear in an earlier wave of texts, written towards the end of British rule, where they serve to visualise Hong Kong's colonial transformation in the nineteenth century. A noteworthy example is Timothy Mo's historical novel *An Insular Possession* (1986), which draws on the image of the floating island to reconstruct Hong Kong's inception during the First Opium War. Although the novel imagines the region in the pre-colonial period as an archipelago (its '[i]slands spread over the waters on both sides', enveloped in ethereal cloud and ambiguously 'locked by islands or continent'), it focuses on the region's rapid transformation in the 1840s.[5] Amid the new watery world of the opium trade, the novel conjures a terraqueous landscape of floating warehouses, floating barges, floating batteries, floating hotels, floating brothels, and floating opium hulks serviced by the smaller vessels of 'fast crabs' and 'scrambling dragons', whose ability to float secures the regime's extra-territorial legality. While, for Mo, the existing 'floating villages' and 'sea-borne cities' of southern China are incorporated into the new circulatory system of an Anglo-American capitalist empire, a different narrative is provided in the Chinese writer Xi Xi's story from the same year, 'Strange Tales from a Floating City'. Here, the island's inception is imagined in mythological rather than historical terms through the sudden, surreal appearance of a city in the sky. Suspended above the ocean but below the clouds, this city 'floats' in a more literal sense, its residents suffering from a water crisis even as they dream, during typhoon seasons, of their separation from the raging waters below.

Read together, these fictions of a floating city articulate anxieties about the region's colonial history and its legacies, encoding political and environmental concerns into their representations of water. In one sense, the language of floating evokes Hong Kong's colonial construction as a process that defied the limits of the currents and tides, registering the 'hydrocolonial' nature of its expansion by way of large-scale land reclamations, hydraulic engineering and steam-powered riparian warfare.[6] Equally, narratives of the floating city affirm the imaginative power of water in the region's fraught political landscape, channelling ideas of separation and integration that anticipate conflicts over the territory's autonomy today.[7] Fictions from the late colonial

---

[5]   Timothy Mo, *An Insular Possession* (1986; London, 2002), pp. 427–8. Subsequent references to this work give page numbers in parentheses in the main text.
[6]   On the term 'hydrocolonialism', see Isabel Hofmeyr, *Dockside Reading: Hydrocolonialism and The Custom House* (Durham NC, 2022).
[7]   This is apparent in recent political slogans such as 'Be water!' and 'Reclaim the city!' It also speaks to such ongoing projects as the Hong Kong government's vast reclamation scheme, 'Lantau Tomorrow Vision', and the PRC government's 'Bay

period invite a closer reading of water's deep historical permeation of the city's political imaginary, just as they call attention to the environmental pressures that continue to exacerbate its political conflicts. Importantly, as literary texts, these fictions of floating cities also harness literary form to dramatise water crisis at private and experiential levels, adopting affective and bodily registers in their representations of individuals who are either cut off from water or linked by its processes of flow and circulation. Deploying water as method, these texts explore the complex relations between individuals and islands, viewing both as interconnected bodies that are enmeshed within, but also floating separate from, surrounding waters.

The role of water in literature, and particularly its ability to make visible the complex entanglements of bodies and environments, has been a subject of attention within the Blue Humanities. Scholars such as Elizabeth DeLoughrey, Isabel Hofmeyr, Astrida Neimanis, Stacy Alaimo, and Sharae Deckard, among others, have examined the literatures of water as they engender alternative modes of theoretical, political, and environmental understanding.[8] For Neimanis, water 'constitutes one of the so-called Anthropocene's most urgent, visceral, and ethically fraught sites of political praxis and theoretical inquiry'. Citing Jamie Linton's study of nineteenth-century hydrological discourses, which conceptualised 'modern water' as a limitless resource, Neimanis takes inspiration from feminist, queer and material ecocriticism to instead emphasise the human body's own watery constitution. The 'constant process of intake, transformation, and exchange', she observes, reveals our enmeshment in hydrosocial relations, complicating a discrete or 'dry' individualism.[9] Her concept of 'bodies of water' enables a theoretical reconsideration of the relationship between matter and consciousness, locating individuals amid the wider ecological systems, circulations, and flows by which they are constituted.

While water's ethical potential as a concept is now well-established in the Blue Humanities, recent scholarship in postcolonial ecocriticism has drawn attention to the way that the flows constituting subjects and environments are striated according to racialised logics and globally uneven levels of per-meability and vulnerability. Neel Ahuja, for example, is critical of those who

---

Area' discourse. Thanks to Jessica Valdez for pointing out the latter context.

[8]   Some of these critics appear in Laura Winkiel, ed., *Hydro-Criticism*, special issue of *English Language Notes* 57.1 (2019). See also Sharae Deckard, '"Waiting for the Master's Dams to Crack": Hydro-dependency, Water Autonomy, and World-Literature', *New Formations* 103 (2021), pp. 134–55.

[9]   Astrida Neimanis, *Bodies of Water: Posthuman Feminist Phenomenology* (London, 2017), pp. 2, 20.

embrace an antihumanist ethic without a corresponding materialist analysis of global ecological entanglements.[10] His own method emphasises the colonial histories that underlie ecosocial processes of consumption and waste as well as contemporary forms of carbon privilege. While a queer ethics of water invites theorists to map circulatory processes across species, scales, and systems, a postcolonial approach remains attentive to the material histories that perpetuate global inequalities in both the circulation of flows and the distribution of social vulnerability and environmental crisis.

Narratives of colonial Hong Kong as a 'floating city', this essay will argue, lend themselves to this postcolonial method, insofar as they combine an interrogation of the ethics of water with a materialist analysis of the circulatory system in which flows 'flow'. In Mo's novel, the British Empire is conceptualised as a vast circulatory system that redirects flows of liquid commodities (including opium, alcohol and tea) as well as elements (hydrogen, nitrogen, carbon) and power (water and steam). While these flows are seen to transform China's riparian environments, they also reconfigure the circulations of nutrients, fluids and stimulants within and between individual bodies. After discussing Mo's hydrocolonial aesthetics, this essay considers the 'floating city' as represented in both Mo and Xi Xi's texts. In the latter, the city's separation from surrounding waters generates a private and collective experience of water crisis, complicating postcolonial narratives of the floating city as a miraculous space. In different ways, then, water operates as a narrative vehicle that illuminates the entanglements of individuals and islands, while making visible the colonial contexts in which such entanglements are formed. Fictions of floating cities, I argue, attest to structurally embedded experiences of ecological vulnerability. In depicting the British Empire as a vast circulatory system that reorganises global flows of resources, these texts link past waves of hydrocolonialism to current struggles over postcolonial and environmental futures.

Hydrocolonialism and imperial circulation in *An Insular Possession*

An Insular Possession explores the historical events leading up to the cession of Hong Kong during the First Opium War (1839–42). Centring on the founding of a press in southern China, it also meditates self-consciously on the complexities of representing this history. Across 700 pages, Mo constructs a vast archive of historical and fictional sources, piecing together fragments

---

[10]   Neel Ahuja, 'Intimate Atmospheres: Queer Theory in a Time of Extinctions', *GLQ* 21.2–3 (2015), pp. 365–86.

from letters, scripts, diary entries, memoirs, court proceedings, and local newspapers (notably the new *Lin Tin Bulletin and River Bee*, as well as its rival, the *Canton Monitor*, which is based on the *Canton Register* founded by the Scottish opium trader James Matheson). Water, from the first chapter, serves as a metaphor and vehicle for the novel's narrative method. This role is prefigured in the lengthy description of the Pearl River (Zhujiang) which takes up the entire first chapter and which, as Elaine Yee Lin Ho notes, echoes the riverine tradition at work in writers such as Dickens, Conrad, and Naipaul, while also tapping into a Chinese novelistic tradition understood as episodic and digressive rather than linear and controlled.[11] The river, returned to compulsively across the novel, allows the narrative to 'float' between various locations on the delta, enabling readers to catch pieces of dialogue in media res as though overheard on its floating vessels, and to read fragments of letters as though intercepted from its passing mailboats. Because of the river's material role in facilitating the narrative, water sets the pace of its events, which flood or trickle according to the tidal forces enabling communication. Given that Mo has, elsewhere, compared writing to an act of hydroengineering, *An Insular Possession* can be read as a decisive example of 'hydrofiction', one that harnesses water as method.[12]

While the first wave of criticism in the 1990s viewed the novel's numerous water metaphors as part of a postmodern negation of historical objectivity, associating the text's tidal imagery with the porous, fluid borders separating history and fiction, past and present, water is also deeply historical and political in Mo's novel.[13] As John McLeod notes, it is important to retain a sense of the novel's critical agenda, which shows how discourses are determined by the power of the colonial archive and are not 'free-flowing'.[14] The two central characters, traders-turned-journalists who attempt to establish an alternative press, find themselves embroiled in the opium trade, despite their best

[11]   Elaine Yee Lin Ho, 'How Not to Write History: Timothy Mo's *An Insular Possession*', *Ariel: A Review of International English Literature* 25. 3 (1994), pp. 51–65.

[12]   Shirley Geok-Lin Lim, 'A Conversation with Timothy Mo', *World Englishes* 29.4 (2012), pp. 557–70 (p. 560). On the concept of 'hydrofiction', see Hannah Boast, *Hydrofictions: Water, Power, and Politics in Israeli and Palestinian Literature* (Edinburgh, 2020).

[13]   For a discussion of postmodernism in the novel, see Jennifer McMahon, 'Postmodernism in Bamboo Scaffolding: Timothy Mo's *An Insular Possession* and Xi Xi's "My City: A Hong Kong Story"', *Ariel: A Review of International English Literature* 32.1 (2001), pp. 119–36.

[14]   John McLeod, 'On the Chase for Gideon Nye: History and Representation in Timothy Mo's *An Insular Possession*', *The Journal of Commonwealth Literature* 34.2 (1999), pp. 61–73.

intentions. Mo depicts these characters boarding opium clippers to distribute print commodities, he imagines the leaves of books and Bibles being used to wrap opium cakes, and he evokes the many ways in which literature and translation are bound up with the production of knowledge used by opium militarists. By imagining literature as a waterborne commodity imbricated in the opium regime, *An Insular Possession* engages with water's material role in channelling discourse and determining its wider political effects.

In this way, the hydraulic imagination of *An Insular Possession* highlights not only water's imaginative possibilities but also literature's political imbrication in a process of 'hydrocolonialism', a term used by Isabel Hofmeyr to refer to the colonisation of water as both a material resource and an idea. While Hofmeyr shows how literature was bound up with maritime colonialism in southern Africa, her rubric can be applied productively to the riparian worlds linking India, China, and Southeast Asia during the opium trade. After Warren Hastings took command of the East India Company's opium monopoly in 1774, he began a project of transforming rivers to facilitate faster shipments; by the mid nineteenth century, steamships conquered the rivers, just as the record-breaking journeys of clippers dominated the oceans, shrinking the distance between Calcutta and Canton. In Mo's novel, the movement of Lord Napier's frigates is initially inhibited by the Pearl (which 'saves' Canton by being 'sinuous, supple, devious, deceptive, opaque, winding, shallow, and treacherous', and having 'more mouths than the Hydra'), yet, as the narrative proceeds, new steam technologies enable Anglo-American forces to overcome the limits of its currents and tides (59; 470). Across the delta, at Canton, Whampoa, Lin Tin Island, and finally Hong Kong, water is further colonised by floating barges weighing up to seven hundred tons, while the transformation of new treaty ports through hydroengineering gives concrete expression to the empire's hydrocolonial ambitions. If the opium trade involves the colonisation of and by water in these examples, it also colonises the idea of water. Just as the East India Company began to see sacred Indian rivers primarily as 'resources for accumulating capital', as Vipul Singh has argued, Mo's traders describe Hong Kong's waters as 'liquid capital'.[15] The novel's opium magnates, Jardine and Matheson, also draw on the narrative of the ocean as a 'lawless' space in an effort to exempt their floating barges from Chinese laws, regulations and taxes. Ironically, these characters also justify displays of force on the basis of their inability to distinguish between Chinese 'river-pirates' and legitimate traders, even as they themselves are depicted as

[15]   Cited in Mark W. Driscoll, *The Whites are Enemies of Heaven: Climate Caucasianism and Asian Ecological Protection* (Durham NC, 2020), p. 7; Mo, *An Insular Possession*, p. 438.

demi- piratical figures in the novel. Water, in this way, is not only central to the construction of an extra-territorial military, economic, and legal system in *An Insular Possession*, but it also channels the discourses through which this system is imagined and legitimised.

While *An Insular Possession* tells a story of hydrocolonialism in the Pearl River, it focuses specifically on a group of men engaged in more indirect forms of hydrocolonial practice. By staging their personal experiences on the river, the novel makes use of the language of flows to connect their bodies to the 'bodies of water' which their actions transform. This emphasis on flows is anticipated in the lengthy description of the Pearl given in the opening chapter. The river, the narrator suggests, is 'pregnant – with silt, with life, and with the opposite of life'; it carries silt and sewage, faeces and fertiliser, the corpses of children and 'drunken sailors', and the 'waste' of human life: 'Along with the rest of the city's effluvia the river sweeps the victims out to sea. Thus for centuries it has fulfilled the functions of road and, as rivers will, cloaca' (p. 9). The river here is not only a sewer or drain but, crucially, a cloaca or orifice serving as the opening for the digestive and reproductive tracts. In 'stain[ing] the clean blue sea yellow-brown, the colour of tea as drunk in London' (p. 9), its waters are linked not only to silt and sewage but also to the yellow-brown stains of tea and the slurry of opium. Through the river's imagistic blend of bodily waste and commodities that form the lifeblood of empire (the flows of tea, opium, and the alcohol imbibed by drunken sailors) the opening of *An Insular Possession* presents readers with a vision of empire as a vast metabolic and circulatory system, one which channels the fluids linking individual and imperial bodies.

Mo's representation of empire as circulatory system is grounded in colonial economic discourse. In 1834 the British East India Company's monopoly over the China trade was abolished by the British parliament, opening up commerce to a new era of 'free trade'. The problem diagnosed by the free traders of that year, when the novel begins, is described as an impediment to 'the proper workings of a new and cleansed system' (p. 103). Discussing the health of the empire, the traders claim that flows of silver are needed to govern India, just as flows of tea are needed to suppress revolt at home (asking '[w]hat would our own dangerous classes do without their precious tea?', p. 19). Their language channels the discourse in the colonial archive, which, as Lisa Lowe shows, was highly critical of the Qing government's prohibition of opium's import, emphasising the need to 'balance exchange' and prevent the so-called 'drain of silver' required in payment for tea.[16] Mo's traders, calling for 'free and unimpeded intercourse' (p. 27), seek to forcibly integrate the Chinese social body into the empire's circulatory system as a way of restoring the balance in the flows of drugs in one direction and stimulants in the other. Yet the novel also shows how ideas of balance for the British traders mean imbalance for the Chinese. For the latter, 'the massive outflows of silver ... [are] comprehended as a flux of life-sustaining fluids from the bowel' (p. 231). While these flows are emitted through Canton, the 'sphincter of the empire', their redirection through opium warfare constitutes a 'deadly stab in the vitals of the Celestial empire' (pp. 231, 483). The Chinese believe that the white men are constipated at an individual level (noting how they request herbs and rhubarb to clear their 'barbarian bowels', p. 34) and also at a national level, as they require the Chinese to relieve them of the blocked-up emissions of opium, wool and cotton. On both sides, the discourse seeks to relieve a blockage in the flows sustaining the imperial body.

Through this language of bodily flows and digestive blockage, *An Insular Possession* depicts empire as a vast circulatory and metabolic system that reorganises consumption and waste across the connected scales of bodies and ecosystems. While this echoes free trade discourse, it can also be seen to channel the language of health professionals and sanitation specialists in nineteenth-century colonial cities such as Hong Kong, where, due to the water-borne diseases exacerbated by shipping and land reclamations, urbanists were attentive to the fluid relations among bodies and environments, conceiving both as interlinked biophysical systems.[17] At the same time, the novel's metabolic language speaks to the specificity of Hong Kong's key commodity, opium, as both an economic and bodily regime. As Lowe writes, 'opium was more than simply an economic commodity. The distribution of the highly addicting drug that induced docility and dependence targeted the biology of the Chinese population'.[18] As with traditional drug commodities such as tobacco, tea, and sugar, opiates were not only a driver of colonial economies in Asia but they also altered biochemical processes within individual bodies, adjusting the rhythms of life and work among the social body. In Mo's novel, opium slows down Chinese bodies just as tea stimulates the English textile worker, so that a 'drug of a kind is at work in all corners of the [Atlantic] triangle' (p. 35). Mo's representation of empire as body is less

---

[16]   Lisa Lowe, *The Intimacies of Four Continents* (Durham NC, 2015), p. 103.
[17]   On the nineteenth-century discourse of urban metabolism, see Matthew Gandy, 'Rethinking Urban Metabolism: Water, Space and the Modern City', *CITY* 8.3 (2004), pp. 363–79.
[18]   Lowe, *The Intimacies of Four Continents*, p. 103.

a metaphor, in this context, than a formal response to imperialism's affective, energetic and biological transformations.

As Rebecca Duncan and Rebekah Cumpsty have argued, the body in postcolonial literature can serve to connect the ideological structures of colonialism to the material conditions with which they are imbricated.[19] Bodily registers and affects, they suggest, open up a materialist perspective on the way in which colonialism is lived and felt. But while they privilege the bodily experiences of marginalised postcolonial subjects, *An Insular Possession* focuses almost entirely on the bodies of white men. Not only does the novel linger graphically on their flesh but it also dwells on their near-constant intake of wine, whisky, beer, tea, milk, sugar, wheat, meat, tobacco, and other nutrients, stimulants, and fluids. Because acts of eating, drinking, smoking, and sexual intercourse occur frequently in the background, the characters' intellectual discussions about economics, politics, philosophy, and the arts are either accompanied or bookended by acts of consumption and excretion. Characters think about their bowel movements before proposing an idea; they discuss egalitarian principles over ludicrously carnivorous breakfasts; and they conclude discussions about the 'intercourse' of trade by visiting brothels, describing the Tanka boat girls as 'fresh meat' (p. 188). Before debating the necessity of war, for example, the men tuck into a 'dainty breakfast of paw-paw, kedgeree, cold fowl, ham, curry, eggs … washed down with a bottle of claret' (p. 77); similarly, they discuss 'the latest issues in Boston, London, Philadelphia, Fort William, Trincomalee, and Peking' over a 'relatively modest' dinner of 'York ham, fowls, beef, abalone, and local crayfish' accompanied by champagne and claret 'to aid digestion' (p. 25). Following a speech celebrating American democracy, to take another example, the narrator notes how '[t]he festivities concluded with a hearty breakfast at which beefsteaks and onions consorted democratically with champagne wine' (p. 355). While the narrator claims that the 'merchant adventurers have the sense of being far removed from the events which will shape their lives and fortunes' (p. 25), their acts of consumption create imperial intimacies that link their bodily actions to the distant events they discuss, connecting the flows of nutrients that sustain their bodies to the imperial commodities in which they trade.

The grammar of such passages is noteworthy. When long arguments about free trade are rounded off with a call for more wine or tobacco from a Chinese servant, these orders frequently form an abrupt end to the entire chapter or section, as in 'Cheong, claret' (p. 78). The grammars of the corpo-

---

[19]   Rebecca Duncan and Rebekah Cumpsty, 'The Body in Postcolonial Fiction after the Millennium', *Interventions* 22. 5 (2020), pp. 587–605.

real in these moments, as demands for food or drink are followed by a blank page, draw attention to the absent source of the commodities which sustain the protagonists' bodies. Through this technique, the text invites the reader to connect the white male body to the empire: both are configured as circulatory systems that rely on fluids, nutrients, and labour flowing in from outside the frame of the narrative itself.

While Mo's attention to colonial discourse makes *An Insular Possession* appear problematically one-sided – prompting several scholars to critique the absence of Chinese voices in the novel – his fixation on the bodies of white men can also be seen to effect a Cartesian reversal, by which the thoughts of those who are supposed to have extracted themselves from nature are reduced back to the demands and desires of the body. If Mo's inclusion of historical and archival documents on the Opium War maintains a Cartesian effect by describing economic ideas or reporting political events in a detached way, the literary dimensions of the novel – its hydraulic and metabolic language, its ability to stage colonial discourses in the empire's tiffin rooms, saloons, and brothels – prevents the reader from separating these ideas from the bodily needs of the speaker. In this way, the novel imagines a colonial world that is organised not so much around the ideas of white men, which are shown to be highly contradictory and shifting, but rather around the needs and desires of their bodies. By focusing on the white male body and the commodities that sustain it, *An Insular Possession* imagines empire as a system for centring precisely these needs and desires: a racialised system of flows.

In a recent study of ecological discourse during the Opium Wars, Mark Driscoll has identified the birth of a new system of 'Climate Caucasianism' in this period. Amid the unprecedented use of steam and coal-powered military technologies and the expanded matrix of shipping, cargo, and finance, the Opium Wars unleashed a new wave of extractivism that not only sped up anthropogenic climate change by causing profound alterations in hydrogen, carbon and nitrogen cycles, but also redirected flows of labour, nutrients, energy, and waste.[20] For Driscoll, this moment was one in which European-derived peoples advanced a racial calculus to justify a second wave of exploitation and indenture after abolition, 'peripheralising' Asia and configuring Asian and Pacific bodies as less valuable than white ones. This racial calculus can be observed in ship's logs through the divergences in the provisions for Asian lascars (who received not only less food but also less water) as well as in

---

[20]   Driscoll, *The Whites are Enemies of Heaven*. See also Andreas Malm on the British Empire's shift from 'flow' energy systems (such as water and wind) to 'stock' (coal-powered steam technology), *Fossil Capital: The Rise of Steam-Power and the Roots of Global Warming* (London, 2016).

the disparities found in insurance policies. It is also apparent in Mo's novel, which regularly depicts the casual devaluation of Asian lives through legal and financial modes of quantification. Throughout *An Insular Possession*, events proceed according to the extractive logic of the boys' adventure novel, as the young men of the trading house spend their days in the treaty ports drinking, eating, wrestling, racing, picking fights with locals, hunting local wildlife and soliciting sex; even the innocuous activities of the protagonists, who paint waterscapes, are marred by rickshaw journeys that reveal the unequal value placed on human energy according to race. Likewise, the white men regularly use 'clearing sticks' to injure passers-by, treating the Chinese as flora to be 'cleared' (pp. 49, 114), and separating singular (white) lives from the undifferentiated (racialised) mass. In the manner of the boy's adventure, everyday racial terror is described flippantly: the violent shattering of a young Chinese boy's skull, for example, is a trivial incident, as are the murders of three Chinese people by one of the traders, in retaliation for their suspected consumption of his dog. In both incidents, it is again worth paying attention to Mo's grammar and typography. The narrator returns to these deaths at the very end of the chapters, lingering on them briefly as if to draw attention to their inconsequentiality. By ending chapters with brief allusions to these moments, the text once again draws attention to what it leaves out; in doing so, it evokes the unequal system of representation, enunciability, and value that render these moments meaningful or interesting to the reader, drawing attention to the novel's (and reader's) own imbrication in the system of Climate Caucasianism it depicts.

Responding formally to the racialised dynamics of Anglo-American imperialism in nineteenth-century Asia, *An Insular Possession* imagines the birth of an imperial circulatory system that redirects flows of resources, depicting white male bodies as individual systems that *miniaturise* empire in this context. Imagining bodies energised by sugar and tea, made impulsive by whisky and beer, bulked up by animal proteins, and puffing smoke like miniature steam engines ('puffing fit to rival the *Jardine* steamer', p. 249), the novel invites a reading of the human as the product of a racialised system of flows. While theorists associated with queer ecology have brought attention to the flows that link humans to wider socio-ecological assemblages, using terms such as 'transcorporeality' to think across scales and systems, postcolonial ecocriticism draws attention to the uneven and racialised striation of these flows.[21] Neel Ahuja, for example, calls for a critical discourse attuned to the way 'racial divisions of climate emerge in the intimate scales

---

[21]   On transcorporeality, see Stacy Alaimo, *Bodily Natures: Science, Environment, and the Material Self* (Bloomington, 2010).

of contact between human social forms and ecologies of production and waste', arguing that '[t]he everyday activities of carbon-dependent industrial living connect one's bodily consumption and waste to the "stranger intimacies" of a shared atmosphere, slowly threatening other far-flung bodies, human and nonhuman'.[22] Attentive to the way that the effects of everyday practices can cause unintentional extinctions, his focus on interconnected biological systems creates problems of knowledge and agency, complicating a Romantic emphasis on feeling and intentionality. For Ahuja, 'queer inhumanism' offers an alternative account of the entangled lifeworlds that exist in 'the background of the everyday', compelling us to rethink 'our casual reproduction of forms of ecological violence that kill quietly, outside the spectacular time of crisis'.[23]

In confronting the spectacular violence of the Opium Wars with the casual violence of imperial consumption, *An Insular Possession* anticipates this queer inhumanism. If the novel's incidents of direct violence are all the more chilling for their casualness, they also highlight the difficulties of addressing systemic or 'slow' forms of violence, of that kind that determine who can eat a carnivorous breakfast or visit a brothel, for example, or who suffers from the wider effects of imperial consumption practices. This is highlighted when one of the novel's two protagonists, Walter Eastman, imagines harnessing the energy of Chinese bodies in the service of hydrocolonialism. He suggests that the Americans should tap into the labour pool opened up by the First Opium War in order to build canals across the U.S. Pacific Coast, sending twenty vessels of Chinese workers (described at the time as 'pig' labour) across the Pacific Ocean, with 'allowance made for the proportion who will perish on the voyage' (p. 162). His idealist co-editor, Gideon, finds this racial calculus repugnant, but Walter responds by asking whether sugar tastes sweet despite slavery, arguing that '[m]erely to exist is to be involved in the system others have created to tend to your daily needs' (p. 162). In one sense, Walter's argument provides a disturbing justification for indenture that appears to excuse his own inaction. Equally, however, his emphasis on the substances that nourish and sustain the human body, and this body's reliance on the exploitation of other subjects and species, draws attention to the indirect forms of violence perpetuated by empire's circulatory system of flows. If, then, *An Insular Possession* diagnoses this system, and shows how it is sustained through hydrocolonialism in the mid nineteenth century, its representational strat-

22   Ahuja, 'Intimate Atmospheres', pp. 369, 372.
23   Ahuja, 'Intimate Atmospheres', p. 372.

egies also anticipate what Neimanis terms a 'meaningful mattering of our bodies', inviting a corporeal mode of reading that responds to this system's global complexities.[24]

The floating city from Mo to Xi Xi

Despite the emphasis on global ecological entanglements in *An Insular Possession,* the title itself evokes a logic of insularity that contradicts these ideas. This title refers specifically to Hong Kong Island. Using militaristic and homophobic language, the editors of the *Canton Monitor* make a case for the acquisition of an 'insular possession' that will defend the imperial body, insisting on the need for 'manly and determined firmness' (p. 41). Paraphrasing Sir George Staunton's call to establish an 'Insular Position' on the Chinese coast, the editors claim that 'an unresisting submission' to 'acts of molestation' would be 'prejudicial to the national honour', declaring Britain's need for 'a floating island' that is less 'impregnable' (pp. 105, 141). Insofar as the logic of the insular possession disavows exchange through the language of impregnability, it echoes what Wendy Brown has described, in a different context, as the masculinist dimension at work in border logic, whose fantasies of impenetrability play out at the level of both the individual body and the collective national body.[25]

Even as the floating island is envisaged as a masculinist sanctuary from pregnancy, penetration and fluid exchange, the free traders write that '[i]t is our duty through the instrumentality of trade, to bring China into the family of nations and, indeed, into a free and unimpeded intercourse with... the rest of mankind' (p. 27). Hong Kong here becomes central to the plan for future 'intercourse', serving as a '*point d'appui* from which all China may in the fullness of time be opened' (p. 534). The heteropatriarchal language of the colonial press echoes one of the novel's main intertexts, Gideon Nye's 'Morning of my Life in China' (1873), which praises the British and Americans for 'breaching [China's] ponderous wall of exclusiveness'.[26] While scholars have viewed the expropriation of Hong Kong Island as less an 'opening' than an enclosure – insofar as it secured the 'trafficking of drugs, arms, and people', and inaugurated a 'new kind of racial capitalist and climate regime', as Driscoll argues – the language of 'opening', 'breeching', and 'intercourse' can

---

[24]   Neimanis, *Bodies of Water*, p. 1.
[25]   Cited by Etienne Balibar, 'Reinventing the Stranger: Walls All Over the World, and How to Tear Them Down', *symploke* 25.1–2 (2017), pp. 25–41 (p. 36).
[26]   Gideon Nye, 'The Morning of My Life in China' (Canton, 1873), p. 25.

be seen to naturalise colonial intervention by promising to integrate China into the heteronormative family.[27] As Anne McClintock has argued, '[t]he trope of the organic family became invaluable' within colonial discourse due to 'its capacity to give state and imperial intervention the alibi of nature'.[28] In the discourse of colonial Hong Kong, the island is imagined as the off-spring or 'progeny' resulting from (forced) intercourse between Britain and China. Esther Cheung has shown how historians as late as the 1990s continued to naturalise this history through 'familial and natal images such as "parents", "offspring" and "birth"'.[29] Yet, if nature operates discursively to authorise the power of those deemed male and mature in colonial discourse, then *An Insular Possession* also traces the ties that bind imperial bodies. Just as intergenerational family networks govern employment practices in both the trading houses and the colonial administration, so military allegiances are forged along racial lines, with the British referring to the Americans as 'brothers' and 'cousins' within the racialised hierarchy of the imperial family. Through the novel's emphasis on the exchange of blood and bodily fluids, empire in *An Insular Possession* is imagined as both a body and a family: one that forges new ties and disrupts existing ones.

Making these disruptions clear, the final chapters of Mo's novel depict the hydrocolonial transformation of the southern Chinese coast as an attempt to separate the region from its surrounding waters. At the end of the narrative, the acquisition of Britain's new 'floating island' is overshadowed by a water crisis: the construction of Hong Kong's fort and deep-water harbour, the levelling of the island's terrain, and the reclamation of the coastline are all imagined as misguided attempts to break free from the region's water ecologies and hydrological cycles. While the *Hong Kong Guardian* dismisses the 'teething pains of the infant dominion' (p. 651), it notes how the island's position makes it highly vulnerable to extreme weather events rather than being impenetrable. As characters are 'carried off' by cholera, typhoid and dysentery epidemics following two major typhoons that devastate the new port in the summer of 1841, the editors speculate on the 'noxious vapours' and 'foul miasmas of the air' (p. 660) collecting on the low, damp ground. Yet they also note how the Chinese are less afflicted: '[t]he natives say that the foreigners have been punished for disturbing the dragon which lives in the valley by their digging irrigation ditches and drawing-channels' (p. 660).

[27]   Driscoll, *Enemies of Heaven*, pp. 13–4.
[28]   Anne McClintock, *Imperial Leather: Race, Gender, and Sexuality in the Colonial Contest* (New York, 1995), p. 45.
[29]   Esther M. K. Cheung, 'The Hi/Stories of Hong Kong', *Cultural Studies* 15.3–4 (2001), pp. 564–90 (p. 572).

The evocation of one of Kowloon's nine dragons here, which echoes references to river deities elsewhere in the novel, is grounded in local knowledge about the effects of hydrocolonialism and its disruption to water cycles. This knowledge derives from the region's Indigenous and fisher communities, who, having already faced the consequences of the Han colonisation of Guangdong's fertile coasts, have experienced previous waves of hydrological instability. Similarly, the Sanyuanli incident, described several chapters earlier, is imagined as a misguided attempt on the part of the colonisers to battle against water. As Britain's sepoys fight against an 'aggravating, fluid enemy' in the rain, they encounter 'soft, self-dispersing, thinking flesh and blood', and attempt unsuccessfully to 'flog a jelly-fish, or the water which is both its element and main constituent' (pp. 619–20). Just as the 'fluid enemy' of the southern Chinese peasantry and the rain combines human and extra-human agencies in this image, so the river itself is described as an agent of hydro-resistance in the novel. Amid the ancient aquaculture of the Zhujiang, where, as Mark Elvin shows, practices of crop and excrement recycling were well in advance of other agricultural practices globally, the river derails the steamer by luring it onto paddies that appear to be water.[30] It is the marginal Chinese voices of the novel, moreover, which insist on respecting the river, warning that '*[t]he tides... are unpredictable and not to be harnessed to man's convenience*' (p. 363). In these moments, water serves both as a narrative force that sutures ecological entanglements across space and time, and as a source of ecological knowledge that encourages one body to learn from the other.

If Mo's novel confronts colonial insularity with the entangled ecologies of the Pearl River delta, a similar tension can be observed in an important work of fiction published in the same year: 'Strange Tales from a Floating City' (alternatively translated as 'The Floating City' and 'Marvels of a Floating City'), by the writer Xi Xi (西西).[31] This story borrows from a series of paintings by René Magritte to depict a city that, as Dorothy Tse explains, 'hangs in the sky between the clouds above and the sea below – that is, China and

---

[30]   Citing but working against Karl Wittfogel's view of China's 'hydraulic despotism', Mark Elvin discusses hydraulics as a complex source of power and even 'proto-democracy' in southern China, *Retreat of the Elephants: An Environmental History of China* (New Haven, 2004), p. 28.

[31]   Xi Xi, 'The Floating City', trans. Linda Jaivin with Geremie Barmé, Geremie Barmé and Linda Jaivin, eds, *New Ghosts, Old Dreams: Chinese Rebel Voices* (New York, 1992), pp. 416–24. The same translation is also titled 'Strange Tales from a Floating City' and published online: https://chinaheritage.net/journal/the-floating-city-浮城/. Subsequent references to this work give page numbers in parentheses in the main text. Xi Xi is the pen name of Zhang Yan.

Britain, respectively'.[32] 'The Floating City' begins by mythologising Hong Kong's colonial inception:

> Only our grandparents' grandparents witnessed how it all began ... There had been a violent collision of clouds lighting up the sky with flashes and roars of thunder. On the sea countless pirate vessels had run up the skull and cross-bones and fired their cannon nonstop. Suddenly the floating city had dropped from the clouds and hung in midair (p. 416).

If the storm clouds symbolise British forces during the First Opium War, the sea and its 'pirate vessels' are equally if not more threatening: '[t]he people of the floating city opened their eyes wide and looked down. The angry waves of the sea surged beneath their feet. The city could be overwhelmed by the waters' (p. 419). By imagining the ocean as a lawless space, the story resurrects anxieties about the floating city's extraterritorial legal status.[33] Importantly, it is not only the city that floats in Xi Xi's story: its residents 'dreamed they were floating in the air, neither rising nor falling. It was as though each of them was a floating city in miniature' (p. 418). While the people dream of ascending to the 'clouds' ('there would be hope for the city if it floated upward'), their dreaming is ultimately presented as compensatory: '[i]n their longing to fly, the people of the floating city keep looking up at the sky. But they can't take off... All they can do is dream' (pp. 420, 423).

Scholars have connected Xi Xi's surreal narrative style to the first Hong Kong novel, *The Drunkard* by Liu Yichang, which depicts the city through the stream of consciousness of the protagonist, whose perceptions include 'dream[s] of Hong Kong sinking into the sea'.[34] Observing how Hong Kong's writers have channelled the private aspirations and anxieties of its inhabitants, Leonard Kwok-kou Chan and Sylvia Chang describe the region as a 'floating city' due to the subjective qualities of its literature, noting how these open a window into the city's uniquely 'in-between' identity.[35] Cognisant of these subjective qualities, Dorothy Tse also remarks on the 'floating' quality of Xi Xi's language, identifying a 'tradition of resistance to the language of daily life' in Hong Kong's 'decadent' literature.[36] Noting

---

[32]   Dorothy Tse, 'Writing Between Languages', *International Writing Program Archive of Residents' Work* 834 (2011), pp. 1–2 (p. 2).
[33]   The story was published after the signing of the Sino-British Joint Declaration in 1984.
[34]   Liu Yichang, *The Drunkard*, trans. Charlotte Chun-lam Yiu, ed. Nick Hordern (Hong Kong, 2020), p. 5.
[35]   Chan, quoted in Chang, 'Floating City in Literature'.
[36]   Tse, 'Writing Between Languages', p. 2.

how 'the image of land or soil seldom appears in Hong Kong's literature', she argues that the city's writers consciously opposed themselves to, and cut themselves off from, the working-class and agrarian literature of mainland China in the 1950s and 60s. Echoing this tradition, 'The Floating City' emphasises the role of dreams in the construction of an insular territory 'cut off' from its surrounding waters.

Importantly, the story's focus on dreams of floating allows it to engage with the late colonial narrative of Hong Kong as a 'miracle city'. Drawing on the intertextual apparatus of the fairytale (an important genre introduced to the region by missionaries who translated Aesop's fables, as Mo also notes), the narrator writes that 'all the fables said that Cinderella would meet her prince on a white horse before midnight. Had the prince of the floating city been waiting close by as midnight approached?' (p. 421). In the 1980s, as colonial Hong Kong consolidated its role as a global financial centre, the language of the fairy tale filtered into discourses of the city's own spectacular 'rise' as a capitalist success story.[37] Echoing these, Xi Xi engages with the city's mythology of self-created wealth: 'With their willpower and faith, the inhabitants of the floating city toiled to create a liveable home. Within a few dozen years their efforts made the city vibrant, prosperous, and wealthy' (p. 417). Just as the city's dizzyingly vertical skyline becomes a symbol for its global ascension (its '[b]uildings stood packed together in rows on the ground; highways and overpasses writhed in the air', p. 417), so the idea of floating serves to illustrate the narrative of the urban miracle, mythologising Hong Kong's heroic ability to lift itself up from its surrounding environment.

Yet 'The Floating City' also goes on to complicate this fairy-tale narrative. Attentive to the problems and gaps in the city's narrativisation, the story, like Mo's novel, undermines the discourse of the floating city by dramatising a water crisis. In the sixth section, 'A Problem', the narrator explains that 'The floating city did not have any rivers, and the sea water was undrinkable. The city had to rely on the bounty of heaven for water' (p. 419). Residents, while afraid of being engulfed in the water below, have no access to life-giving fluids and must rely on the whims of the clouds. The section incorporates Magritte's 'Hegel's Holiday', a painting of a glass of water balanced atop an umbrella. While the painting dramatises a break with teleology, as the rain (cause) comes after the glass of water (effect), it also enacts a reversal of externality and internality, as the glass of water externalised for human consumption is placed on top of the umbrella. The narrator writes that '[p]eople treat

---

[37]   The story, as critics have noted, was written during a boom in local manufacturing in the 1970s and 80s, when Hong Kong 'transformed itself', Cheung, 'Hi/Stories of Hong Kong', p. 572.

water in different ways at different times ... people want to drink water when they are thirsty, they want it inside them. But on rainy days they use umbrellas to keep it out' (pp. 419–20). If residents attempt to distance themselves from fluids, thus maintaining what Neimanis calls a 'dry individualism', the story invites a psychoanalytic reading of the condition of both desiring and disavowing water, a condition evoked in the text as a collective 'neurosis' (p. 418). Confronting dreams of ascension with experiences of water crisis, 'The Floating City' provides a critical window into the psychic and affective complexities of inhabiting an 'insular possession'.

By emphasising water crisis, Xi Xi also shows how the late colonial narrative of the urban miracle depends on the separation of the city from its gestational waters and the flows that sustain it, from the resources that make financial accumulation possible, to the social-reproductive labour of the mothers and grandmothers who give birth to, and care for, urban migrants. Equally, narratives of the miracle city can be seen to repress the Indigenous water histories of a city that was less a single island than an archipelago of islands, islets, fishing villages, and 'floating' boat communities. Complicating the story of the city's sudden 'birth', the delta had been a regional centre of pearl fishing whose histories of settlement extended back at least nine centuries. In his essay 'Rediscovering the Rural in Hong Kong's History', Ho-Fung Hung argues that the Hakkas, Puntis and Tanka fishermen were 'sacrificed under the Hong Kong miracle and were repressed in the developmental discourse on Hong Kong's past'. As Hung notes, Hong Kong is regularly described as a 'fishing village-turned-metropolis', yet the residents of its floating villages and fishing communities were never 'a residual category in the social formation of a metropolitan Hong Kong, but an essential part of it'.[38] Read in this context, 'The Floating City' reproduces but also interrogates colonial and settler–colonial discourses that erase the city's water histories through their mythical construction of the urban miracle.

Xi Xi ends 'The Floating City' by drifting out of the city and gazing back at its residents from the outside. In this final image of a mediated city, the floating island becomes a fishbowl whose meaning is determined from both inside and outside. In floating beyond the city, the story draws the reader's attention to the relational meanings and circulations of images (including its own references to European surrealism and fairy tales) which contribute to the imaginative construction of both the city and the story itself. As with the floating narrative style of Mo's novel, which stages colonial discourses

---

[38]   Ho-Fung Hung, 'Rediscovering the Rural in Hong Kong's History: Tankas, Hakkas, Puntis, and Immigrant Farmers under Colonialism', *Hong Kong Cultural Studies Bulletin* 8–9 (1998), pp. 2–16 (pp. 2, 11).

by drifting across the river, 'The Floating City' can be read as another example of hydrofiction. Water, for Xi Xi as for Mo, becomes key to the narrative incorporation of multiple perspectives on the British Empire's hydraulic transformations, their political and environmental effects, and their modes of representation.

While *An Insular Possession* draws attention to the circulatory systems linking bodies of water at individual and imperial scales, as this essay has argued, 'The Floating City' offers insights into the subjective and experiential worlds that these hydrocolonial histories bring into being. In deploying water as method, both texts prefigure a postcolonial and queer-ecological attention to the unequal flows, circulations, and relationships that connect and separate bodies and territories, individuals and islands. Adopting a relational method, both writers interrogate and complicate fictions of floating cities by channelling the narrative and imaginative possibilities of water. In this way, they speak to the broader capacity of postcolonial literatures to reflect back on the fragile ecologies of the British Empire, allowing the reader to learn both from past waves of hydrocolonialism and from pre-existing bodies of ecological knowledge.

3

Sweet Food to Sweet Crude: Haunting Place through Planet

SAM SOLNICK

Merseycene Hauntings

At the University of Liverpool, we teach a module called 'Literature and Place' in which first-year undergraduates read a horror short story by one of our alumni, Clive Barker. 'The Forbidden' is a tale of urban decline, where an ambitious academic researcher visits a dilapidated housing estate and discovers that the city is haunted by a hook-handed killer, who smells of sweets and whose rotting torso swarms with honeybees.[1] This monstrously saccharine horror is known as the 'Candyman'. 'The Forbidden' might seem an odd choice of text for a module designed to encourage students to think about their degree programme and their chosen city of study in relation to questions of environment and decolonisation. They tend initially to see the Candyman as an overdetermined metaphor for the dangers of desire: for sexual fulfilment, for academic success, or, for those who pick up on the story's nods towards Merseyside's 1980s heroin crisis, for drugs. But there is, hiding in plain sight, another way to interpret the Candyman's candy. As Barker himself later explained, the Candyman's apian torso draws inspiration from the bee-infested lion's corpse on the front of tins of Golden Syrup, a product manufactured by the most famous corporation from Liverpool: the sugar behemoth, Tate & Lyle.[2] So perhaps the walking hive of the Candyman is a horrifying body politic: a beehive version of Thomas Hobbes's Leviathan, but with a distinctive additive? Maybe the Candyman is the spectre of sugar which haunts Merseyside: its original sin, its one-time sustenance, and, perhaps, its future doom?

---

[1]   Clive Barker, 'The Forbidden', *The Books of Blood. Volumes 4–6* (London, 1985), pp. 1–37.
[2]   Barker, cited in Jon Towlson, *Candyman* (Liverpool, 2018), p. 71.

This chapter takes Barker's image of a commodity-haunted city as entry point (and exit wound) to show that Merseyside is a particularly compelling site through which to think about the trans-scalar dimensions of environmental crisis, where the slow violence of political and infrastructural histories haunts landscapes, bodies and climate. As Elizabeth DeLoughrey argues, it is necessary to 'provincialize' the geological and ecological transformations of the Anthropocene, because a 'planetary scale needs to be placed in a dialectical relation with the local to render [both] their narratives meaningful'.[3] Such a dialectical relationship between part (place) and whole (planet) must be diachronic as well as spatial, necessarily 'entangled with the *longue durée* of empire and ecological imperialism'.[4] With its extensive relationships with both sugar plantations and the oil industry, Merseyside is more entangled than most.

Ecocriticism is often most generative when the environment is read (and taught) through place as well as text. This chapter provincialises the Anthropocene by analysing it through the Mersey-scene (or even, quasi-allegorically, as a 'Merseycene'). It puts work from different periods, regions, and genres in conversation with each other to offer new ways of reading texts *from* Liverpool in environmental terms. It also analyses texts or artworks created elsewhere but encountered *in* Liverpool, to offer new ways of thinking about the city's history and infrastructures in relation to broader environmental contexts. It does so first by offering an environmental long view on how writing from Liverpool represented the plantations at the high point of the triangular trade of European goods, enslaved peoples from Africa, and plantation cash crops from the Americas. Eclogues by the eighteenth-century abolitionist poets Edward Rushton and Hugh Mulligan conceive the revenge of the enslaved against the sugar trade in meteorological terms, by employing the image of the spirit-haunted storm. This figuration, binding together colonial enslavement and anthropogenic weather, is read alongside an awareness of the direct relationship between the racialised violence of plantation monocultures and the emergence of hydrocarbon capitalism and climate change. As Donna Haraway puts it, 'the slave plantation system was the model and motor for the carbon-greedy machine-based factory system that is often cited as an inflection point for the Anthropocene'.[5] The middle sections of the chapter then examine three examples of the long legacy of

---

[3]   Elizabeth M. DeLoughrey, *Allegories of the Anthropocene* (Durham NC, 2019), p. 10.
[4]   *Ibid.*, p. 10.
[5]   Donna Haraway, 'Anthropocene, Capitalocene, Plantationocene, Chthulucene: Making Kin', *Environmental Humanities* 6 (2015), pp. 159–65 (p. 160).

ecological imperialism, in and through Merseyside. Unequally distributed vulnerabilities to (un)natural disasters appear in a poem by the Jamaican poet Ishion Hutchinson, featured in a reading given in Liverpool in the wake of Hurricane Matthew in 2016. Public sculpture on the Liverpool docks memorialises oil and violence on the Niger Delta, reflecting on the Mersey Estuary's ongoing role in neo-colonial extraction and the petrochemical industry. A Frantz Fanon-inspired art-garden, nurtured with the community in one of the most deprived and diverse areas of Liverpool, explores the migration of plants and peoples to foster resilience. Finally, the chapter returns to Barker's Candyman, and in particular to his bees, to reflect on how they – like the city they spawn from – offer a way to think through the colonial, infrastructural, and ecological entanglements which haunt place and planet.

'Vengeance is mine', Sayeth the Storm

Writing about the figure of the storm in world literature, Sharae Deckard explains that 'if storms served throughout the imperialist imaginary as an intertextual, transhistorical metaphorics for rebellion, mutiny, and colonial insurgency, then in the postcolonial imaginary tempests, cyclones, hurricanes and typhoons have been linked to insurrection, slave rebellions, labour unrest, general strikes, anti-colonial liberation movements, nationalist movements, and socialist revolution'.[6]

What happens to the long literary history of the Caribbean storm in the light of what Jennifer Wenzel has described as 'reading under duress', her coinage to describe the struggle of literary criticism in the Anthropocene? To analyse texts with a long environmental perspective, we need to 'read and write in a mode adequate to history, answerable to the future' and in a manner alive to 'multiple forms of force at work in human and natural history'. There is a political sense of 'duress' at play here as the 'force of the state: political repression or coercion', such as the plantocratic violence of the colony. But, explains Wenzel, duress 'derives from *dūritia*, Latin for "hardness"; it shares this root with "endure."'[7] 'Reading under duress' therefore also refers to a 'hard', lithographic awareness of the planet-shaping geological forces that write human activity into the rock strata in the Anthropocene.

---

[6]   Sharae Deckard, 'The Political Ecology of Storms in Caribbean Literature', Chris Campbell and Michael Niblett, eds, *The Caribbean: Aesthetics, World-Ecology, Politics* (Liverpool, 2016), pp. 25–45 (p. 26).

[7]   Jennifer Wenzel, 'Stratigraphy and Empire: Waiting for the Barbarians, Reading under Duress', Tobias Menely and Jesse Oak Taylor, eds, *Anthropocene Reading: Literary History in Geologic Times* (University Park PA, 2017), pp. 167–83 (p. 170).

Some of the most important geological and ecological disruptions of the Anthropocene emerge with and through the linked processes of plantation colonialism and hydrocarbon capitalism.

The poetic figure of the hurricane-as-revenge swirls with different agencies and temporalities in eighteenth-century discussions of plantation violence, which endure and ramify still, in an era of climate change. Hugh Mulligan and Edward Rushton were part of a circle of poet abolitionists in Liverpool, a group which also included the minister William Shepherd and the lawyer William Roscoe. Rushton's 1787 'West Indian Eclogues' was his first major poem. It drew on his experience of the slave trade, gained working in the merchant navy from the ages of ten to nineteen, before he was blinded by an infection (probably trachoma) contracted while tending to the enslaved at sea. He returned to Liverpool to become an abolitionist and radical bookseller. Less is known about Mulligan, who came to Liverpool from Ireland and (Rushton's dedicatory poem indicates) died in the 1790s in relative obscurity.[8] Despite having no previous publications, two of his poems appeared in the major periodical *Gentleman's Magazine*, in 1783. Here, I focus on one version of 'American Eclogue', part of a sequence of four anti-slavery eclogues collected in his only published volume, *Poems Chiefly on Slavery and Oppression* (1788).

For Franca Dellarosa, both Rushton's and Mulligan's poems are examples of how the eclogue form allowed 'interaction with a disquieting and unstable present, where individual, local experience was materially intertwined with a global context'.[9] The centrality of the slave trade to the explosion of Liverpool's size and wealth meant that its citizens' experience of locality was haunted by an awareness of its human cost elsewhere, a sense of the city built on the bodies of others. As Mulligan put it in another poem, 'Epistle to Varro',

Where'er I turn, that trade I trace
Which marks Britannia with disgrace;
Suburbean gardens feast the eyes,
And blood-cemented villas rise.[10]

---

[8]   Edward Rushton, *The Collected Writings of Edward Rushton (1756–1814)*, ed. Paul Baines (Liverpool, 2014), p. 122. For a useful summary of Rushton's activities in Liverpool, see Baines's introduction.

[9]   Franca Dellarosa, *Talking Revolution: Edward Rushton's Rebellious Poetics, 1782–1814*, 2nd edn (Liverpool, 2021), p. 145.

[10]   Hugh Mulligan, *Poems Chiefly on Slavery and Oppression with Notes and Illustrations* (London, 1788), p. 34, lines 49–53.

Dellarosa describes both poets as writing in a context which 'short-circuited space and complicated time perception, suggesting the existence of multiple, simultaneous relations between the realities of Liverpool, England, and "Jamaica" [for Rushton], or "a plantation in Virginia" [for Mulligan]'.[11] The eclogue's quasi-dramatic form allows these abolitionist poets to ventriloquise the horrifying violence of plantations through their enslaved speakers. They use the desire for revenge to generate sympathy and foster abolitionist sentiment.

Three different types of revenge are present in 'West Indian Eclogues' and 'American Eclogue': 'plantocratic revenge' against the enslaved, the revenge of the enslaved against their abusers, and a sense of retribution which comes from 'on high' and is coded by storms. John Kerrigan describes 'plantocratic revenge' as violence against Black bodies, 'used to punish rebellious behaviour or to make an example of someone in order to deter revolt'.[12] Rushton's second eclogue instances this, when the enslaved Pedro is gibbetted for a week as punishment for rebellion, and left to die without food or water. Some of Rushton's contemporary reviewers felt 'West Indian Eclogues' should have focused more on these sorts of punishments than on the desire for revenge they prompted:

> there is some impropriety in making the Negroes, the interlocutors in these Eclogues, chiefly employ themselves in venting imprecations, and planning revenge, against their oppressors. It is doubtless extremely *natural* for them to do so: but as the principal design of this performance is to excite pity for the unhappy slaves, their various calamities, not their impatience, should have been chiefly dwelt upon.[13]

The criticism here actually reflects a central feature of Rushton's approach: to show the enslaved as feeling subjects, who desire revenge, rather than simply as victims. As Grégory Pierrot says of the poem, revenge 'is a passion any person with feeling can understand'. But, he explains, any such sympathy is complicated by anxieties about the morality of actually exacting revenge.

Most abolitionist writers (though, notably, not Rushton) pulled back from actually 'condoning, or even quite portraying retributive violence'. Instead, 'by imagining retribution spoken by the enslaved but performed by the "Most High"', especially in the form of the storm, poets could 'endorse

---

[11]   Dellarosa, *Talking Revolution*, p. 145.

[12]   John Kerrigan, 'Slavery and Revenge', *London Review of Books* (22 October 2020), https://www.lrb.co.uk/the-paper/v42/n20/john-kerrigan/slavery-and-revenge.

[13]   *The Critical Review, Or, Annals of Literature* 64 (December 1787), p. 434 [my italics].

the punishment of enslavers but retain moral righteousness and avoid being accused of stoking the fires of slave revolt'.[14] Take the start of 'American Eclogue', where ghosts haunt weather and landscape:

> Whilst the loud storm amidst the mountains howls
> And light'ning gleams, and deep the thunder rolls.
> Beneath the leafless tree, ere morn arose
> The slave ADALA thus laments his woes:
> "Ye grisly spectres, gather round my feet,
> From caves unblest, that wretches groans repeat!
> Terrific forms from misty lakes arise!
> And bloody meteors threaten thro' the skies!
> Oh ! curs'd destroyers of our hapless race,
> Of human-kind the terror and disgrace!
> Lo! Hosts of dusky captives, to my view,
> Demand a deep revenge! Demand their due![15]

Adala's individual inflamed passion mingles with the force of a murdered multitude that arises from the landscape to demand vengeance. Elena Spandri describes the passage as a kind of 'gothicized mindscape' where the speaker's self-reflective narrative 'opens up a distance between the real pain of the sufferers and the vicarious pain of the spectators involved in the dynamics of sympathy'.[16] In Mulligan's eclogue both justice and revenge remain unfulfilled. Adala displays a passivity that longs for revenge, but does not enact it. Rather the poem revolves around an abolitionist sensibility which is clearest in Adala's plea:

> Oh hear a suppliant wretch's last sad prayer!
> Dart fiercest rage! Infect the ambient air!
> This pallid race, whose hearts are bound in steel,
> By dint of suff'ring teach them how to feel.[17]

The words are directed to the 'pallid race' living in Liverpool and other cities enriched by enslavement. Spandri argues that the transmutation of Adala

---

[14] Gregory Pierrot, '*Droit du Seigneur*, Slavery, and Nation in the Poetry of Edward Rushton', *Studies in Romanticism* 56.1 (2017), pp. 15–35 (p. 19).
[15] Mulligan, *Poems Chiefly on Slavery and Oppression*, p. 2, lines 13–24.
[16] Elena Spandri, '"Can fancy add one horror more?" Radical Sympathy in Hugh Mulligan's Eclogues Against the Empire', *La Questione Romantica* 8.1–2 (2016), pp. 31–48 (pp. 37–8).
[17] Mulligan, *Poems Chiefly on Slavery and Oppression*, p. 6, lines 143–6.

from 'dehumanized captive' into 'sentimental man of feeling' complicates 'the compassionate, but potentially reifying, gaze of the far-off European citizen'.[18] This is true, but it is a move that both undermines Adala's agency to take revenge and attenuates the force of that imagined retribution. In this, 'American Eclogue' reflects other poems of the time, such as William Cowper's 1788 'The Negro's Complaint', which saw in the storm an image of retribution from on high against enslavement, for 'Vengeance is mine, sayeth the Lord' (Romans 12.19). As Pierrot explains, in 'surrendering revenge to divine agency expressed in the elements, speakers in these poems find for their pain a form acceptable to all that allows them not to stain the moral righteousness of their anger'.[19]

However, coding revenge in elemental terms removes agency from the enslaved. What marks Rushton's eclogues out from many other poems of the period is that the enslaved have both subjectivity and, at least for the character of Loango, in the final eclogue, retaliatory agency. Revenge is not just imagined but plotted and, eventually, enacted. It is interesting that some of this plotting occurs while the enslaved characters are preparing their food. Loango mentions the yams and plantains grown, presumably, in his garden, and other characters celebrate the cultivation of these staples in Africa. As Sylvia Wynter argues, the cultivated 'plots' of the enslaved provided not only sustenance outside of the plantation monoculture, but a space to plot revolt (and hence a space, later, for the plot of the Caribbean novel).[20] In recent discourse around the concept of the 'Plantationocene', the plot, and the tradition of cultivation it reflects, serves as an icon of Black agency as 'a creative source of hope, vision, and perseverance. Within the plot, we find relational modes of being central to the emergence of radical foodways enabling survival and social cohesion'.[21]

Rushton's eclogue closes with two lines where Loango, 'with frenzy fir'd', takes revenge for the rape of his wife.[22] His vengeance is wrapped up, however, in the pathetic fallacy of the storm. In a long speech before he acts, he pleads with the elements to wreak a broader violence on the people and technologies of the plantation itself:

---

[18] Spandri, 'Can fancy add one horror more?', p. 38.
[19] Pierrot, 'Droit Du Seigneur, Slavery, and Nation', p. 18.
[20] Sylvia Wynter, 'Novel and History, Plot and Plantation', *Savacou* 5.1 (1971), pp. 95–102.
[21] Janae Davis *et al.*, 'Anthropocene, Capitalocene, ... Plantationocene? A Manifesto for Ecological Justice in an Age of Global Crises', *Geography Compass* 13.5 (2019), p. 8.
[22] Rushton, *Collected Writings*, p. 55, lines 111–12.

Roar on, fierce tempests: – Spirits of the air
Who rule the storms, oh! Grant my ardent pray'r.
Assemble all your winds, direct their flight,
And hurl destruction on each cruel White: –
Sweep canes, and Mills, and houses to the ground,
And scatter ruin, pain, and death around.[23]

Rushton's spirit-haunted hurricane is shot through with different temporalities, where the present and the possible swirl together. For Deckard, this
is a central feature of the storm trope in Caribbean literature: tempests (as
denoted by their Latin root *tempus*, 'a time of occasion and opportunity')
often indicate a particular moment of *kairos*, a moment of critical reconfigu-
ration which ruptures the smooth progress of chronological time (*chronos*).[24]
The storm that reflects Loango's revenge also gestures towards a broader
moment of political transformation, insurrection against oppression, which
anticipates the Haitian revolution a few years later.

When I first encountered 'West Indian Eclogues', after a colleague had
set Rushton's text on 'Literature and Place', I found myself unable to read
it without seeing his sense of rebellion-*as*-weather haunted by my own sense
of a revolution *in* the weather, which typifies our own kairotic moment of
climate crisis. This strange, anachronistic experience of encountering the
poem reflects an aspect of Wenzel's 'reading under duress'. She asks us to
consider the ways 'meaning and justice' are 'connected to the shapes we
assume time and history to have', but also to consider what happens when
we extend this across a geological or climatological scale.[25] To think about
Rushton or Mulligan in these terms is to see their meanings, and especially
their powerful sense of injustice, ramify and distort across scales which
rupture conventional notions of temporality and causality. Loango's vision
of the apocalyptic storm reaches into the present.

Resource extraction from the plantations 'underwrote the birth of industry
and urban settlement and arguably provided the impetus and even model for
factory production' that inaugurated the shift to hydrocarbon capitalism.[26]
The sugar flowing through Liverpool was a vital ingredient in the emergence
of the coal-fired infrastructure of North-West England at the time Rushton

[23]   *Ibid.*, pp. 53–4, lines 29–34.
[24]   Deckard, 'Political Ecology of Storms', p. 25.
[25]   Wenzel, 'Stratigraphy and Empire', p. 168.
[26]   Wendy Wolford, 'The Plantationocene: A Lusotropical Contribution to the
Theory', *Annals of the American Association of Geographers* 111.6 (2021), pp. 1622–39
(p. 1623).

and Mulligan were writing, not just financing the factories but fuelling those who worked within them. Sidney Mintz has argued, for instance, that factory labour was supported by newly affordable sugar-based foodstuffs which offered quick calories, and, when sweetening tea and coffee, functioned as appetite suppressants, thereby enabling an often undernourished workforce to labour for longer.[27] Moreover, the plantations inaugurated fundamental transitions in agriculture and the world-food-system which continue to shape the climate, initially through the shift to monocropping, and then intensified through the emergence of other forms of extractive, input-intensive farming, including the growth of fertilisers and the methane emissions and rainforest destruction of large-scale meat production.[28] The violence of the plantation endures as climate change.

Unnatural Disaster

The spirit-haunted storms of the Liverpool abolitionists offer an allegory for thinking about climate change. In his study of 'geohistorical poetics' in eighteenth-century poetry, Tobias Menely finds what he calls a 'climatological unconscious' that typifies contemporary criticism (and society at large). Such a climatological unconscious relies on 'suppositions about literary mediation and historical context premised on the analytic separation of society from the Earth', which is itself based on a misplaced sense of human agency, 'a symptom of the fossil-fuel-enabled fantasy of an escape from planetary vicissitude'.[29] To read 'under duress' is to rupture that separation. Rushton and Mulligan's storms are a striking image for climate change, but not in the trivial sense that they imagine human-forged changes in the weather, nor even because in uncanny fashion, they locate a driver for anthropogenic environmental change in the radical upheavals of colonialism and enslavement, but because hurricanes are not what they once were.

Carbon emissions mean that hurricanes are no longer easily thought of as natural disasters (indeed, as discussed below, no disaster is ever truly natural). Their increasing frequency and intensity have come to embody a changing climate that, like the storms themselves, amalgamates human and nonhu-

---

[27]   Sidney W. Mintz, *Sweetness and Power: The Place of Sugar in Modern History* (London, 1986).

[28]   For a useful summary of the relations between land use and climate emissions, see Natalie M. Mahowald *et al.*, 'Are the Impacts of Land Use on Warming Underestimated in Climate Policy?', *Environmental Research Letters* 12.9 (2017), pp. 1–10.

[29]   Tobias Menely, *Climate and the Making of Worlds: Toward a Geohistorical Poetics* (Chicago, 2021), p. 35.

man agencies, and therefore remains fundamentally resistant to control. As Menely explains,

> What appeared to be a vast increase in human productive power turned out to be a disruption of Earth system processes that catastrophically rebounds on human world making, exposing the limits of our agency, the vulnerability of our infrastructure, and the inadequacy of our political institutions. The shock of the Anthropocene is not the geologic scaling up of the human – which is, after all, a story we have been telling for two centuries – but the fact that human societies have succeeded in intensifying planetary processes in ways that reveal our inability fully to control, contain, and capture the Earth's energies.[30]

Due to the hydrocarbon energy regime it helped unleash, the plantation violence that Rushton and Mulligan's poems sow into the wind is reaped in the whirlwinds of the present and future storms which dominate the climate-change imaginary.

My reading of abolitionist storms here harbours an elision. It transmutes quasi-apocalyptic visions of future revenge against colonial oppression into an uncanny anticipation of climate change. But to turn global heating into a planetary punishment for the sins of the past – to see it as just desserts for the barbarity of the sugar trade – is both compelling and grotesque: those desserts are unjust, because they are unequally distributed. Climate change may indeed one day sweep away the apparatus of neo-colonialism, but generally it is those territories least responsible, and which have already experienced the political and environmental violence of colonialism, who will be – are being – hit hardest and first. Discourse about the Anthropocene always needs to be wary about emphasising the global and the future eco-apocalyptic without recognising how specific inequalities and injustices emerge at different places and times. Scaling-up from plantation to planet too quickly risks evacuating the geographical and historical particularity of colonialism in the Caribbean.

Scholars writing from decolonial and indigenous perspectives have pointed out that the reality of the Anthropocene and climate change '–or at least all of the anxiety produced around these realities for those in Euro-western contexts – is really the arrival of the reverberations of that seismic shockwave into the nations who introduced colonial, capitalist processes across the globe in the last half-millennium in the first place.'[31] Reading

---

[30] *Ibid.*, p. 211.

[31] Heather Davis and Zoe Todd, 'On the Importance of a Date, or Decolonizing the Anthropocene', *ACME: An International E-journal for Critical Geographies* 16 (2017), pp. 761–80 (p. 774).

the long tradition of hurricanes in Caribbean literature in terms of future
climate change risks downplaying the specificity of these storms' 'provincial'
impact, in favour of how they reflect planetary shifts in weather systems.
It embodies how discourse around climate change and the Anthropocene
gets stuck on 'novelty of crisis rather than being attentive to the historical
continuity of dispossession and disaster caused by empire'.[32] The arts' particular capacity to foster forms of attentiveness does not rest in their conveying information about environmental crisis (though they can sometimes do
this). Attentiveness emerges through the affective and cognitive processes of
reading, viewing, or listening. Consequently, where, and indeed when, we
encounter a poem, performance or artwork matter.

In late 2016 my university department invited the Jamaican poet Ishion
Hutchinson to Liverpool. One of the poems he read was his 'After the Hurricane':

> After the hurricane walks a silence, deranged, white as the white helmets
> of government surveyors looking into roofless
>
> shacks, accessing stunned fowls, noting inquiries
> [...]
> they draw tables to show the shore
>
> has rearranged its idea of beauty for the resort
> villas, miraculously not rattled by the hurricane's[33]

Hutchinson has described the poem as an attempt to render the experience of
living 'with and through' the 'double apocalypse' of the hurricane and of past
enslavement in an area of Jamaica still associated with sugar production.[34]
This doubleness is reflected in the connotations that swirl around the eerie
whiteness at the poem's opening: white colonialism, the whiteness of sugar,
a 'deranged' white 'silence' in the face of Caribbean suffering, and the 'white
helmets' of government surveyors who are mostly concerned with the still-
standing resorts catering to white tourism (the infrastructure for emissions-

---

[32]   DeLoughrey, *Allegories of the Anthropocene*, p. 2.
[33]   Ishion Hutchinson, *House of Lords and Commons: Poems* (New York, 2016),
p. 15. A full version of the poem can be found at https://www.poetryinternational.
com/en/poets-poems/poems/poem/103-28374_AFTER-THE-HURRICANE. The
reading took place in 19 Abercromby Square, a building which was, ironically, initially intended to be an unofficial embassy for the Confederacy during the American
Civil War.
[34]   Ishion Hutchinson, 'After the Hurricane', Lift Every Voice project (2020), https://
www.africanamericanpoetry.org/media-library/ishion-hutchinson-after-the-hurricane.

spouting holidaymakers is built of sterner stuff than local housing is). Their rationalising tables and inquiries function as a reminder that a logic-based bio-politics incommensurate with the scale of threat is, in fact, what Achille Mbembe would describe as a deathly necropolitics, which dictates who matters and who perishes.[35]

What made Hutchinson's November 2016 reading particularly poignant was the awareness of Hurricane Matthew tearing through the Caribbean a month earlier. The storm left Jamaica relatively unscathed, but Haiti was hit hard (with over five hundred deaths and hundreds of thousands of destroyed homes), due to its limited recovery from the cataclysmic earthquake of 2010, which lead to over 220,000 deaths. Unlike hurricanes, tectonic activity is not linked to climate change, but the human factors which made both into a disaster overlap. Neither earthquakes nor hurricanes are 'natural disasters'; both are better described as 'social disasters', says geographer Neil Smith, describing how 'in every phase and aspect of a disaster – causes, vulnerability, preparedness, results and response, and reconstruction – the contours of disaster and the difference between who lives and who dies is to a greater or lesser extent a social calculus'.[36] Haiti is profoundly vulnerable in this way because of a variety of linked factors: a crippling debt-cycle (initiated as punishment for the Haitian Revolution of 1791–1804), which affects its capacity for maintaining levels of medical care, sewage, and housing; the population displacements and land clearances of the Haitian American Sugar Company (HASCO) who began production in 1918 and left in 1987; 98 per cent deforestation tied to industrial agriculture, and the use of wood for fuel which leaves the landscape prone to infrastructure destroying mudslides; and, finally, Haiti's position in one of the most hurricane-prone areas on the planet, where the intensity and frequency of storms are only likely to increase in a climate warmed by carbon emissions from elsewhere.[37]

Near the entrance of Liverpool's International Slavery Museum stands a sculpture entitled *Freedom!* where distorted faces loom out of junk and metal. Created by Haitian sculptors from the Atis Rezistans collective, in collaboration with Port-au-Prince artist Mario Benjamin, the artwork was commissioned to mark the bicentenary of abolition and, the museum's website indicates, to highlight slavery's after-effects of global inequality,

[35] Achille Mbembe, *Necropolitics* (Durham NC, 2019).
[36] Neil Smith, 'There's No Such Thing as a Natural Disaster', *Items: Insights from the Social Sciences* (2006), https://items.ssrc.org/understanding-katrina/theres-no-such-thing-as-a-natural-disaster.
[37] On Haiti after the earthquake, see Junot Diaz, 'Apocalypse', *Boston Review* (2011), https://bostonreview.net/articles/junot-diaz-apocalypse-haiti-earthquake.

debt, food injustice, and the slow violence of millions working 'in unhealthy, dangerous – even life-threatening – conditions'.[38] One effect of positioning the sculpture within the dockside memorialisation of colonialism's triangular trade is a reminder to be attentive to the ways that the Mersey Estuary is not merely a key historic site of colonial extractivism (with all its planet-shaping aftershocks), but is also intimately bound up with ongoing neo-colonial environmental and political violence.

Oil's Living Memorials

With every sugar rush there is a sugar crash. In the mid-1980s Liverpool suffered mass unemployment and depopulation. The increasing use of containers for transport reduced the numbers employed on the docks, and both union activity and shifts in commodity prices led to the exodus of major manufacturers (including the car company British Leyland, and, significantly, Tate & Lyle). Core to attempts to regenerate Liverpool city centre, which began in the 1980s and strengthened after the city became the European Union's 'Capital of Culture' in 2008, was the transformation of the Albert Dock warehouses into a cultural and tourist space, which now houses the Tate Liverpool gallery, the International Slavery Museum and, on the adjacent Pier Head (ironically, near where a group of sailors tried to murder the abolitionist Thomas Clarkson), the Museum of Liverpool.

We encourage our 'Literature and Place' students to visit the docks and museums to help them understand the violent history of Liverpool, and in particular the long processes of extractivism which helped forge the city and the university where they find themselves, and which are still in operation.[39] One of the key works we show them, alongside the Liverpool docks, is photo documentation of a large bus sculpture called 'The Living Memorial', by Nigerian-born, British artist Sokani Douglas-Camp, which was installed outside the International Slavery Museum in 2009.[40]

The sculpture, commissioned by the activist group *Platform*, was topped with oil drums featuring the names of the so-called Ogoni 9: Baribor Bera, Saturday Dobee, Nordu Eawo, Daniel Gbooko, Dr Barinem Kiobel, John Kpuinen, Paul Levera, Felix Nuate, and, most famously, the writer-activ-

---

[38]   Photo and commentary at 'Freedom! Sculpture', National Museums Liverpool (2007), https://www.liverpoolmuseums.org.uk/freedom-sculpture.
[39]   The course convener, Dr Natalie Hanna, instigated this process.
[40]   Photograph at Platform, 'Release the Bus Memorial NOW: Artists, Campaigners and Others Speak Out!' (2015), https://platformlondon.org/2015/11/06/release-the-bus-memorial-now-speak-out.

ist Ken Saro-Wiwa. These were members of a non-violent protest group, 'Movement for the Survival of the Ogoni people' (MOSOP), which stood against environmental degradation on the Niger Delta, and was particularly critical of both the Nigerian Government and Royal Dutch Shell. The nine were executed by hanging on the 10 November 1995, after a highly criticised trial which led to Nigeria's suspension from the Commonwealth. After a lawsuit brought by Saro-Wiwa's son, Shell paid over fifteen million dollars as a settlement, though without admitting guilt.[41]

In bringing the bus to sites with histories of migration and colonialism, such as Peckham and Liverpool, Platform conceived of it as a 'travelling memorial', an 'antidote to the colonial notion of fixed, figurative monuments'.[42] Part of its function, argues Christiane Scholte, was to dramatise what Amitav Ghosh famously calls the 'muteness of the oil encounter', particularly in relation to the experience of indigenous populations.[43] Douglas-Camp herself said that she also wanted to foreground a broader sense of interconnection, and that the sculpture showed 'oil, transport, environment ... how vulnerable we all are ... tying Nigeria and the UK together'.[44]

The central thrust of the so-called 'infrastructural turn' in the humanities is that 'it would be folly to imagine knowing ourselves without also knowing our embeddedness in a network of large and sophisticated technological artifacts'.[45] It is here that the arts provide a crucial role, not just in mapping that embeddedness but also in *feeling* it, particularly in a port city whose maritime position and historical proximity to manufacturing leave it deeply embedded within the UK's energy infrastructure. As an exercise designed to challenge my students to think about different types of vulnerability and connectivity, I ask them to go and stand at Pier Head (or, better still, the deck of the Mersey Ferry) and to look back to where the 'Living Memorial' had stood, outside the International Slavery Museum. Then I ask them to spin around, to let their eyes pass Tate Liverpool (funded by sugar wealth and, until Platform and others forced them to relinquish it, oil sponsorship from BP) and the dockside railway (reminding them that the 1830 Liverpool to Manchester

---

[41]   See Rob Nixon, *Slow Violence and the Environmentalism of the Poor* (Cambridge MA, 2011), pp. 120–44.

[42]   Cited in Christiane Schlote, 'Oil, Masquerades and Memory', Gordon Collier *et al.*, eds, *Engaging with Literature of Commitment. Volume 1: Africa in the World* (Leiden, 2012), pp. 241–61 (p. 252).

[43]   *Ibid.*, p. 250.

[44]   Cited in Victoria Brittain, 'Ken Saro-Wiwa: A Hero for Our Times', *Race & Class* 56.3 (2015), pp. 5–17 (p. 8).

[45]   Michael Rubenstein, Bruce Robbins, and Sophia Beal, 'Infrastructuralism: An Introduction', *Modern Fiction Studies* 61.4 (2015), pp. 575–86 (p. 585).

passenger line is the origin of hydrocarbon-fuelled mass transit). Then they look out over the water to Tranmere Oil Depot (built by Shell, owned by them until recently, and one of the main landing sites for sweet crude from Nigeria), past Port Sunlight (built by Lever Brothers, beneficiaries of twentieth-century enslavement in the Congo, and which, as Unilever, have been accused of using suppliers which destroy forests to plant palm oils). Then students gaze towards Runcorn (key site of the UK's petrochemical industry), Ellesmere Port (where Innospec are one of the world's last manufacturers of leaded petrol), and the UK's second-largest oil refinery, Stanlow (also built by Shell). I tell them to take in that information; then to breathe in and out, to imagine the emissions in their lungs, to feel themselves embedded in these living memorials of the estuary, as a planet-shaping landscape. It is only after doing this, I tell them, that they should look down at the Mersey's water, and ask themselves how far it might rise.

Cultivating Resilience

Anyone who has taught undergraduates or schoolchildren about the environmental crisis has most likely encountered a common pedagogical challenge. On the one hand, there is a desire to provoke engagement through communicating the urgency, causes, and complicities of the situation. On the other, there is the need to be wary of overloading students with the negative affects which may then arise, with anxiety, anticipatory grief, or melancholia. This difficult negotiation is itself reflected in a 'tic' which Heather Houser identifies in fiction and non-fiction about climate change: the obligatory note of hope at the end.[46]

Yet while compensatory hopefulness always risks false (or indeed, following Lauren Berlant, 'cruel') optimism, environmentally aware art and literature can articulate cautious hopes for the future without erasing the long history of ecological-imperial violence and environmental crisis. As part of the 2018 Liverpool Biennial, the artist Mohamed Bourouissa built a garden in south Liverpool with an accompanying film (part of his broader ongoing project, 'The Whispering of Ghosts'). The project was inspired by the work of the writer and psychiatrist Frantz Fanon at the Blida-Joinville Psychiatric Hospital (Blida, Algeria), where one of his patients, Bourlem Mohamed,

---

[46] Lauren Berlant, *Cruel Optimism* (Durham NC, 2011). See also Heather Houser, 'Is Climate Writing Stuck?', *Literary Hub* (2022), https://lithub.com/is-climate-writing-stuck. For an example of leading readers into climate activism, see the paratext of the climate novel by Jenny Offill, *Weather* (2020), (www.obligatorynoteofhope.com).

was encouraged to approach occupational therapy through gardening. Bourouissa's garden in Liverpool was co-created with artists, children, and the local community, who sowed both local plants and those from an Algerian herbarium. It was conceived as 'a space of resilience', drawing on the term's varied uses in 'psychology, ecology and natural science'.[47]

The site and process of the art-garden is significant. Toxteth is one the most diverse and deprived areas of Liverpool, with high numbers of children living in poverty. Kingsley Community School, which housed the project in its grounds, educates children from thirty-five countries, who together speak over thirty languages.[48] The school lies a five-minute drive south of Wavertree Botanical Gardens, formed to house a collection built by Rushton's abolitionist friend Roscoe, and which, for all Roscoe's good intentions, still embodies aspects of the extractivist legacies of colonial botany. 'Resilience Garden' offered participants a different interaction with plant biology: not seen as samples from the colonies but as maps of migration and of diaspora in the most literal sense of the word, a 'scattering of seeds'. Residents were encouraged to bring their own plants, including those used in the culinary traditions of the area, to think about the relationship between production, consumption and culture. As a member of Granby Community Land Trust explained, 'There's also lots of herbs to reflect the cooking which goes on in the area, and that's another thing that is important about the garden; it helps people to create a connection with what they eat and what they grow'.[49] The species which Bourouissa himself introduced also drew unexpected connections between roots and routes. The mimosa tree he planted was not, as he had thought, native to Algeria but rather Australia – whence the English took it to plant in other colonies. After territorial exchanges between imperial powers, it was eventually brought to Algeria by French colonialists. Its presence in an English garden 'reflects on the circular notion of colonial movement; how this has shaped the current national identities of countries like Britain and formed the psychological make-up of African countries like

[47] Project description at Mohamed Bourouissa, 'The Whispering of Ghosts' (2018), https://www.mohamedbourouissa.com/the-whispering-of-ghosts.
[48] Kingsley Community School, 'Welcome' (2022), https://www.kingsley.liverpool.sch.uk/welcome.
[49] Cited by Liverpool Biennial, 'How the Resilience Garden in Granby Came to Life' | Liverpool Biennial of Contemporary Art' (2018), https://biennial.com/blog/09/10/2018/biennial.com/blog/09/10/2018/how-the-resilience-garden-in-granby-came-to-life.

Algeria'. But this process also disrupts 'fixed perceptions of national identity, by revealing the transient nature of nationality'.[50]

Analysing Bourouissa's recent practice, Carlos Basualso argues that 'The Whispering of Ghosts' (both the garden and an accompanying film, which melds footage of Fanon's words with those of his patient) might be read as a kind of 'allegory',

> understood in the sense that Walter Benjamin referred to [...] when describing the German Baroque Drama; a collection of fragments that stands for the ruinous result of that long siege which is our recent history, the history of our times. Fanon's voice, the skeletal armature of an institution of oppression, the endless loop of a disjointed and painful narrative, the weathered physiognomy of Bourlem Mohamed, all fragments, irredeemable, that engulf us in their pull toward a center of pure devastation. It is in that inaccessible center that the garden of resilience, nonetheless, continues to grow.[51]

While perhaps overly neat in its optimism, such a reading of 'Resilience Garden' in terms of Benjaminian allegory is fitting. In a Benjamin-inspired argument that allegory is a particularly generative literary form for thinking about the Anthropocene, DeLoughrey points to the figuration of the garden from Caribbean writers such as Jamaica Kincaid and Olive Senior, who have used 'the allegory of the island garden and "excavated" the soil to explore the violent process of sedimentation and creolization', where 'the complex diasporas of plants and peoples in the Caribbean problematise the notion "natural" history and its segregation from human agency'.[52] Bourouissa's garden also offers a way of thinking through eco-imperialistic processes across scales and across time. It takes the psychoanalytic work of Fanon, a Caribbean writer, undertaken in a French African colony, and re-seeds both its plants and ideas into, and with, a multi-ethnic urban community, in one of the most significant ports of empire. As with the Caribbean gardens DeLoughrey analyses, 'The Whispering of Ghosts' articulates a 'history of empire, diaspora, and resettlement' that 'foregrounds the ways in which the violence of plantation societies ruptured continuous human relationships to place and thus to earth (soil) and Earth (planet)', but it does so by looking to the future as well as the past.[53]

[50] Jess Cole, 'The Community Garden in Liverpool Built as a Site for Resilience', *Dazed* (2018), https://www.dazeddigital.com/art-photography/article/40749/1/mohamed-bourouissa-community-garden-liverpool-has-become-a-site-for-resilience.

[51] Carlos Basualdo, 'Bourouissa's Method', *ArtAsiaPacific* 113 (2019), pp. 113–18 (p. 118).

[52] DeLoughrey, *Allegories of the Anthropocene*, pp. 36–7.

[53] *Ibid.*

Hope in the Horrorcene

To return to the start: Barker's story 'The Forbidden', which takes place during Liverpool's nadir in the 1980s. Perhaps the most iconic pop-cultural rendering of the city in that period was Alan Bleasdale's television drama *The Boys from the Blackstuff* (1982). This hugely popular BBC series closed with shots of the characters walking past the shell of Tate & Lyle's abandoned refinery, as it is being torn down; the substance which sustained Liverpool for so long was now leaving a decaying cavity in the cityscape. The company left Liverpool in the wake of Britain's entry into the European Economic Community, where the Common Agricultural Policy (CAP) 'guaranteed prices and protectionism against imports [...] for EEC-produced commodities'.[54] European sugar beet would be favoured over the sugarcane from the Caribbean (and elsewhere) which had been a mainstay of Tate & Lyle's operations. For Michael Niblett, the CAP is part of a series of agricultural upheavals from the 1960s and 1970s which are reflected in the emergence of British 'Folk Horror' at the time: an instance of how 'irrealist' or EcoGothic forms often emerge in territories impacted by the ecological disruption of the capitalist-world-system.[55] 'The Forbidden' might be read as a corresponding, urban irruption of irrealist or gothic aesthetics, with the Candyman reflecting the upheavals foisted upon Liverpool by globalisation and the world-food-system.[56] He embodies social unrest after the loss of the sugar industry as well as the violence of the colonial past.

Anna Tsing and her collaborators, in the influential *Arts of Living on a Damaged Planet: Ghosts and Monsters of the Anthropocene*, differentiate between monstrosity and spectrality as ways of thinking environmentally. Ghosts are revenants, they return the past to the present (and future). Anthropocene ghosts remind us that to live in the Anthropocene is to be haunted by knowledge: by an awareness of past trauma, by the violence of

---

[54] Tony Weis, *The Global Food Economy: The Battle for the Future of Farming* (London, 2007), p. 66.
[55] Michael Niblett, '"The Landscape Heaved with Unspeakable Terror": The Weird Presence of the World-Food-System in the Cultural Imaginaries of England and the Caribbean', Michael Niblett, Chris Campbell and Kerstin Oloff, eds, *Literary and Cultural Production, World-Ecology, and the Global Food System* (Basingstoke, 2021), pp. 65–92. This volume has a variety of examples of irrealism as an aesthetic response to upheavals in ecology and economy.
[56] On how critical irrealism can be applied in a British context, see Sam Solnick, 'Critical Climate Irrealism', Adeline Johns-Putra and Kelly Sultzbach, eds, *The Cambridge Companion to Literature and Climate*, Cambridge Companions to Literature (Cambridge, 2022), pp. 296–306.

genocide and enslavement cementing cities and infrastructure, by the vulnerability of particular communities and territories to (un)natural disasters. It is also to be materially haunted: by weather-shaping emissions, or by the enduring impact of toxins secreted into landscapes. By contrast, monstrosity articulates 'life's symbiotic entanglement across bodies', including, though not limited to, ecosystemic enmeshments of human and nonhuman life.[57]

Barker presumably did not intend his Candyman to be read in environmental terms, but, like so many horror stories, the Candyman prefigures the kind of gothic economy re-animating that which capitalism would obfuscate. A murderous, animated tin of Golden Syrup, Candyman embodies the spectre of sugar which haunts Merseyside. Yet the bees nestling in his rotten flesh also reflect Anna Tsing and colleagues' description of Anthropocene monstrosity as 'bodies tumbled into bodies'.[58] To read Candyman in terms of actual candy is to dissolve the long environmental history of sugar into the series of allusions and metaphors for the body politic which swarm around his torso.

The instance of *bugonia* on the front of Tate & Lyle's Golden Syrup tin (where bees are shown hatching in a carcase of the dead lion) actually comes from the story of Sampson, which is a tale about the revenge of an enslaved person against his captors.[59] The bees within the chest cavity also recall the homunculi depicted on the title page of Hobbes's *Leviathan* (a favoured figure within Barker's short fiction), in which the many come together to form the one, *(be)e pluribus unum*.[60] But there are other political images of bees at play: the use of apian comparisons to explore hierarchy and productivity in Plato's *Republic*, Virgil's description of *bugonia*, where carcase-spawning bees are a model for co-operation in the *Georgics*, the many associations of bees with labour or citizenship, including the bee as civic symbol of Liverpool's neighbouring city, the Industrial Revolution's 'Cottonopolis', Manchester.

Therefore, to read the political metaphorics of Candyman's bees in a sugar-fuelled environmental context is to ask questions about who (and what) is considered part of the *polis* and who is reduced to bare life. It raises

---

[57]   Anna L. Tsing *et al.*, *Arts of Living on a Damaged Planet: Ghosts and Monsters of the Anthropocene* (Minneapolis, 2017), p. M2.

[58]   *Ibid.*, p. M2.

[59]   Sampson is an important figure within both abolitionist and Black Nationalist discourses, and his story is a presence in the plot of the *Candyman* films (set in Chicago, not Liverpool).

[60]   Thomas Hobbes, *Leviathan, or, the Matter, Forme, and Power of a Common Wealth, Ecclesiasticall and Civil* (London, 1651). See, for example, Barker, 'In the Hills the Cities', *The Books of Blood. Volumes 1–3* (London, 1984), pp. 122–49.

ideas about the social organisation of energy production (honey is, after all, a calorific resource that might be equitably distributed for the good of the collective, or, to mix the metaphor, violently extracted and spread on toast).[61] The Candyman is both monstrous and spectral, a revenant borne from the legacy of sugar and from the loss of bees that now comes back to haunt us. As such, the character can be seen as a kind of undead memorial to the city's key commodity, which drove its boom and helped cause its bust. Given the planet-shaping processes the plantations unleashed, the Candyman and his swarming bees now seem a little like the return of the environmental repressed. But, like hurricanes, bees are not only metaphors. What is really horrifying about a monstrous entanglement of human and apian *à la* Candyman is the reminder that humans rely on bees to survive.

Along with other pollinators, their numbers are collapsing, whether that be through neonicotinoid pesticides or parasites picked up when entire bee colonies are shipped out to water-hungry almond megafarms in California.[62] We have to be wary of any ecocritical analysis in which 'multispecies assemblages of "plants, animals, microbes, and people" are flattened and simply appear as cogs in the wheels of capitalist destruction'.[63] Such flattening risks downplaying the specific types of racial-sexual oppression that shaped the plantations. Even so, one can recognise the current pollinator crisis as a long-term consequence of the plantation monoculture where the violence of enslaved labour and proto-industrialisation operated alongside an epistemological and ecological violence that saw nature as malleable to (some) humans' profit and use. As Laura E. White puts it in her Derridean analysis of 'ecospectrality', the figure of the environmental ghost is sometimes not only a 'revenant that returns the past to attention', it is an 'arrivant that announces possible futures'.[64] Bees are ecospectral too, these days. While sometimes ghosts of the past (as with the famous example of the bee orchid, whose appearance is a living memorial to an extinct pollinator), sometimes

[61] As Stuart Hall suggests, nothing embodies the history of commodity violence quite like breakfast products, 'Old and New Identities, Old and New Ethnicities', Les Back and John Solomos, eds, *Theories of Race and Racism*, 2nd edn (Abingdon, 2009), pp. 199–208.
[62] Annette McGivney, '"Like Sending Bees to War": The Deadly Truth Behind Your Almond Milk Obsession', *The Guardian* (8 January 2020), https://www.theguardian.com/environment/2020/jan/07/honeybees-deaths-almonds-hives-aoe.
[63] Davis *et al.*, 'Anthropocene, Capitalocene, ... Plantationocene?', p. 5, citing Donna Harraway.
[64] Laura A. White, *Ecospectrality: Haunting and Environmental Justice in Contemporary Anglophone Novels* (London, 2020), p. 8.

bees are icons of future loss, the possibility of apian (and therefore, perhaps, human) extinction.[65].

But bees can also be icons of potential endurance; of resilient futures. While writing this conclusion, I walked back to Granby to visit a new Winter Garden, built by Granby Community Land Trust in the shell of the sort of derelict housing that Barker's Candyman haunts. A plaque inside explains how (along with Bourouissa's "Resilience Garden" and Millennium Road Community Garden) it forms a symbolic memorial to 'the "Triangular Slave Trade". Representing our people in Afrika, Caribbean and Europe within the "Toxteth Triangle" to Commemorate, Venerate, Conciliate, Honour and Heal'.[66] These three small plots provide spaces of contemplation, sites for intercultural community activities, pockets of ecological diversity within an urban landscape, including pollinating plants around which urban bees now hum. Tiny reminders of the power of environmentally orientated culture to not only imagine change but to enact it.

An obligatory buzz of hope.

[65] Robot pollinators in recent science fiction are testament to this, for example 'Hated in the Nation' (dir. Hames Hawes), Black Mirror (2016), series 3, episode 6.
[66] Michelle Peterkin-Walker, 'Politics of Plants' plaque, Cairns Street Winter Garden.

4

Nonhuman Entanglements in Adam Roberts's Science Fiction: Bête *(2014) and* By Light Alone *(2012)*

NORA CASTLE

Science fiction (sf) is notoriously hard to define. As Sherryl Vint explains, it is a genre which is ostensibly interested in science, but also, importantly, in the 'mythologies of science'.[1] Alongside being a literary genre which has evolved over time – often propelled, especially in the early years, by the idiosyncratic visions of editors and publishers – it is also 'a cultural mode that struggles with the implications of discoveries in science and technology for human social lives and philosophical conceptions'.[2] As Adam Roberts describes in his book, *Science Fiction* (2000), one of the fundamental markers of sf tends to be an 'encounter with difference'.[3] Drawing on Darko Suvin's foundational concept of the 'novum', he continues:

> This encounter is articulated through a 'novum', a conceptual, or more usually material embodiment of alterity, the point at which the SF text distils the difference between its imagined world and the world we all inhabit. This serves as the basis of many critics' affection for the genre, the fact that SF provides a means, in a popular and accessible fictional form, for exploring alterity.[4]

While the most recognisable forms of alterity in sf might be the 'final frontier' of outer space and the otherworldly others to be found there, a growing body of research has been focused on alterity closer to home: the hidden lifeworlds and subjectivities of nonhuman animals (NHAs) and plants. This 'nonhuman turn' in sf operates in tandem with a contemporary wave of sf and sf criticism focused on environmental concerns. These strands have

---

[1]   Sherryl Vint, *Science Fiction: A Guide for the Perplexed* (London, 2014), p. 4.
[2]   *Ibid.*
[3]   Adam Roberts, *Science Fiction*, 2nd edn, The New Critical Idiom (London, 2006), p. 28.
[4]   *Ibid.*; Darko Suvin, *Metamorphoses of Science Fiction: On the Poetics and History of a Literary Genre* (New Haven, 1979).

coalesced in the shadow of imminent anthropogenic climate catastrophe in our current geological epoch, which has been (controversially) termed the Anthropocene.[5] As plants and NHAs are increasingly entangled with technoscience and biotechnological inventions, sf accordingly struggles with the implications of those inventions not only for human lives, but also for the lives of the nonhuman others themselves. And as phenomena like global warming and pandemics disrupt supply chains and food systems, the need to acknowledge human entanglements with the nonhuman world is becoming undeniable. Importantly, then, sf also struggles with humans' philosophical conceptions of how to relate to and understand the lives of nonhuman others, often questioning species boundaries and hierarchical relationality.

This chapter draws on critical animal studies and critical plant studies (particularly the work of theorists such as Sherryl Vint and Katherine E. Bishop, which unites those fields with sf studies) to argue that sf is the perfect staging ground for analysing human entanglements with NHAs and plants. It takes seriously Roberts's claim that sf can 'provide a symbolic grammar for articulating the perspectives of normally marginalised discourses of race, of gender, of non-conformism and alternative ideologies', focusing in this case on the subversion of anthropocentric and species-hierarchist views of the world.[6] The chapter focuses on close readings of two novels by Roberts, who is a creative writer as well as sf critic: *Bête* (2014) and *By Light Alone* (2012).[7]

The two novels I explore here are characterised by their focus on the tensions and contradictions that are provoked by a single technological change. Like many sf stories, they examine societies in flux after the introduction of life- or world-changing tech. In these tales, technology that was intended to benefit marginalised populations – in the case of *Bête*, nonhuman animals, and in the case of *By Light Alone*, the poor – provokes unintended consequences that in some cases complicates and even worsens their lot. In *Bête*, this technology takes the form of an implanted chip which allows NHAs to

[5]   Drawing on an understanding of sf as a mode (that is, not just a genre but a way of seeing the world), theorists like Rebecca Evans and Ursula K. Heise claim that the Anthropocene can be read as science fiction, Rebecca Evans, 'Nomenclature, Narrative, and Novum: "The Anthropocene" and/as Science Fiction', Special issue: SF and the Climate Crisis, *Science Fiction Studies* 45.3 (November 2018), pp. 484–99; Ursula K. Heise, 'Terraforming for Urbanists', *Novel: A Forum on Fiction* 49.1 (2016), pp. 10–25; Ursula K. Heise, 'Science Fiction and the Time Scales of the Anthropocene', *ELH* 86.1 (Summer 2019), pp. 275–304.

[6]   Roberts, *Science Fiction*, p. 28.

[7]   He is Professor of English at Royal Holloway, University of London, and a prolific author of science fiction, fantasy, parody fiction, and critical texts, including *Science Fiction, The History of Science Fiction* (2006), and *Rave and Let Die: The SF and Fantasy of 2014* (2015).

communicate using human speech. In *By Light Alone*, it takes the form of New Hair, a biotechnological adaptation which allows humans to photosynthesise through their hair. These technologies blur species boundaries, but the novels simultaneously resist the collapsing of species difference and the a-historicising of multispecies relationality. The hybridity of the human-like animals and plant-like humans in these respective novels not only tells a story about multispecies entanglements, but also illuminates the webs of power and privilege undergirding humans' social, political, and legal systems and the ways these systems entrench certain intra- and inter-species relationships, both in the novels and in the real world.

The chapter begins with a section on critical animal studies and its relationship to sf. This passage incorporates a reading of *Bête*, focusing especially on what constitutes consciousness – human, animal, or otherwise – and, in turn, questions of who (or what) can count as a person.[8] The subsequent section focuses on critical plant studies and its relationship to sf, incorporating a reading of *By Light Alone*. It focuses especially on what happens when the concept of 'becoming-plant' becomes literalised in plant–human hybrids, and what changes this might provoke in structures of society. It includes a discussion of the overlap between the aesthetics of a pastoral nostalgia and a politics of exclusion. The chapter argues that these two texts, which each include a novum that has the potential to create more just multispecies futures, demonstrate on the one hand the inadequacy of the technofix, and on the other the need for intersectional ethical and political frameworks that afford ethical consideration to (human and nonhuman) others, without eliding or ignoring their differences.

Critical Animal Studies and *Bête*

The study of the relationship between humans and NHAs has a long history in philosophical and scholarly thought, including in the writings of Pythagoras and Aristotle. However, Kenneth Shapiro traces the beginning

---

[8]   I use 'person' here in reference to legal frameworks that divide entities into 'persons' and 'things'. Within these frameworks, certain entities can be granted the status of 'nonhuman persons' and afforded certain moral and legal rights, often based on assessments of sentience. For example, in 2008 the Spanish Parliament granted 'human' rights to great apes, and in 2015 an orangutan was granted legal personhood by a judge in Argentina. The former ruling included a prohibition on experimentation on any great apes, and the latter ruled that the orangutan was entitled to better living conditions. A number of animal rights groups have argued that legal personhood should also be granted to cetaceans (a category which includes dolphins and whales). Personhood rights have historically not only been extended to NHAs, but also to other nonhuman entities, such as corporations in the US.

of Human-Animal Studies (HAS) – the interdisciplinary exploration of the relationship between humans and NHAs in the humanities and social sciences, often with a particular focus on the 'falsely polarizing differences between "human" and "animal"' – to the early 1970s.[9] Shapiro considers critical animal studies (CAS) merely another name for HAS; elsewhere, Richard Twine argues that CAS is HAS's more politically charged counterpart. CAS explicitly foregrounds a critique of capitalism, and advocates for ethical lifestyle change (for instance, to diet) and social action, alongside scholarly investigation.[10] CAS is interested in the social, cultural, (geo)political, economic, institutional, and infrastructural dynamics and their resultant power structures that govern human relationality to NHAs.

The way humans treat NHAs also has implications for how certain humans treat other humans; CAS must be understood within an interspecies and intersectional context. Joshua Bennett, for example, traces the way 'antiblack thought [has] maintained the fissure between human and animal', arguing that 'the black aesthetic tradition provides us with the tools needed to conceive of interspecies relationships anew'.[11] Through close readings of figures such as the mule and the shark in twentieth and twenty-first century Black writing, he argues that authors such as Zora Neale Hurston and Robert Hayden use the fraught kinship between NHAs and African Americans as a method of deconstructing traditional Western philosophical ideas of personhood. Rather than denying the connection with the animal that has historically been used to oppress them, these authors instead embrace a politics and poetics of interspecies empathy. Maren Tova Linett, drawing on the work of Sunaura Taylor, argues that ableism has helped maintain that same fissure (for instance, NHAs cannot be considered 'people' due to their lack of certain capacities that some disabled people may also lack), and argues for interspecies solidarity: 'if, when we [disabled people] are animalized, we seek to distance ourselves from other animals in order to claim just treatment, we leave unchallenged the assumption that it is acceptable to exploit nonhuman animals'.[12] The conceptions that align Black people or disabled people with

[9]   Kenneth Shapiro, 'Human-Animal Studies: Remembering the Past, Celebrating the Present, Troubling the Future', *Society & Animals* 28.7 (2020), pp. 797–833 (p. 805), citing Richard Twine, *Animals as Biotechnology: Ethics, Sustainability and Critical Animal Studies* (New York, 2010), p. 2.

[10]   Twine, *Animals as Biotechnology*, p. 9.

[11]   Joshua Bennett, *Being Property Once Myself: Blackness and the End of Man* (Cambridge MA, 2020), p. 4.

[12]   Maren Tova Linett, *Literary Bioethics: Animality, Disability, and the Human* (New York, 2020), p. 19. See also Sunaura Taylor, *Beasts of Burden: Animal and Disability Liberation* (New York, 2017), p. 43.

animals are also part and parcel of the sociopolitical formations that have spurred on anthropogenic destruction of the environment. For example, as Jason Moore argues, the early modern plantation system worked to reframe some people (for example, enslaved Africans) – alongside NHAs, plants, and microbes – as resource inputs, aligning them with capital-N Nature rather than capital-H Humanity.[13] Donna Haraway, Anna Tsing and their colleagues, through their conception of the Plantationocene, understand this system as a central figure in a lineage of extractivist sociopolitical systems which have led to climate and planetary crisis.[14]

The exploration – and critique – of the line(s) between humans and NHAs, between person, pet, meat, and pest, forms part of the strength of sf that incorporates NHAs. This is especially true considering increasing technological intervention into the lives and bodies of NHAs in the real world, for example through genetic engineering, cloning, and experimentation into xenotransplantation, as well as through farm management solutions like Precision Livestock Farming, which uses sensors, cameras, and machine learning software to automate farm processes and transform animal behaviour into analysable data.[15] As Sherryl Vint explains, 'Technoculture is deeply implicated in the reshaping of human/animal interactions; and sf, as a literature concerned with the social impact of science and technology, can contribute to a necessary rethinking of responsibility and ethics'.[16] Interventions like xenotransplantation especially require 'that we hold the contradictory beliefs that animals are sufficiently like humans to provide useful biological matter, yet sufficiently unlike us that their slaughter in these pursuits is not an ethical issue'.[17] Sf investigates what is at the crux of these contradictory beliefs: that despite being our kin, and deserving of ethical consideration, NHAs will always remain in some ways opaque to us. It does so through novums like writing from the point of view of NHAs (as in Adrian Tchaikovsky's *Children of Time,* 2015), allowing humans to 'jump' into the bodies of NHAs and experience their different forms of embodiment (for instance, in Emma Geen's *The Many Selves of Katherine North,* 2016),

[13]   Jason W. Moore, 'The Rise of Cheap Nature', Jason W. Moore, ed., *Anthropocene or Capitalocene? Nature, History, and the Crisis of Capitalism* (Oakland, 2016), pp. 78–115.
[14]   Donna Haraway *et al.,* 'Anthropologists Are Talking – About the Anthropocene', *Ethnos* 81.3 (2016), pp. 535–64.
[15]   Xenotransplantation is the transplantation of organs or tissues from one species to another, such as from a pig to a human.
[16]   Sherryl Vint, '"The Animals in That Country": Science Fiction and Animal Studies', *Science Fiction Studies* 35.2 (2008), pp. 177–88 (p. 178).
[17]   Vint, '"The Animals in That Country"', p. 178.

or 'uplifting' NHAs to have human-like speech and sentience (as in *Bête*).[18] Our efforts to understand NHAs in real life necessarily transform them, and filter them through an anthropocentric worldview. These methods tend to assume that NHAs' ability to conform to ways of making them legible to us (for example, the capacity for dogs to learn to press assistive-speech buttons to communicate) is equivalent to their capacity for intelligence or communication more generally. As Vint explains, 'Sf's critical engagement with the cultures of science is also a critical engagement with the constitutive relationship between science and what we know of animal-being'.[19]

Roberts's *Bête* is an especially interesting exploration of the constitutive relationship to which Vint refers. Its novum is a microchip that allows nonhuman animals to use human speech. Originally developed by Deep Blue Deep Green, an animal rights activism organisation, the chips in their earliest iterations predominantly caused the NHAs to regurgitate propaganda, but in later iterations seem to actually allow them to speak their own thoughts – although the protagonist, Graham Penhaligon, refuses to believe this. In the novel, NHAs who can speak are prohibited from being killed, whereas those who cannot speak can still be killed and consumed as food. Graham is a British butcher who loses his farm when he kills a 'canny' cow, and who then becomes an itinerant, travelling from town to town to do back-alley butchery. The novel follows Graham and his interactions with other humans and especially with chipped beasts (known as bêtes), including the cow that he kills, a cat called Cincinnatus, and a prophet known as the Lamb. It tracks the movement from (some) humans' initial acceptance of the bêtes, and of legal protections given them, to a reversal of both acceptance and protections, and an eventual war against them. The novel is narrated by what the reader eventually learns is a posthuman/postanimal assemblage of Graham, Cincinnatus, and a vixen, due to Graham's ingestion of a chip towards the end of his life.[20] Graham is generally presented as a cantankerous old man, who is enraged by the new laws which have eliminated his livelihood, but eventually he forms a begrudging alliance with a group of bêtes, who want him to help them broker a peace treaty with the humans. He spends a disproportionate amount of the novel arguing with

[18]   Adrian Tchaikovsky, *Children of Time* (2015; London, 2016); Emma Geen, *The Many Selves of Katherine North* (London, 2016).

[19]   Vint, *"The Animals in that Country"*, p. 180.

[20]   The chips retain (a copy or version of) the consciousnesses of their former connections. For more on the posthuman/postanimal narration, see Liza B. Bauer, '"Four Legs in the Evening": Postanimal Narration in Adam Roberts' *Bête* (2014)', *SubStance*, Special issue: Ecocriticism & Narrative Form, 50.3 (2021), pp. 53–73.

various bêtes, and it is to one of these arguments (with Cincinnatus) that the chapter will turn, after examining the opening pages of the novel.

In *Bête*, it is not just the line between 'person' and 'animal' that is being interrogated, but also the line between those and 'machine'. The first lines of the novel make this clear: 'As I raised the bolt-gun to its head the cow said: "Won't you at least Turing-test me, Graham?"'[21] In a bid for its life, the talking cow references a test used to determine whether a computer can convincingly imitate a human respondent, with the implication that this would prove that it is conscious, and therefore to slaughter it would be immoral. This leads into a rumination on the idea of consciousness:

> 'There's nothing magical or spiritual about consciousness, Graham,' said the cow. 'Any cortical architecture which can support learning and recall and which involves multiple, hierarchically organized loops of axonal projections converging on nodes out of which projections also diverge to the points of origin of convergence is functionally conscious' (pp. 4–5).

This response, whose difficulty to parse perhaps detracts from its effectiveness, is immaterial to Graham, who retorts, 'I don't feel like I'm talking to a cow, even a really smart one. I feel like I'm talking to a spokesperson from the Deep Blue Deep Green organization. I think that ought to figure in the Turing test, too. Suchlike considerations' (p. 7). Graham believes that any human speech coming from an NHA is a result of the AI in their chip and completely separate from the animal itself. This stems from his belief that 'talk' is a distinctly human mode of communication, and that imposing such communication on NHAs is just that – an imposition, an anthropomorphising that denies or obscures something fundamental about the way NHAs function differently (pp. 113–14). This take is actually quite sophisticated, though through most of the novel Graham's viewpoint comes across more as stubborn conservatism. Nevertheless, what is at stake in this discussion is nothing less than the future of the animal – both nonhuman and human. As both humans and NHAs are increasingly entangled with technology, and especially biotechnology, the novel asks, what will happen to an understanding of 'human' and 'animal'? At what point does an animal cease to be animal, and to become something else? And what happens when that animal becomes more 'human', or the human more 'animal'? This problematic is literalised in the narration of the story by the Graham/Cincinnatus/vixen hybrid, but is also discussed explicitly through the concept of *tertium quid*.

---

[21]   Adam Roberts, *Bête* (London, 2014), p. 3. Subsequent references to this work give page numbers in parentheses in the main text.

Tertium quid, a Latin phrase derived from Greek for 'some third thing', refers to '[s]omething (indefinite or left undefined) related in some way to two (definite or known) things, but distinct from both'.[22] In the novel, it refers to the 'chip meld[ing] with the animal mind' to create something 'special [, ...] a new thing' (p. 278). The possibility of this 'third thing' is discussed in a conversation between Graham and Cincinnatus, in which the cat differentiates his 'radically different intellect' from simple chips made to do basic tasks:

> 'And the difference here, my dear Graham, is that my chip both acts and is acted upon. The mysteriously lacking ingredient x that means your laptop is never going to become conscious [...] is supplied by the animal mind into which it is lodged. It's miraculous, really.'
> 'You're not a miracle,' I returned. 'You're a chess-playing algorithm that happens to use words instead of chess moves. You're an illusion.'
> 'My consciousness being precisely as illusory as yours ...' said the cat, smugly [...] 'Or perhaps you can point to the metaphysical bedrock upon which the proof stands that I am talking to a human being?' (pp. 64–5)

In this discussion, and throughout the novel, Roberts plays with conceptions from the philosophy of mind to provoke questions not only about animal intelligence and animal consciousness, but also *human* intelligence and consciousness. He posits the possibility of a posthumanism that is actually post*animal*. It is only from a human perspective that our capacities are exceptional; from the perspective of a cat (or a spider, as in Adrian Tchaikovsky's novel, *Children of Time*), we must seem incompetent in many basic skills.[23] Roberts explicitly applies arguments made about 'sentient' robots/androids and AI to living creatures, transforming the 'uncanny irruption of the *in*human into the sphere of the human' into the uncanny irruption of the *non*human into the sphere of the human – or rather, perhaps, bursting our bubble that there is a solely 'human' sphere at all.[24] In this way, the bêtes in the novel seem to epitomize Haraway's conception of the 'cyborg', a figure that breaks down the boundaries of human and NHA, and of human/NHA and machine. She explains that 'a cyborg world might be about lived social

---

[22]   'Tertium quid, n.', in *Oxford English Dictionary*, https://www.oed.com/view/Entry/199636.

[23]   For an excellent example of humans appearing unintelligent due to their different embodiment and ways of communicating, see Tchaikovsky, *Children of Time*, pp. 236–7. This passage has parallels with *Bête* (pp. 114–15) as both deploy spiders as their example.

[24]   Roberts, *Science Fiction*, p. 159 [my italics].

and bodily realities in which people are not afraid of their joint kinship with animals and machines, not afraid of permanently partial identities and contradictory standpoints'.[25] In *Bête*, Roberts creates a cyborg world in which people are, in fact, *very* afraid of their joint kinship with animals and machines, afraid enough to wage war against them. He uses his story world to highlight the tensions and difficulties inherent in attempting to dismantle a human/NHA binary, rather than creating a world in which that dismantling has already taken place.

As Roberts notes through the character of Cincinnatus, humans 'don't like admitting [they] don't recognize something; so when [they] see something that is genuinely baffling [they] misrecognize it as something else' (p. 309). The humans in the novel struggle to see the bêtes as people of a different kind, as complex others with differing interior lives and senses of embodiment, instead over-simplistically misrecognising them as either inscrutable, hostile foes or emancipated, anthropomorphised companions. The novel puts pressure on the contradictory beliefs that NHAs are sufficiently like us that we can utilise biotechnology to make them legible to us, yet also unlike us enough that they will remain inferior creatures over whom we will still have control. In doing so, it critiques not only HAS but also CAS, questioning what sort of solidarity is actually possible, or even desirable, from a nonhuman point of view. *Bête* forces the reader to reconsider NHAs as kin but also as opaque. NHAs have a right to opacity (and I use this phrase deliberately to invoke the intersectional implications of animal studies discussed above) and also to moral standing. By using a novum of talking animals, but one in which the NHAs and humans often talk *past* rather than *to* one another, Roberts stakes a claim that 'There is no recognition; there is only misrecognition' – but this does not mean that humans and NHAs are not inextricably entangled. Our relationship to NHAs is complex, the novel argues, and cannot simply be reduced to an issue of translation solved by a technofix.

Critical Plant Studies and *By Light Alone*

Buoyed by work in the sciences in the early 2000s, especially Anthony Trewavas's pivotal work which sparked intense debate about whether plants could be understood as intelligent, critical plant studies (CPS) began to coalesce in the early 2010s.[26] This is not to say that this was the first instance of

[25]   Donna Haraway, *A Cyborg Manifesto: Science, Technology, and Socialist-Feminism in the Late Twentieth Century* (Minneapolis, 2016), p. 15.
[26]   See Anthony Trewavas, 'Plant Intelligence: Mindless Mastery', *Nature* 415.6874 (2002), p. 841; Anthony Trewavas, 'Aspects of Plant Intelligence', *Annals of Botany*

thinking theoretically with plants – far from it. But it was in this period that an explosion of theoretical work on plant agency, plant thinking, and the moral status of plants began to be published. Perhaps the most influential figure in the field is Michael Marder, whose *Plant-Thinking: A Philosophy of Vegetal Life* (2013) has remained essential reading. Marder's goal is to articulate a kind of 'vegetal phenomenology', and to recuperate the plant from its abjection in Western thought, historically and through to the present, without diminishing or disregarding its alterity.[27] The concept of plant-thinking, which attempts to see plants as plants, as much as possible from their own point of view, is related to the concept of 'becoming-plant', which Karen L.F. Houle derives from Gilles Deleuze and Félix Guattari's understanding of 'becoming'. She explains that 'becoming-plant *forces us* to think [...] the complex ways that *plantness composes us*', while it also forces a shift in perspective away from the hierarchical mode of understanding human relationships with the nonhuman world that characterises a capitalist world-ecology.[28] This is because

> plant communication is neither strictly individual nor even species-specific but is accomplished in and through radical kinships, through a fantastically versatile and multi-directional capacity to harmonize a multiplicity of actions. Whatever plants are up to, it is complex being-together in the world, an original sociality going beyond any simple sense of between.[29]

Becoming-plant, then, means understanding the world otherwise. It entails seeing intra- and inter-species relationships as 'transient alliances rather than strategies'.[30] It means recognising our inextricable connectivity with nonhuman others, a connectivity which Moore has called the 'web of life', and which Timothy Morton refers to as 'the mesh'.[31]

92.1 (July 2003), pp. 1–20.

[27] Michael Marder, *Plant-Thinking: A Philosophy of Vegetal Life* (New York, 2013), p. 10.

[28] Karen L.F. Houle, 'Animal, Vegetable, Mineral: Ethics as Extension or Becoming? The Case of Becoming-Plant', *Journal for Critical Animal Studies* 9.1–2 (2011), pp. 89–116 (p. 111).

[29] *Ibid.*, p. 111.

[30] *Ibid.*, p. 112.

[31] See Jason W. Moore, *Capitalism in the Web of Life: Ecology and the Accumulation of Capital* (London, 2015); Timothy Morton, 'The Mesh', Stephanie LeMenager, Teresa Shewry, and Ken Hiltner, eds, *Environmental Criticism for the Twenty-First Century* (New York, 2011), pp. 19–30. Houle refers to the interrelation between humans and nonhuman others as an 'assemblage', a term that has become popular in new materialist analysis, 'Becoming-Plant', p. 111.

Recent sf scholarship has begun incorporating the ideas of critical plant studies, including plant-thinking and becoming-plant, into critical readings of science fiction texts. This includes work by Natania Meeker and Antónia Szabari, and a collection edited by Katherine E. Bishop, David Higgins and Jerry Määttä, as well as a slightly earlier collection edited by Dawn Keetley, which contains material on sf.[32] Meeker and Szabari, for example, ask whether we can '*become* plants in order to become critically postconscious, posthuman, feminist or queer subjects'.[33] They argue that plants, as agential beings, actively co-create futures with humans and other nonhuman others, especially as they become unruly.[34] The unruliness of plants, as Keetley notes, forms part of why they are so fruitfully incorporated in works of horror – and, I would add, sf – as monstrous 'others'.[35]

One of the most consistently cited observations in recent critical writing about plants, both within sf studies and outside it, is the 'radical alterity of plant being'.[36] The alien-ness of plants, as Bishop notes in her introduction to *Plants in Science Fiction*, makes them perfect subjects for sf. She explains that '[o]ne of the greatest boons of sf is the way it allows us to confront that which is alien to us – worlds, thoughts, experiences, desires and lives that are not our own [...] And what alive is more alien to humans than plants?'[37] Bishop locates the specific power of plants in sf as that of shifting dominant paradigms; 'plant life in sf transforms our attitudes towards morality, politics, economics, and cultural life at large, questioning and shifting many traditional

[32] There are also significant slippages between horror and sf as genres more broadly, and between the use of plants in horror and sf more specifically.

[33] Natania Meeker and Antónia Szabari, *Radical Botany: Plants and Speculative Fiction* (New York, 2020), p. 27.

[34] For more on the idea of 'unruliness' and the nonhuman world, see Siddharta Krishnan, Christopher L. Pastore, and Samuel Temple, eds, 'Unruly Environments', *RCC Perspectives* 3 (2015), pp. 1–77.

[35] Dawn Keetley articulates six theses on why plants are the fodder of horror: '(1) Plants embody an absolute alterity; (2) Plants lurk in our blindspot; (3) Plants menace with their wild, purposeless growth; (4) The human harbors an uncanny constitutive vegetal; (5) Plants will get their revenge; and (6) Plant horror marks an absolute rupture of the known', 'Introduction: Six Theses on Plant Horror; Or, Why Are Plants Horrifying?', Dawn Keetley and Angela Tenga, eds, *Plant Horror: Approaches to the Monstrous Vegetal in Fiction and Film* (London, 2016), p. v. Many, if not all, of these are also applicable to sf depictions of plants.

[36] Matthew Hall, 'In Defence of Plant Personhood', *Religions* 10.317 (2019), pp. 1–12 (p. 1).

[37] Katherine E. Bishop, 'Introduction', Katherine E. Bishop, David Higgins, and Jerry Määttä, eds, *Plants in Science Fiction: Speculative Vegetation* (Cardiff, 2020), pp. 1–8 (p. 3).

parameters'.[38] Like CPS work in sf more generally, Bishop's contributors 'ask
how plant-based characters or foci shift our understandings of institutions,
nations, borders and boundaries, erecting – and dismantling – new visions of
utopian and dystopian futures'.[39] Creatures like plant-human hybrids, anthropomorphic plants, seductive plants, plant-like aliens, and invasive plants all
challenge human positionality in terms of our relationship with plants, and by
extension, the wider nonhuman (and hierarchised human) world.

In *By Light Alone*, Roberts explores what happens when becoming-plant,
which is meant to be a radical departure from the paradigmatic exploitative and extractivist philosophy of the capitalist world-system, is instead
co-opted into the very capitalist, hierarchical structures it seeks to subvert.
The novel's novum is New Hair, a technology which allows human to photosynthesize through their hair follicles. Taken orally, the 'Neocles Bug'
releases 'millions of fantastically small machines' into the blood stream,
which then stimulate the growth of New Hair.[40] The photosynthesis can
then be passed to infants through breastfeeding.[41] The Bug effectively eliminates world hunger, but stark wealth disparity remains; as a status symbol,
the rich shave their heads and eat only 'real' food. The narrative itself is not
about the development and implementation of this technology, which is
already a given in the world of the novel. Rather, the novel details the story
of the opportunistic kidnapping of a wealthy New York couple's daughter,
Leah, from a vacation ski resort.[42] It encompasses the daughter's supposed
recovery, the couple's divorce, and the daughter's actual reappearance, facilitated by her participation in an attempted revolution. Through this narra-

---

[38]   *Ibid.*, pp. 4–5.

[39]   *Ibid.*, p. 5.

[40]   Adam Roberts, *By Light Alone* (London, 2012), pp. 168, 190. Subsequent references to this work give page numbers in parentheses in the main text.

[41]   This invention could potentially be inspired by the scientific discovery that
the green sea slug (*Elysia chlorotica*) is able to transfer genes from the algae it eats
into its genome. This causes it to develop the ability to photosynthesize, an ability
which it then passes on to its offspring, Sidney K. Pierce, Nicholas E. Curtis, and
Julie A. Schwartz, 'Chlorophyll a Synthesis by an Animal Using Transferred Algal
Nuclear Genes', *Symbiosis* 49.3 (December 2009), pp. 121–31; Sidney K. Pierce *et
al.*, 'Transcriptomic Evidence for the Expression of Horizontally Transferred Algal
Nuclear Genes in the Photosynthetic Sea Slug, Elysia Chlorotica', *Molecular Biology
and Evolution* 29.6 (June 2012), pp. 1545–56.

[42]   Child theft is apparently a common occurrence (though children are taken less
often from the upper classes) because of the difficulty of carrying a pregnancy for the
poor of the story world. Leah's height is also cited as a potential factor, as tallness and
body fat are markers of beauty.

tive frame, the reader is shown how New Hair has completely reconfigured labour relations in the story world.

In a conversation with Leah's father, George, Dot, a woman hired to help find the kidnapped Leah, explains how

'Once upon a time, even the lowest of the low had a *little* bit of money, because in the old days peasants had to eat. Had to eat or die. A dead peasant isn't any good to a village boss. You can't get any work out of a dead peasant. So village bosses had to make sure the peasants got substance monies – in cash or kind. Enough to eat, enough to live.'

'The New Hair freed people from that,' observed George.

'Just so. Now, you might think it would have freed up the peasants to spend their small money on something else, to better themselves, whatever. All that utopian jibberjabber. But it didn't. Instead it freed up the *bosses* to stop giving peasants any money at all. You drink water from the canal; you soak up sunlight from the ever-generous air, and you never need to eat. [...] if you're an honest-to-goodness peasant, all it does its free the bosses to squeeze more money for themselves from your labour' (pp. 88–9).

In this conception, Roberts demonstrates that becoming-plant, which tends to be framed as a panacea for the harm done by exploitative, hierarchical modes of viewing the world, is not effective if it is not accompanied by political, structural change. The technofix of New Hair, an invention meant specifically to alleviate the plight of the poor and food insecure, in fact makes the gap between the ultra-rich and the extreme poor *even worse*.[43] Rather than people on more equal footing, the Bug is considered a distasteful drug of the masses, who are maligned as lazy and called 'leafheads' (p. 7).[44] Dot goes on to explain why the peasants don't just 'rise up and throw the oppressors in the canal' (p. 89) but instead still work for the bosses. She understands their reasoning as threefold: 'a deep-dyed ontological inertia' (p. 89), the threat of violence (that is, head shaving), and the needs of pregnant women, who cannot carry a pregnancy to full term solely on sunlight.[45] Not only has the technofix not alleviated oppression, it has in

[43]   As Dot explains, 'It used to be that the bosses paid peasants just enough to stop them starving; now they pay peasants considerably less – just enough to keep one fraction of a family in milk-powder for a year or two. The bosses make more money and keep more money. Which means that people like you or I, higher up the pyramid, have more money' (p. 93).

[44]   Visibly displayed long hair is also considered distasteful. Waitstaff at the resort, for example, are expected to braid their hair and tuck it into their uniform so it is largely hidden from the guest's view, pp. 24–5.

[45]   The inertia is attributed particularly to the men. Dot also notes that 'that sounds

fact exacerbated gender inequality alongside wealth inequality. Dot names this as '"the most important of Mad Nic's unintended consequences. His invention made men idle and made sure that all the heavy lifting passed to women. Not," she added, looking darkly at George, "that that wasn't pretty much the case before"' (p. 93).

Alongside its implications for gender relations for those of lower socioeconomic status, the becoming-plant of the poor is also mobilised by the rich for their own ideological purposes. Raphael, a leader of a hippie-esque counterculture group (albeit one with personality cult vibes), who grow their hair in defiance of social convention and with whom George becomes involved, claims that the mass of idle labourers constitutes exactly the conditions for a revolution: 'absolute poverty is absolute freedom!' (p. 174) Raphael intellectualises and romanticises the plight of the poor in order to produce content for his followers, but his predictions of a revolution prove true, with riots in Florida, for example. While all this is going on, however, the majority of the rich are only vaguely aware of the dissent below, as it is not fashionable to watch the news or be cognizant of current events. Whether the photosynthesising poor are an actual threat becomes a matter of debate between Leah's mother, Marie, and her lover, Arto, who are both involved in the Queens Rewilding Project. While their reasoning differs, both treat the poor as weeds to be cleared away. For them, this new interconnection with plants is not a radical redefining of human/nonhuman kinship, but rather a confirmation of their view of the poor as effectively nonpersons. The Rewilding project does not have the political valence one might expect from the term 'rewilding', which in the real world is used to refer to progressive efforts to restore land to a state in which it is uncultivated and can be used as a habitat for wild animals, especially those that have had their previous natural habitats destroyed by human infrastructure. Rewilding is meant to encourage biodiversity and sustainability, and ideally remove human intervention. The Queens Rewilding Project, however, is instead a massive gardening project. It does involve reforesting, but, according to Arto, 'the project was pure politics – a twenty-second-century Clearances – to move a population of potentially dangerous low-earning types further *away* from the city itself' (p. 209). Roberts here refers to the Highland Clearances, but the term is

---

a bit racist. Peasantist. [...] So people don't like talking about it' (p. 89). It also reflects the idea that plants, because they are rooted in one spot, are less 'alive' and active than NHAs or humans. The issue around pregnancy means that 'women are prepared to work, indeed *eager* to work, in a way the men aren't. If a boss wants a ditch dug, he goes to a woman' (p. 92).

also reminiscent of the 1850s clearance of Seneca Village, a predominantly African American community, to create Central Park in New York.[46]

Arto refers to the project as 'a buffer zone', a term which can refer to border or demilitarised zones, but which in agricultural cultivation and conservation refers to areas which cannot be sprayed with pesticides or other contaminants in order to protect adjacent areas.[47] What is being protected, however, are not the plants or plant-like people, but rather an elite enclave. Arto wants to '[r]ing the city with wilderness – and some farmland too, since we need food. Fence the wilderness about; police the whole zone. Then *let* the longhairs swarm all over the Midwest for all I care! We'll have *our* sanctuary' (p. 212). The plant-like poor here are analogous to invasive plants and noxious weeds which threaten to endanger the crops and gardens. Marie, on the other hand, believes that the project is '*art*', and emphasises its 'aesthetic value as nature' (p. 209). The clearing of the poor is not because they are dangerous weeds but rather because they are unsightly; they are not sufficiently beautiful flowers for her garden. Marie's view of the project involves discussions of activeness and agency, but not on the part of the plants, nor on the part of the plant-like poor. She explains that both she and Arto were drawn to the project because 'they wanted to remake the world', albeit in different ways:

> When her daughter was returned Marie knew that she could never be passive again. She must *do*, must create, must produce. Gardening was the finest and purest articulation of this creative urge, a literal remaking of worldly chaos into beauty. And the Queens project was the biggest gardening scheme in the world! (p. 210)

Marie wants to 're-Eden' the world, to make it more beautiful for her and her ilk to enjoy – and to rule over. The emphasis is on 'Man' (or here, woman) acting on 'Nature' (of which the photosynthesising poor are considered a part), on control and power. It is not a mutual becoming and coevolving, as, for example, Michael Pollan highlights in his discussion of gardeners in *The Botany of Desire* (2001), which leaves 'neither the plants nor the people taking

---

[46]   Despite misconceptions that the residents of Seneca Village were poor squatters, many of the residents owned their own two-story homes and were employed, Central Park Conservancy, 'Before Central Park: The Story of Seneca Village', *Central Park Conservancy Magazine* (18 January 2018), https://www.centralparknyc.org/articles/seneca-village.

[47]   'Buffer strips' is also a term used for these zones in agriculture. These can be used for wildlife habitats, as well as to protect crops and surrounding areas. Buffer strips often consist of perennial plants, like shrubs, which are hardier than the crops they border.

part in it unchanged'.[48] This is especially true as the reader rarely, if ever, sees Marie engaging in actual gardening, rather than merely overseeing such work. The opposing views held by Marie and Arto are only apparently so. The aesthetic view of nature has its roots in a long history of pastoral writing and reimagining of the countryside. The countryside in this vision is idealised, abstracted, and tinged with a compounding nostalgia that eventually harks back to Eden. It is, as Raymond Williams explains, reframed as a place of quiet, innocence, and simple plenty. This pastoral imaginary relies simultaneously on the exploitation of nature and of labourers in the countryside, and on the obscuring of any labour taking place beneath an aesthetic of unmediated and perfect nature.[49] In the novel, the aesthetic reordering of 'worldly chaos into beauty' simultaneously enacts a policing of the unwaged masses. Arto's vision of a 'buffer zone' through which the distasteful (and potentially revolutionary) underclasses are held at arm's length and Marie's vision in which the unsightly chaos of active and uncontained nature is tamed go hand in hand. The dual subjugation of plants and people implied here, through the historical context of plantation agriculture and its transformation of labour practices, also forms part of the basis for the concept of the Plantationocene.[50] The fact that this pastoral imaginary manifests as a garden rather than as an agricultural site also highlights its connection with a violent, hierarchised view of certain other humans and nonhuman others, as botanic gardens have historically been linked to imperialism and empire.[51] It is worth noting that Marie's description of a 'literal remaking' also invokes sf tropes of geoengineering and terraforming. Terraforming narratives, especially early ones, often have roots in a similar conservative view of Humanity's mastery of

[48] Michael Pollan, *The Botany of Desire: A Plant's-Eye View of the World* (New York, 2001), p. 265.

[49] Raymond Williams, *The Country and The City* (New York, 1975). See, for example, pp. 36–8.

[50] See Gregg Mittman, *Reflections on the Plantationocene: A Conversation with Donna Haraway and Anna Tsing* (Madison, 2019), p. 6.

[51] See, for example, Tom Bristow, '"Wild Memory" as an Anthropocene Heuristic: Cultivating Ethical Paradigms for Galleries, Museums, and Seed Banks', in *The Green Thread: Dialogues with the Vegetal World*, ed. Patrícia Vieira, Monica Gagliano, and John C. Ryan (Lanham, 2016), pp. 81–106; Franz Broswimmer, 'Botanical Imperialism: The Stewardship of Plant Genetic Resources in the Third World', *Critical Sociology* 18.1 (1991), pp. 3–17; Xan Sarah Chacko, 'Stringing, Reconnecting, and Breaking the Colonial "Daisy Chain": From Botanic Garden to Seed Bank', Special Section: Global Fertility Chains and the Colonial Present of Assisted Reproductive Technologies, *Catalyst: Feminism, Theory, Technoscience* 8.1 (2022), pp. 1–30.

Nature. As Chris Pak explains, 'Terraforming is thus a method for creating via technological means anachronistic worlds rooted in the pastoral ideal'.[52] While *By Light Alone* is not about colonisation *per se*, it is about the subjugation and exploitation of a class of peoples (that is, the poor). Its novum is, therefore, part of a lineage of sf that registers historical (ecological) regimes as a 'conflation of plants and people', which, as Jerry Määttä explains, aligns with the 'already established literary trope of associating monster plants with indigenous or colonised peoples'.[53] The radical possibilities of 'becoming-plant' that are made possible in the text by a literal hybridisation of plants and people are undercut by a system which actually reads the plant-like people as even more exploitable. The 'leafheads' are seen as more passive and less worthy of moral consideration (in line with a 'Cartesian paradigm that sees "social" forces imposing their will upon an exogenous nature'), rather than their hybridity provoking an understanding of plants as more active/agential, and more interconnected with humans.[54] In this way, Roberts's novel demonstrates that while new materialist philosophies of human–nonhuman relations (which advocate for an understanding of plants as vibrant and agential) are attractive in theory, in practice they fall short without a historical materialist understanding of the world-system (and its attendant sociopolitical power structures) into which those theories are being introduced.

Conclusion

In *Bête* and *By Light Alone*, Roberts uses novums that blur the lines between humans, nonhuman animals, and plants. In terms of issues of ethical intra- and inter-species relations, these novums highlight the likelihood of unintended consequences in our own well-intended technoscientific solutions (such as cloning or genetic modification). In *Bête*, the novum of technologically enhancing NHAs to be able to converse in human speech, in order to prove their right to ethical consideration, does not eliminate the hierarchy between humans and NHAs. Instead, the existence of these 'human-like' animals eventually provokes military action and further divides NHAs and humans,

---

[52] Chris Pak, *Terraforming: Ecopolitical Transformations and Environmentalism in Science Fiction* (Liverpool, 2016), p. 66.

[53] Jerry Määttä, '"Bloody Unnatural Brutes": Anthropomorphism, Colonialism and the Return of the Repressed in John Wyndham's *The Day of the Triffids*', Katherine E. Bishop, David Higgins, and Jerry Määttä, eds, *Plants in Science Fiction: Speculative Vegetation* (Cardiff, 2020), pp. 32–55 (pp. 44, 47).

[54] Jason W. Moore, 'Madeira, Sugar, and the Conquest of Nature in the "First" Sixteenth Century. Part II: From Regional Crisis to Commodity Frontier, 1506–1530', *Review (Fernand Braudel Center)* 33.1 (2010), pp. 1–24 (p. 4).

even as the postanimal-assemblage narrator demonstrates the entanglement of NHAs and humans in a cyborgian future. The novel highlights the ways in which humans tend to over- or under-attribute characteristics associated with personhood to NHAs based on human philosophical frameworks. It resists a collapsing of species categories even as it questions the efficacy and meaning of categories of 'human' and 'animal', even and especially as they increasingly intersect with (bio)technology. In *By Light Alone*, the novum of New Hair, which makes humans more 'plant-like' by allowing them to photosynthesize, eliminates world hunger and food insecurity but does not result in a sociopolitical configuration in which the poor have more freedom. Instead, it exacerbates the discrimination and alienation they face. By virtue of the 'Bug' being used as a class marker, the radical possibilities of 'becoming-plant' are largely foreclosed; instead of forcing society to recognize 'the complex ways that *plantness composes us*', the plant-human hybridity merely gives the elite in the novel more grounds, in their view, to see the poor as passive or unruly resources unworthy of ethical consideration.

Through these two sf imaginaries, Roberts demonstrates that intensifying the similarities or overlap between humans and nonhuman others, through the development of 'human-like' animals or 'plant-like' humans, *does* have effects on humans' feelings of kinship with nonhuman others (and with other humans). Those effects, however, are not necessarily ones that lead to more caring multispecies (or intraspecies) relationships. Certain humans have long animalised others they deem 'inferior', and have long disregarded plants as unworthy of consideration. The mutability of the category of Humanity has historically been used to exclude, rather than include. Figures like the cyborg, which upset existing hierarchies and power structures, are threatening to the current social order of the world-system. As this chapter has shown, it is not enough to literalise human–nonhuman entanglements through hybrid-ising biotechnology. The technofix in isolation does not work. Instead, such technology needs to be accompanied by sociopolitical change in order to be effective in creating futures of multispecies justice. A shift in ontological perspective requires revolution.

5

Sum deorc wyrd gathers: *Dark Ecology, Brexit Ecocriticism, and the Far Right*

AIDAN TYNAN

Referring to a poem by Bertolt Brecht, Hannah Arendt wrote that the dark times of early-twentieth century Europe were characterised not by an occlusion of the brightly lit world of public affairs but by the capacity of this world to hide its atrocities out in the open. Dark times, whenever they occur, happen in this way through the medium of some supposedly transparent rationalisation, Arendt writes.[1] In Brecht's 'To Those Born Later', written in exile in the late 1930s, the speaker appeals to future generations not to blame him too harshly for having failed to avert the catastrophe:

> You who will emerge from the flood
> In which we have gone under
> Remember
> When you speak of our failings
> The dark time too
> Which you have escaped.[2]

Thinking about the impasses of environmental politics today often feels like being in the position of Brecht's speaker, striving to explain to some future society that the darkness did not look so dark, that it all seemed to happen in the plain light of day. It is a matter of learning to see the darkness for what it is. James Bridle has argued that this is a 'new dark age' precisely because our current, massively distributed, networked technologies cannot give the fully illuminated picture of the world that we believe technoscientific reason should do. Bridle argues that the task, then, must be to learn to live in the absence of enlightenment's certainty, to inhabit the darkness as a space of

---

[1]   Hannah Arendt, *Men in Dark Times* (New York, 1968), pp. viii–ix.
[2]   'An die Nachgeborenen' (1939), 'To Those Born Later', *Bertolt Brecht: Poems 1913–1956*, trans. and ed. John Willett and Ralph Manheim, with Erich Fried (London, 1976), p. 319.

possibility in which unknowing is not only unavoidable but necessary.[3] This
is a profoundly ecological position, and so it is no surprise that he refers to
ecocritical theorist Timothy Morton's concept of the 'hyperobject' to characterise technological networks.[4] Environmentalists have long understood that
we live in a lighted clearing surrounded by a much greater, denser, darker
mass of planetary life. The sunny optimism of 'bright green' environmentalism, with its faith in technological solutions, is frequently criticised.[5] This is
an ecological critique of light, in which the public world of politics (what
Arendt describes as a 'space of appearances') is decentred by an appeal to
something fundamentally withdrawn from the *lumen naturale* of human
reason.[6] The chromatics or shades of ecopolitics, ranging from dark to bright,
suggest degrees of commitment to this position.

But how should the ecological critique of light be understood at a time
when all sorts of dark politics, disturbingly reminiscent of Brecht's 1930s,
are looming? Neo-fascist tendencies towards white ethnonationalism and
anti-immigrant racism have appeared in the early twenty-first century in the
context of a warming Earth in which the political itself is adapting to vola-
tile new environmental conditions.[7] The climate denial that has long been
the position of the right and far right is mutating into a violent, exclusionary, and nihilistic environmental politics.[8] Fascism is returning as ecofascism,
fossil fascism, or what Christian Parenti calls the 'armed lifeboat' scenario, in
which 'green authoritarianism [emerges] in rich countries, while the climate
crisis pushes the Third World into chaos'.[9] The ecopolitical question is not
simply how to make our world more sustainable but how to avert 'climate

[3]   James Bridle, *New Dark Age: Technology and the End of the Future* (London,
2018), p. 15.
[4]   *Ibid.*, p. 73. Timothy Morton defines hyperobjects as 'things that are massively
distributed in time and space relative to humans', *Hyperobjects: Philosophy and
Ecology After the End of the World* (Minneapolis, 2013), p. 1.
[5]   Derrick Jensen, Lierre Keith, and Max Wilbert, *Bright Green Lies: How the
Environmental Movement Lost Its Way and What We Can Do About It* (New
York, 2021).
[6]   Arendt, *Men in Dark Times*, p. viii.
[7]   See Joel Wainwright and Geoff Mann, *Climate Leviathan: A Political Theory
of Our Planetary Future* (London, 2018). See also Andreas Malm and the Zetkin
Collective, *White Skin, Black Fuel: On the Danger of Fossil Fascism* (London, 2021).
[8]   For an international overview of these trends, see Bernard Forchtner, ed., *The Far
Right and the Environment: Politics, Discourse and Communication* (Oxford, 2021).
[9]   Christian Parenti, *Tropic of Chaos: Climate Change and the New Geography of
Violence* (New York, 2011), p. 11. On ecofascism, see Sam Moore and Alex Roberts,
The Rise of Ecofascism: Climate Change and the Far Right (Cambridge, 2022). On
fossil fascism, see Malm and the Zetkin Collective, *White Skin, Black Fuel.*

barbarism'.[10] If scientific enlightenment is held to be insufficient to bring about salvation, then we necessarily enter into a dark political terrain in which a desire for environmental justice must confront the most repressive forces.

I will draw out some consequences of this for the politics of ecocriticism by analysing the concept of 'dark ecology', which has been espoused independently by Morton and environmentalist-turned-novelist Paul Kingsnorth.[11] These are vastly different figures – the former a cutting-edge cultural theorist and philosopher with communist leanings, the latter a disillusioned ex-activist seeking new narratives of ecological belonging through English nationalism – so it is important not to conflate their positions. Nevertheless, their convergence on the theme of darkness tells us a lot about the situation of environmental politics today. In what follows, I analyse Kingsnorth's novel *The Wake* (2014) in the context of his non-fiction writings, before moving on to look at Morton's ecocritical theory in some detail. For both authors, dark ecology is a political and aesthetic framework that moves us from the Gaian holism of deep ecology towards somewhere gloomier, but it also aims to avoid simple despair by turning the dark affects of melancholy, loss and separation into modes of ecological inhabitation in their own right.[12] It is only in a melancholy mood that the sheer scale and extent of the impasses we face can be properly lived. Morton writes that

> Dark ecology undermines the naturalness of the stories we tell about how we are involved in nature. It preserves the dark, depressive quality of life in the shadow of ecological catastrophe. Instead of whistling in the dark, insisting that we're part of Gaia, why not stay with the darkness?[13]

[10] Naomi Klein, *On Fire: The Burning Case for a Green New Deal* (New York, 2019), pp. 49–50.

[11] Timothy Morton asserts ownership of the concept, dating its invention to 2004, in *Dark Ecology: For a Logic of Future Coexistence* (New York, 2016), p. 163; his first publication on it was *Ecology without Nature: Rethinking Environmental Aesthetics* (Cambridge MA, 2007). Paul Kingsnorth, 'Dark Ecology', *Confessions of a Recovering Environmentalist* (London, 2017), pp. 119–49, originally appeared in 2013. Kingsnorth had already established the Dark Mountain Collective with Dougald Hine in 2009.

[12] The term deep ecology originated with Norwegian philosopher Arne Naess in the 1970s, and was developed by Bill Devall and George Sessions in *Deep Ecology: Living as if Nature Mattered* (Salt Lake City, 1985). The left-anarchist social ecologist Murray Bookchin famously used the term ecofascism to denigrate the kind of ecocentric holism which deep ecology emphasised. On this history, see Keith Makoto Woodhouse, *The Ecocentrists: A History of Radical Environmentalism* (New York, 2018).

[13] Morton, *Ecology without Nature*, p. 187.

There are divergent ways of doing this, of course, and darkness is irreducibly ambiguous. Though Morton and Kingsnorth's politics tend in opposing directions, they both seek political positions based on an *aesthetics* of darkness, and thus, I argue, have more in common than either would probably care to admit. While Kingsnorth seems happy to court accusations of right-wing and even far right tendencies in his appeals to econationalism, Morton insists that dark ecology is sufficient to avert the calamitous intersection of environmentalism and far right extremism gaining ground today. The specific role of ecocriticism in this respect needs to be interrogated, since it too often assumes a left-liberal orientation as the default setting of ecological consciousness. This article will explore some of the questions raised by Greg Garrard's article 'Brexit Ecocriticism' in this respect to suggest that ecocritics must engage with the aestheticisation of environmental politics, and with the dangers attendant on this.[14] Given that Walter Benjamin, in the 1930s, famously defined fascism as an aestheticisation of politics, and communism as a countervailing politicisation of art, dark ecology, whatever else it may mean, emerges from the kind of penumbral historicity evoked in Brecht's poem.[15] Within this shadowy space, framings of political identity and historical time become warped, or, to use a term invoked similarly by both Morton and Kingsnorth, *weird*.

An English Twilight

The Irish writer Fintan O'Toole has argued that the form of nationalism which drove Brexit involved 'the fever-dream of an English Resistance, and its weird corollary: a desire to have actually been invaded so that one could – gloriously – resist. And not just resist but, in the ultimate apotheosis of masochism, die'.[16] O'Toole's main literary example of such dark English dreaming is Robert Harris's alternative history novel *Fatherland*, which depicts a contemporary Britain in which Nazi Germany won the War. But, as Christian Schmitt-Kilb notes, O'Toole could just as easily have referred to Kingsnorth's Booker-longlisted novel, *The Wake* (2014).[17] This is the first in a trilogy of novels,

---

[14] Greg Garrard, 'Brexit Ecocriticism', *Green Letters: Studies in Ecocriticism* 24.2 (2020), pp. 110–24.
[15] Walter Benjamin, *Illuminations*, trans. Harry Zohn (New York, 1968), p. 242.
[16] Fintan O'Toole, *Heroic Failure: Brexit and the Politics of Pain* (London, 2018), p. 44. See also Robert Harris, *Fatherland* (London, 1992).
[17] Christian Schmitt-Kilb, 'A Case for a Green Brexit? Paul Kingsnorth, John Berger and the Pros and Cons of a Sense of Place', Ina Habermann, ed., *The Road to Brexit: A Cultural Perspective on British Attitudes to Europe*, pp. 162–78 (p. 164).

including *Beast* (2016) and *Alexandria* (2020), which presents a long speculative history of England, from the Norman Conquest of 1066 to the present day, and then to the year 3000. I focus on *The Wake* since it most directly captures how Kingsnorth imagines the converging destinies of national identity and ecological crisis.

Two key features lend the book its undeniable appeal and dramatic power: the way it sets an ecoapocalyptic narrative in the eleventh century and the ingenious, made-up version of Old English in which the entire text is written. Buccmaster of Holland, the first-person narrator who leads a futile effort to resist the 'frenc' invaders who have come to 'angland', speaks to us in a language both rooted in place and broken into scattered fragments which reach us across a gulf of time:

> songs yes here is songs from a land forheawan folded under by a great slege a folc harried beatan a world brocen apart. all is open lic a wound unhealan and grene the world open and grene all men apart from the heorte. deofuls in the heofon all men with sweord when they sceolde be with plough the ground full not of seed but of my folc [...] so it is when a world ends.[18]

With some help from a glossary provided by the author, the reader understands that 'forheawan' means 'cut down' and 'slege' means 'slaughter' but is left to decipher 'folc' as 'folk', 'sceolde' as 'should', 'deofuls' as 'devils', and so on. The effect is reminiscent of Russell Hoban's science fiction dystopia *Riddley Walker*, which forces the reader to engage with a shattered English vernacular that has slowly emerged in the centuries following nuclear Armageddon.[19] In both cases, linguistic and historical estrangement effects function side-by-side in an apocalyptic narrative. For Kingsnorth, the dismemberment of English organic community by the invading Normans is an ecological catastrophe as much as a genocide, the wounds inflicted on the 'folc' an inversion of the generative act of ploughing and sowing. Green wounds are mirrored in the green land. Through the myth of the Norman Yoke, the history of environmental crisis is woven into the *longue durée* of what Kingsnorth sees as the destruction of native English society, which was small-scale and rooted in place rather than global and imperialistic.[20] But

[18]   Paul Kingsnorth, *The Wake* (London, 2014), p. 2.
[19]   Russell Hoban, *Riddley Walker* (London, 1980).
[20]   The Norman Conquest has, for centuries, been a contested part of English cultural memory. The myth of the Norman Yoke, particularly strong in the seventeenth and nineteenth centuries, denotes the idea that the conquest amounted to a brutal dispossession of a more democratic Anglo-Saxon society. For a discussion of the myth, its various deployments and historical contexts, see Siobhan Brownlie,

this is not, despite appearances, just an historical novel. Kingsnorth's fiction is directly inspired by a crisis of environmental politics, and what he sees as a deleterious global and technocratic turn in the green movement's orientation. In a 2017 article in the *Guardian*, he explained that his support for Brexit was motivated by the pursuit of a 'benevolent green nationalism' (which he describes elsewhere as 'ecological Englishness'), opposed both to the 'rootless ideology' of neoliberal capitalism and the left-liberal mainstream of contemporary environmentalism.[21]

Buccmaster's Old English vernacular is arrived at through a careful excision of words and letters which would not have existed before Norman society imported its Latinate French. The method is inconsistently deployed, as Kingsnorth admits in *The Wake*'s explanatory note, but his goal is much less historical accuracy or linguistic authenticity than to 'project a ghost image of the speech patterns of a long-dead land', to evoke a 'shadow tongue' still haunting modern English.[22] The narrator's stentorian, repetitive voice springs from this spectral persistence of something dead within living speech. Language is rooted in place, Kingsnorth is suggesting, but this also means that it can be uprooted, lost, and destroyed along with the living landscape itself.

Buccmaster, a free tenant farmer in the Lincolnshire fens or wetlands, represents a folk already doomed at the point the narrative begins. This is reflected in his eschatological obsession with omens of the impending 'blaecness' which many of his fellow 'anglisc' in their folly fail to heed: 'none wants to see all wants to haro and plough and drink and fucc lic the blaec will nefer cum'.[23] Buccmaster knows himself to be 'last of the anglisc' standing in 'anglands dyan light'.[24] 'Sum deorc wyrd gathers' on the horizon and within his people, even if they refuse to see it.[25] The Old English 'wyrd' is glossed by Kingsnorth as 'fate' or 'destiny', but it can also mean 'event' or 'phenomenon', and is derived from the verb *weorðan*, to 'become' or 'turn'.[26] Morton,

Memory and Myths of the Norman Conquest (Woodbridge, 2013), pp. 111–30.

21   Paul Kingsnorth, 'The Lie of the Land: Does Environmentalism have a Future in the Age of Trump?', *Guardian* (18 March 2017), https://www.theguardian.com/books/2017/mar/18/the-new-lie-of-the-land-what-future-for-environmentalism-in-the-age-of-trump; Paul Kingsnorth, *Confessions of a Recovering Environmentalist* (London, 2017), p. 212.

22   Kingsnorth, *The Wake*, pp. 356, 353.

23   *Ibid.*, p. 22.

24   *Ibid.*, pp. 333–4.

25   *Ibid.*, p. 45.

26   *Ibid.*, p. 351; J. R. Clark Hall, *A Concise Anglo-Saxon Dictionary*, fourth edn (Toronto, 1960), p. 427.

in *Dark Ecology*, also develops this idea: ecological knowledge or 'ecognosis' is 'knowing in a loop – a *weird* knowing. *Weird* from the Old Norse *urth*, meaning twisted, *in a loop* [...] The term *weird* can mean *causal:* the winding of the spool of fate'.[27] Here lies the key to understanding the novel's aims.

Buccmaster is, in fact, never really convinced of the English resistance, organised first by King Harold II and then by guerrillas such as the actual historical figure Hereward, whose nickname 'the Wake' (the watchful) lends the book its title. Buccmaster, for all his talk of killing 'ingengas' (foreigners) and his own attempts to raise a 'werod' or band of resistance fighters, is frequently sceptical of such efforts, and initially tries to talk his sons out of joining Harold's army. Even after his sons' deaths, he never seeks to join with Hereward, who, in some genuinely comic passages, Buccmaster furiously disparages, out of jealousy for Hereward's greater fame. A large part of what motivates Buccmaster's anger (and, towards the end of the book, his bloodlust) is what he feels to be the mistaken belief that fate, which is essentially dark, can be known and resisted. This is much less a historical novel, then, than one about the *weirdness* of history, its tendency to exceed disenchanted linear temporality as it turns back on itself through the hauntings and echoes of destiny. Instead of taking 1066 as the starting point of English history, as Kingsnorth notes is generally done, *The Wake* takes it as the end.[28] By looping history back on itself in this way, he conjures up what could be called an English Twilight.

For O'Toole, the entire Brexit project is about an image of Englishness modelled on the romantic notion of heroic failure, an approach he adapts from Stephanie Barczewski's book *Heroic Failure and the British*. Barczewski notes that some 'Britons felt that their nation's best qualities emerged in its moments of greatest duress, and that the celebration of heroic failure reflected an admirable embrace of perseverance, resilience and stoicism'.[29] This is embodied in famous episodes of noble defeat, such as the Charge of the Light Brigade at Balaclava and Captain Scott's doomed expedition to the Antarctic. Adapting Barczewski's idea, O'Toole reinterprets Brexit as a collective masochistic fantasy generated by a specifically English experience of the end of the British Empire, in the post-War period, and the devolution of power in Northern Ireland, Scotland and Wales in the late 1990s. While these nations found their postcolonial identity validated by their devolved parliaments and the degree of self-governance they were granted, English nationalism was experienced by many as degraded and taboo. In

---

27   Morton, *Dark Ecology*, p. 5.
28   Kingsnorth, *Confessions of a Recovering Environmentalist*, p. 207.
29   Stephanie Barczewski, *Heroic Failure and the British* (New Haven, 2016), p. vi.

his 2015 article 'Rescuing the English', which reads like a pro-Brexit manifesto, Kingsnorth writes that, following devolution, 'England remained the only UK nation to which power was not devolved, and whose people were not consulted about their governance'.[30] This, of course, is nonsense: devolution was implemented precisely in order to address the imbalance of a Westminster government which was overwhelmingly concerned with the affairs of England, and in which those of the other nations of the Union have always been seen as peripheral. Nevertheless, Kingsnorth, a year before to the Brexit referendum, hit on something crucial about the public mood: at the turn of the twenty-first century, the story of Englishness found itself without dramatic power because it featured no struggle for independence, no imperial yoke from which freedom could be heroically wrested. This is why a novel such as *Fatherland* can be seen to resonate with the fervour of Brexit nationalism, in which the European Union was depicted as a totalitarian monolith. Kingsnorth follows this logic but takes it even further: if we accept the established narrative that Britain as such begins with the invading Normans, were not the English 'the first victims of the British Empire' and its global ambitions?[31] And if Britain invented industrial capitalism, were not the English the first victims of that too?

The fantasy of liberation portended by this anti-imperialist story of English identity is masochistic, as O'Toole observes, because Brexit is fundamentally lacking, is real only insofar as it spurs the fantasy on, and any attempt to actualise it can only entail suffering. This is not to deny the historical significance of the Norman Conquest (or the EU) but Kingsnorth – despite the list of historical sources he references in his appendix to *The Wake* – only wants it as a mythic grand narrative of dispossession and acculturation. Ecological Englishness demands the pathos of loss.

It is not that he is romanticising Anglo-Saxon society in order to construct an Arcadia. The idea of a lost rural idyll, as Raymond Williams famously argued, goes back down the escalator of history as far as one is willing to follow it.[32] Kingsnorth somewhat gleefully observes that his mode of localist, vernacular environmentalism and his veneration of small-scale organic community will inevitably be critiqued as nostalgic and conservative by the middle-class liberals who dominate today's green movement.[33] But there is something much more going on in *The Wake* than simple nostalgia. The collapsing Anglo-Saxon world of the novel is not really idyllic at all, and in any

---

30   Kingsnorth, *Confessions of a Recovering Environmentalist*, p. 201.
31   *Ibid.*, p. 207.
32   Williams, *The Country and the City* (London, 1973), p. 11.
33   Kingsnorth, *Confessions of a Recovering Environmentalist*, p. 125.

case, Kingsnorth is much too good a novelist to trot out clichéd visions of a golden age. In fact, Buccmaster's devotion to his place in the fens, and the violence he wreaks against all who threaten it, is nihilistic and misanthropic in its intensity:

> i wolde haf folcs cnaw of the yfel what has been done to our land and of the yfel what cums on them who worcs to right it. all my lif i has worced to right yfel i has worced to waecen men to mac them see and all my lif i has been beat in the guttas for it. trust none but the treows the meres the ground trust none but the dead.[34]

Buccmaster attempts to gather a band of 'grene men' to live in the woods and fight a guerrilla campaign against the invaders, but he ultimately only trusts the land, its gods and its ancestors, discerning that the essence of rootedness is a deathly communion with the dark earth and its 'mares' or waters. This is an unhappy book, then, despite the moments of humour that tend occasionally to deflate Buccmaster's nativistic bombast and delusions of grandeur. Garrard argues that Kingsnorth's narrator should be understood with a degree of irony, as his claims about the 'triewe anglisc' are surely undercut by the fact that his own Anglo-Saxon ancestors were once colonists, or his admission that the Danish King Cnut had come to England and reigned benevolently.[35] Is Kingsnorth complicating the simplistic nativism of his own conceptions of ecological Englishness here, or criticising the undeniable dangers inherent in such political mythmaking? Perhaps. But then again, Kingsnorth may also be saying that ecological attachment is important precisely because it *is* politically dangerous, because it does *not* necessarily translate into the normative terms of acceptable political discourse. Ecocritics have long understood that literature, and art more generally, can offer a mode of provocation inaccessible to other kinds of discourse. Kingsnorth is deliberately provoking his readers by making them wonder just how ironic or serious he is being in his portrayal of a character whose devotion to the ecology of his homeplace becomes a murderous, delirious and ultimately self-destructive project.

Dark Politics

As Garrard points out, *The Wake* can be regarded as part of a broader contemporary moment in Britain and across Europe, when 'myths of national origins and sovereignty are no doubt coalescing and diverging from domi-

---

34   Kingsnorth, *The Wake*, p. 269.
35   Garrard, 'Brexit Ecocriticism', pp. 118–19.

nant stories of ecological dwelling in distinctive, yet parallel, ways'. He adds
that 'there is work to be done here that further engages, but also elevates,
the times we inhabit'.[36] The character of this work is suggested in his co-
written volume *Climate Change Scepticism: A Transnational Ecocritical
Analysis* (2019), which uses ecocritical methods to analyse right-wing anti-
environmentalist, anti-climate science rhetoric.[37] By scrutinising discourses
beyond the liberal and leftist positions often assumed as the default of
environmental awareness, ecocritics may be able to help depolarise climate
politics and foster consensus on urgent questions of mitigation. In this way,
Garrard maintains, ecocriticism should become both more and less political:
less focused on translating the goals of green activism into critical practice
but more engaged with a wider spectrum of positions and modes of political
analysis. Brexit ecocriticism, then, 'would set out to consider the relationship of conservative, and Conservative, cultural politics to the politics of the
environment, both before 2016 and in the aftermath'.[38]

Kingsnorth is a fascinating case study in this respect precisely because he
does not fit the conservative (or Conservative) mould. He is a former radical
green activist, whose politics were shaped by the anti-globalisation protests of
the 1990s, and, around the same time, the anti-roads actions which occurred
in places such as Twyford Down and Newbury, in the south of England.
Recalling his time in the direct action camps in these rural areas, he writes
that 'there was a Wordsworthian feel to the whole thing: the defence of the
trees simply because they were trees'.[39] But he argues that this period also
marked the conclusion of the kind of ecocentric activism he cared about.
From the end of the millennium to the present, the environmental movement has become less and less nature-centred, and more and more concerned
with things like carbon, sustainability, and renewable energy. This is not environmentalism but 'neo-environmentalism', he complains, little more than an
adjunct to global capitalism in its race to obliterate wild nature with technologies intended to sustain human appetites.[40] Worst of all was the invasion
of the environmental movement by socialists, especially since environmentalism was always supposed to be an alternative to 'the seized up politics of left
and right'.[41] In Kingsnorth's view, the end of the Soviet Union prompted

[36]   *Ibid.*, p. 123.
[37]   Greg Garrard, Axel Goodbody, George Handley, and Stephanie Posthumus,
Climate Change Scepticism: A Transnational Ecocritical Analysis (London, 2019).
[38]   Garrard, 'Brexit Ecocriticism', p. 111.
[39]   Kingsnorth, *Confessions of a Recovering Environmentalist*, p. 74.
[40]   *Ibid.*, p. 131.
[41]   *Ibid.*, p. 75.

leftists to migrate opportunistically to the ecopolitical arena, bringing with them their anthropocentric commitments to social justice:

> Now it seemed that environmentalism was not about wildness or ecocentrism or the other-than-human world and our relationship to it. Instead it was about (human) social justice and (human) equality and (human) progress and ensuring that all these things could be realised without degrading the (human) resource base that we used to call nature.[42]

As a result of this baleful coalescence of capitalists and socialists, 'today's environmentalism is about people', he exclaims, as if there could be no greater betrayal of green principles.[43]

How do we get from the bitterness of disillusionment to the politics of ecological Englishness and the apocalypticism of *The Wake*? The connecting thread lies in Kingsnorth's account of dark ecology. Dark ecology is, in part, a process of grieving for the hope and enthusiasm green activism once inspired, but it also stems from a hard-won realisation that ecology's proper affective register is melancholy, not the optimism that neo-environmentalists draw from the prospect of technological salvation. Kingsnorth provocatively refers to Ted Kaczynski (more commonly known as the Unabomber), not in order to advocate ecoterrorism but to suggest that our environmental situation is so dire that a collapse of 'technological society' may be our only viable path.[44] Drawing on Ronald Wright's concept of the progress trap (the idea that technological solutions to short-term problems generate longer-term problems, requiring more technological solutions), Kingsnorth argues that technology has an inbuilt tendency towards crises. When humans perfected hunting in the Palaeolithic era, this caused extinctions of megafauna and the loss of the food sources provided by big game. This in turn led to the end of large-scale hunter-gatherer societies, and the emergence of agricultural society in the Neolithic period. The emergence of fossil capitalism and the Anthropocene follows the same logic: solutions are found which only intensify the problems they were supposed to solve. Each improvement of knowledge or technology leads recursively to more problems, requiring new improvements, in a runaway process.[45]

Kingsnorth's is not a simplistic anti-technology or primitivist position, then, but a recognition that contemporary ecological crisis is bound to a

---

42   *Ibid.*, p. 76.
43   *Ibid.*, p. 78.
44   *Ibid.*, p. 121.
45   *Ibid.*, p. 138. See also Ronald Wright, *A Short History of Progress* (Toronto, 2004).

long history of human social evolution, in which nature is externalised in response to demands for greater security for ever greater numbers of people. Society becomes trapped and then imperilled within the form of ecological accumulation on which it depends. This is comparable to what Gregory Bateson called a 'double bind', a communication paradox in which a message is refuted by its own context.[46] Rather than dissipating itself, the paradox maintains the subject of communication within a divided state. Morton argues that 'agrilogistics', or the 'technical, planned and perfectly logical approach to built space' which emerged with agricultural society at the end of the last Ice Age, is a similarly paradoxical process.[47] The more agrilogistic consciousness renders nature an externalised resource, the more we are drawn into an ecological web that binds us to it inextricably. For Morton, this weirdly looping form of ecological awareness is manifest in the very agrilogistic consciousness which tries to straighten the loop out through the linear, anthropocentric temporalities of technological reason.[48] The 'machine' of human domination of the Earth becomes unstoppable.[49] But it is also weirdly wired to destroy itself, as if possessed by a nihilistic death drive. And yet dark ecology, for both Kingsnorth and Morton, is also an acknowledgement that if technological society becomes ecologically devastating at planetary scales, that devastation nevertheless emerges from a fundamentally ecological relationship which can provide some kind of path through the ruins. A politics of affect emerges here for both authors: 'you find the sweetness inside the depression', writes Morton.[50] Moving beyond simple despair while confronting the darkness of inevitable collapse, Kingsnorth suggests, in a similar vein that 'there is something beyond despair too; or rather, something that accompanies it, like a companion on the road. This is my approach [...] a dark time; a dark ecology. None of this is going to save the world – but then, there is no saving the world'.[51]

Read in terms of *The Wake*, though, dark ecology's sombre apocalypticism can be said to underpin a political narrative of rebirth or palingenesis. Ecological Englishness is constituted through the annihilation that obliterates the 'anglisc folc', but also brings them back as a spectral presence. Ecocentric hyperlocalism, for all its hostility to anthropocentrism, thus becomes part of

[46]   Discussed in Anthony Chaney, *Runaway: Gregory Bateson, the Double Bind, and the Rise of Ecological Consciousness* (Chapel Hill, 2017).
[47]   Morton, *Dark Ecology*, p. 42.
[48]   *Ibid.*, p. 57.
[49]   Kingsnorth, *Confessions of a Recovering Environmentalist*, p. 141.
[50]   Morton, *Dark Ecology*, p. 117.
[51]   Kingsnorth, *Confessions of a Recovering Environmentalist*, p. 147.

a highly human political project, based in geographical rootedness, a kind of *volkish* environmental populism done up in funereal colours. Kingsnorth's condemnation of 'citizens of nowhere', a phrase subsequently taken up by Theresa May's anti-immigrant Brexit rhetoric, is redolent of antisemitic discourse about rootless cosmopolitanism.[52] This takes us into a very dark political terrain indeed. In Roger Griffin's influential analysis, mythic narratives of collapse and rebirth were characteristic of the fascist ideologies of the early-twentieth century. But the political myths of fascism were themselves symptomatic of a wider context in which modernity was reacting against itself, in a manner that might be called 'autoimmune'.[53] This is reflected extensively in the aesthetic cultures of modernism, as Griffin shows, but the development of ecological politics is deeply implicated, too. The Nazi Party deployed the language and aesthetics of nature protection in various ways to insist upon ethnic purity, organic integrity, and geographical rootedness.[54] What Hitler's minister of food and agriculture Richard Walther Darré called 'blood and soil' was an attempt to align ethnonationalism with a romanticised appeal to the stability and durability of pre-modern agrarian life.[55] The unstable term 'ecofascism' has been used to characterise both Nazi appropriations of environmentalism in this vein and those forms of ecocentrism which appear misanthropic in their exclusion of questions of social justice.

Recently, ecofascism has become an identifier for some within the violent extremes of the contemporary far right.[56] In Europe and elsewhere, political groups are deploying forms of neo-Malthusian environmentalism to demonise immigrants and insist on territorial integrity in the face of climate collapse. Marine Le Pen's National Rally (formerly the National Front) is one of the most prominent examples of contemporary far-right ecopolitics. In 2019, Le Pen targeted immigrants as causing environmental harm: 'environmentalism

[52]   Paul Kingsnorth, *Real England: The Battle Against the Bland* (London, 2008), p. 7. For a history of the antisemitic discourse of the rootless cosmopolitan, see Cathy S. Gelbin and Sander L. Gilman, *Cosmopolitanisms and the Jews* (Ann Arbor, 2017).
[53]   Roger Griffin, *Modernism and Fascism: The Sense of a Beginning under Mussolini and Hitler* (Basingstoke, 2007), p. 8. On the concept of autoimmunity, see Jacques Derrida, *Rogues: Two Essays on Reason*, trans. Pascale-Anne Brault and Michael Naas (Stanford, 2005).
[54]   Janet Biehl and Peter Staudenmaier, *Ecofascism: Lessons from the German Experience* (Edinburgh, 1995).
[55]   See Ursula K. Heise, *Sense of Place and Sense of Planet: The Environmental Imagination of the Global* (Oxford, 2008), pp. 47–8. See also Greg Garrard, 'Heidegger Nazism Ecocriticism', *Interdisciplinary Studies in Literature and Environment* 17.2 (2010), pp. 251–71 (p. 256).
[56]   Moore and Roberts, *The Rise of Ecofascism*.

[is] the natural child of patriotism, because it's the natural child of rootedness [...] if you're a nomad, you're not an environmentalist'.[57] The links made here between national identity, nature protection, and the ecological essentialism of place are not very different from Kingsnorth's, though his tone is loftier. Andreas Malm and the Zetkin Collective argue, scathingly, that Kingsnorth's belletrist rhetoric of national nature is the mere flipside of a brutal climate apartheid in which the global North prioritises its own survival above all else.[58] Love of nature and climate barbarism merge.

Given these troubling similarities between Kingsnorth's supposedly 'benevolent' green nationalism and the more extreme variants of far-right ecopolitics at work today, Garrard's conciliatory approach might appear misplaced. But it is crucial that ecocritics be able to offer some response, other than simple dismissal or blissful ignorance, of far-right environmental discourse, past and present. We should acknowledge how fascism has, in a sense, been part of the history of ecology, even ecocriticism itself, since arguably one of the key founders of ecocritical practice was Martin Heidegger, who joined the Nazi Party in 1932 and never officially renounced his membership. Heidegger's post-war studies of the poetry of Hölderlin and Rilke have been hugely influential for work on the relationships between literature and place. Essential dwelling, for Heidegger, meant the inhabitation of a place of revelation that poetry, in opposition to technological consciousness, makes possible.[59] These kinds of ideas have become embedded in ecocriticism. Foundational texts in the field, such as Jonathan Bate's *The Song of the Earth* (2001) and Lawrence Buell's *The Future of Environmental Criticism* (2005), engage with the problem of Heidegger's fascism obliquely and evasively by regarding the German philosopher's love of rustic place (famously, the Black Forest) as ultimately separable from his unfortunate political views.[60] Garrard, on the other hand, has suggested that ecocritics have little to lose by dispensing with Heidegger altogether.[61] But Morton's dark ecology suggests a different and more interesting, though fraught, path. It is insufficient to segregate Heidegger from politics or to disregard him

[57]   Cited in Joe Turner and Dan Bailey, '"Ecobordering": Casting Immigration Control as Environmental Protection', *Environmental Politics* 31.1 (2022), pp. 110–31 (p. 120).
[58]   Malm and the Zetkin Collective, *White Skin, Black Fuel*, p. 149.
[59]   Martin Heidegger, *Poetry, Language, Thought*, trans. Albert Hofstadter (New York, 1971), p. 213.
[60]   Jonathan Bate, *The Song of the Earth* (London, 2000); Lawrence Buell, *The Future of Environmental Criticism* (Oxford, 2005).
[61]   Garrard, 'Heidegger Nazism Ecocriticism'.

altogether, rather 'ecognosis must traverse Heideggerian-Nazi space, descend below it: through nihilism, not despite it'.[62] In the final section of this article, I give an account of this remarkable claim, showing how Morton's version of dark ecology relates to Kingsnorth's, and what all of this means for the politics of ecocriticism.

Aesthetic Agencies

For Morton, whose most well-known book is still probably *Ecology Without Nature* (2007), the aesthetic problem of 'Nature' is also a political problem, one that relates specifically to fascism. The kinds of aestheticised natural environments beloved of Heidegger (and others besides) are too indebted to Nature as an aesthetic-political framing device to be able to properly engage with ecological realities, which are often dark, depressing and abject.[63] 'Nature' – externalised and romanticised, projected onto wilderness areas and places like the Black Forest – is yet another piece of agrilogistic engineering designed to straighten out the weird loop of ecological awareness, to separate humans from their nonhuman contexts by a neat dividing line, to seek some purified version of humanity by purging it of its ecological others. Nature is over there, we are over here.[64] The Nature of romantic environmentalisms and the Nature of technoscientific Enlightenment reason are really the same thing. Furthermore, if fascism's appeals to a racially homogenous pre-modern society are just part of modernity's own autoimmune reaction, then this itself is part of a longer history, beginning in the Neolithic, in which agrilogistics attempts to escape its own progress traps.[65] There is nothing particularly special about fascism in this sense. Morton writes that

> Nazis are trying to maintain the normative subject–object dualism in which I can recognize myself as decisively different from a nonhuman or, to be more blunt, a non-German, a recognition in which everything else appears as equipment for my Lebensraum project. So there is little point in denigrating ecological politics as fascist. But there is every point in naming some Nature-based politics as fascist. Here is a strong sense in which ecology is without Nature.[66]

---

[62]   Morton, *Dark Ecology*, p. 52.
[63]   Morton, *Ecology without Nature*, p. 58.
[64]   *Ibid.*, p. 8.
[65]   Morton, *Dark Ecology*, p. 38.
[66]   *Ibid.*, p. 138.

The Heideggerian Nature of essential dwelling is projected outside of the turmoil of modern technological society to become a reservation for Being, just as agrilogistic reason projects a concept of matter as an inert resource available for unlimited human consumption. Heidegger's fascism, accordingly, can be regarded as part of the same error that leads us to annul ecological entanglements through a rigid nature/society dualism that segregates humans from nonhumans in arbitrary and often racist ways.

But – and this is key – Morton holds on to a certain version of Heideggerianism, one filtered through Graham Harman's object-oriented ontology, which maintains that reality is itself fundamentally withdrawn into its own dense obscurity and that we glimpse only momentary clearings, partial unconcealments within the thicket.[67] This does not simply mean that reality is withdrawn from consciousness and that we only perceive a representation of it, as asserted by traditional Kantian philosophy, but that all objects – from material things to human minds – withdraw from each *other*, interrelating only partially and in a way that never constitutes the holism of totality. 'Withdrawal – the fact that no access mode can exhaust a thing – bestows upon things their flickering, spectral quality'.[68] The *lumen naturale* of what Heidegger called Dasein (human existence) is only one mode of access in a vast constellation of interconnected objects. A 'hyperobject', for example, is a massively distributed thing that only manifests a partial side of itself at any given moment, as climate does through local weather events, or factory farming through the meat on the plate.[69] Ecological interconnectedness is never exhausted by any particular mode of appearing, but is a flickering half-light of object encounters. Holism is always incomplete (that is, non-Gaian), because there is always a shadowy gap between what an object is and how it appears to another object. This gap is the space of appearance (the aesthetic dimension) and the space of action or agency (the political dimension) combined. The weird is not just related to causality, the web of becoming and fate, then, but also to the 'strange of appearances' – things never appear as they are and are ontologically incapable of doing so.

This 'weird weirdness' is what makes ecology dark.[70] Objects are *aesthetic* as well as political (causal or agentic), and in this respect Morton's work is of a piece with the new materialism that has been crucial for developments in ecocritical theory

[67]   On Graham Harman's influence, see Timothy Morton, *Realist Magic: Objects, Ontology, Causality* (Ann Arbour, 2013), pp. 1–39.
[68]   Timothy Morton, *Humankind: Solidarity with Nonhuman People* (London, 2019), p. 98.
[69]   Morton, *Hyperobjects*, p. 12.
[70]   Morton, *Dark Ecology*, p. 7.

over the last few years.[71] But we need to interrogate carefully what this ecological aestheticising of agencies means for questions relating to the critique of power, theories of the state, and populist social movements, including new nationalist movements and the politics of territories. It is important to insist that there is no guarantee that a dissolution of the nature/society dualism will necessarily give rise to liberatory forces. One way of understanding ecological politics today is to observe that the Arendtian space of appearance, which she quite deliberately defined in anthropocentric terms, is dissipated into the vast aggregation of objects constituting human and nonhuman reality.[72] What historical forces does this leave us open to? Kingsnorth's econationalism, which indigenises a historically privileged group through a compelling narrative of ecological crisis, is only one example. More extreme forms of blood and soil politics is another, taking shape across the world in ways conjugated with climate change.[73] These syntheses of nature, nation and ethnic identity are often only possible through a cultural imaginary, that is to say, an ecoaesthetic politics.[74] Ecocritics generally believe in the symbolic power of cultural representations to change the world for the better.[75] However, they are less likely to take notice of such far-right adoptions of ecoaesthetic agencies.

Morton's ecocommunism could be thought of as a counterexample, a politicisation of the aesthetic as opposed to an aestheticisation of politics, in the Benjaminian sense. But the correspondences noted between the two versions of dark ecology discussed here should cause us to ask questions about Morton's project. In the latter's view, fascism is nothing more than an attempt to annihilate the weird penumbral space between an object and its partial manifestation in an attempt to make the whole a complete presence. The antisemitic figure of the Jew comes to embody everything abject and strange which prevents the closure of the totality, and is targeted with exterminatory violence for this reason.[76] Indeed, all racism might be said to stem from a hatred of ecological otherness. The Nazi nation state and the organic whole of nature fetishised by Nazi nature worship are just reflections of one another.[77] In this sense, Morton insists that dark ecology, stripped

[71]   See, for example, Serenella Iovino and Serpil Oppermann, eds, *Material Ecocriticism* (Bloomington, 2014).

[72]   Hannah Arendt, *The Human Condition* (Chicago, 1998), pp. 198–9.

[73]   Peter Staudenmaier, *Ecology Contested: Environmental Politics between Left and Right* (Porsgrunn, 2021), p. 149.

[74]   Christoffer Kølvraa and Bernard Forchtner, 'Cultural Imaginaries of the Extreme Right: An Introduction', *Patterns of Prejudice* 53.3 (2019), pp. 227–35.

[75]   Timothy Clark, *The Value of Ecocriticism* (Cambridge, 2019), p. 2.

[76]   Morton, *Humankind*, pp. 134–5.

[77]   Morton, *Ecology without Nature*, p. 97.

of the concept of Nature, ensures that we can avoid the political disaster of fascist environmentalism, since dark ecology focuses on the abject, spectral weirdness of human-nonhuman kinships and solidarities.[78] 'Humankind' is Morton's name for the space of human solidarity with nonhumans: 'human-kind is flickering, displaced from itself, ecstatic, rippling and dappled with shadows'.[79] Marxism is still too anthropocentric to grasp this shadowy realm properly, which is why an anarchistic mode is necessary.[80]

The problem, however, is that there is no guarantee that the aesthetic agencies of ecology alone are sufficient to guard against the kinds of dark econationalism we have seen in Kingsnorth's work, or indeed other forms of far-right ecopolitics emerging today. 'Nature' is the key problem for Morton because it remains an illuminating framework, a means of clarifying differences and dispelling spectral ambiguities. But this may be to grant too much saving power to darkness. Morton has argued that Kingsnorth's version of dark ecology 'delete[s] the strangeness' and gives in to 'bleak certainty'.[81] But this is not true. The weird, uncanny, or spectral are equally part of Kingsnorth's project. In *The Wake*, the English landscape is full of supernatural entities and uncanny places, in particular the dark waters of the fens, Buccmaster's *Mare Tenebrarum*, where the 'eald gods' call upon him to fight for England.[82] What is perhaps most fascinating about Buccmaster is that he speaks to us as a ghost, a spectral presence who refuses to be moved from our modern vernacular.

The 'Spectral Plain' is Morton's name for the space of egalitarian, anar-chistic, non-totalisable co-existence in which politics is to be conducted.[83] It can be reached only by descending through the nihilism of racist biopolitics and their strict demarcations of living and dead, clean and unclean, human and nonhuman, to a place where all of these oppositions collapse. Ecological reality is 'undead' in this precise sense.[84] Kingsnorth's notion of ecological Englishness complicates this, however, since it is exclusionary by default, and *The Wake* demonstrates how a palingenetic nationalism can make use of spectral ecology. Indeed, Morton severely underplays the degree to which fascism was fascinated by, and deployed, ideas of the undead and the uncan-

[78]   Morton, *Humankind*, p. 83.
[79]   *Ibid.*, p. 84.
[80]   *Ibid.*, p. 28.
[81]   Timothy Morton, *Being Ecological* (Cambridge MA, 2018), p. 15.
[82]   Kingsnorth, *The Wake*, p. 108.
[83]   Morton, *Dark Ecology*, p. 137.
[84]   *Ibid.*, p. 97.

ny.[85] It is also well known that some fascist authors, both before and after the First World War, were in thrall to the occult in ways that amount to a kind of spiritual ecofascism pitted against scientific rationalism. The Italian writer Julius Evola (who influenced Benito Mussolini and Steve Bannon, among others) is probably the most famous of these figures. In *Revolt Against the Modern World* (1934), Evola espouses a dark ecology in order to ground notions of hierarchy and tradition:

> Traditionally speaking, the notion of 'nature' did not correspond merely to the world of bodies and of visible forms – the object of research of contemporary, secularized science – but on the contrary, it corresponded essentially to part of an invisible reality. The ancients had the sense of a dark netherworld, populated by obscure and ambiguous forces of every kind (the demonic soul of nature, which is the essential substratum of all nature's forms and energies) that was opposed to the suprarational and sidereal brightness of a higher region. [...] Only the nonhuman dimension constituted the essence and the goal of any truly traditional civilization.[86]

Subverting the bright, illuminating framework of Nature with a darker one capable of admitting uncanny nonhuman agencies is not necessarily sufficient to ward off fascism.

While the esotericism of Evolan fascism is unlikely to become widespread enough to warrant a political threat, more populist varieties of such thinking are making themselves felt in the ethnonationalisms now forming in the context of climate collapse. Bruno Latour – a key influence on Harman and Morton – argued that a new kind of politics of the local must emerge, as the cosmopolitanism of global capitalism falls apart.[87] Returning to Earth, to the terrestrial (as opposed to Nature), involves reconceptualising territorial attachments entirely. Ecocriticism should see itself as deeply entangled in these epochal political questions, since place has been for it such a crucial and contested category.[88] A critique of place, rather than an unrelenting aestheticisation of it, is needed now more than ever, but it is also crucial to understand to what extent places are aesthetic constructions with specific histories, aesthetic agents in their own right. Indigenous peoples have long known how

---

[85]   Mark Neocleous, *The Monstrous and the Dead: Burke, Marx, Fascism* (Cardiff, 2005), p. 77.

[86]   Julius Evola, *Revolt Against the Modern World*, trans. Guido Stucco (Rochester, 1995), p. 4.

[87]   Bruno Latour, *Down to Earth: Politics in the New Climatic Regime*, trans. Catherine Porter (Cambridge, 2018), p. 92.

[88]   See Heise, *Sense of Place and Sense of Planet*.

entire worlds have been destroyed in the ruthless establishment of a single capitalist world-system.[89] Dark ecology, for both Morton and Kingsnorth, amounts to a recovery of the local in the ruins of the global, but neither seem interested in trying to comprehend, for example, the world loss suffered by victims of the transatlantic slave trade.[90] Morton argues that dark ecology's commitment to the weird agencies of ecological entanglement can provide a 're-enchantment' of place and the local.[91] Yet, in the absence of a properly contextualised historical and political understanding, the re-enchantment of place can lead down some very dangerous political paths. Rather than fleeing the shattered remnants of the world in search of smaller worlds – little Englands, for example – ecocriticism should insist, all the more strongly, on the irreducibility of a common Earth.

[89]   See Deborah Danowski and Eduardo Vivero de Castro, *The Ends of the World*, trans. Rodrigo Nunes (Cambridge, 2017).
[90]   Malcolm Ferdinand, *Decolonial Ecology: Thinking from the Caribbean World*, trans. Anthony Paul Smith (Cambridge, 2022), p. 35.
[91]   Morton, *Dark Ecology*, p. 17.

6

Literature, Literary Pedagogy, and Extinction Rebellion (XR): The Case of Tarka the Otter

KARÍN LESNIK-OBERSTEIN

Extinction Rebellion's 'fifth principle' states that 'We value ... [f]ollowing a cycle of action, reflection, learning, and planning for more action'.[1] This chapter will examine what this may mean in relation to literature (and the teaching of literature) and what implications it may have outside the classroom. XR activist academics have argued that the environmental emergency demands, as Tema Milstein says,

> [r]adical modes of sustainable education (including regenerative pedagogy, which tends to the global shift to restore, respect, and regenerate ecological and societal balance, and inside-out pedagogy, which helps learners take their inner seeds, sprouts, and blossoms of good ecocultural intentions to stages of external fruition) [that] speak both to educating learners and engaging the public.[2]

The Extinction Rebellion Universities group similarly states in its 'Declaration of Rebellion' that

> We celebrate all forms of learning; opening our hearts and minds to the diverse perspectives and experiences within human understanding; amplifying the voices of those long teaching the inherent value and knowledge within the Earth's life-systems; and exploring the role of the arts alongside the sciences in tackling climate change, the spiritual alongside the material.[3]

---

[1]   Extinction Rebellion, 'About Us' (no date), https://extinctionrebellion.uk/the-truth/about-us.

[2]   Tema Milstein, 'Blooming in the Doom and Gloom: Bringing Regenerative Pedagogy to the Rebellion', *The Journal of Sustainability Education* (9 April 2020), http://www.susted.com/wordpress/content/blooming-in-the-doom-and-gloom-bringing-regenerative-pedagogy-to-the-rebellion_2020_04.

[3]   Extinction Rebellion Universities group, 'Extinction Rebellion Universities Group Calls for Degree Overhaul to Mark Start of Global Climate Strikes' (20 September 2019), https://extinctionrebellion.uk/2019/09/20/extinction-rebellion-

The urgency of the issues at stake inevitably militates for such a language of effect and affect and morality.[4] However, as Timothy Clark argues in *The Value of Ecocriticism*, such aims have embedded in them both the language of a neo-liberal agenda of agency, impact, choice, voices, story, and experience, which are elsewhere held to be deeply implicated in the production of the environmental catastrophe.[5] Helena Feder, in her introduction to *Close Reading the Anthropocene*, similarly warns that '[i]n the Age of "Man," the question of signification may all too easily reify the systems it claims to challenge, if not describe'.[6] This article will discuss what is less often raised about the trap of reification: the question of representation, frequently assumed to be the grounding for activism, literary reading, and pedagogy. Representation also tends to operate in tandem with the critical languages of affect, especially in relation to empathy, attention, and imagination.[7] As Julian Henriques and colleagues argue in their classic analysis of neo-liberalism, *Changing the Subject: Psychology, Social Regulation and Subjectivity*,

> The notion of the unitary, rational subject survives not so much in explicit defences of the model as in the implicit assumptions of various dualisms: social and cognitive, content and process, the intentionality of agents and determination by structures, the subject as constituted or constitutive [...] Some of the same problems apply to the new interest in 'narrative' as a conceptual and empirical tool, an interest based on the [idea] that people tell stories in order to make sense of their experience, past, present and imagined future.[8]

universities-group-calls-for-degree-overhaul-to-mark-start-of-global-climate-strikes.

[4]   The question of how 'urgent' the 'issues' may be, and to whom and how, has been raised in ecocriticism, especially in relation to claims of how 'we' are constituted. See, for example, Sojourner Truth, 'Ain't I A Woman?', *Anti-slavery Bugle* (21 June 1851), https://chroniclingamerica.loc.gov/lccn/sn83035487/1851-06-21/ed-1/seq-4/; Paul Gilroy, *The Black Atlantic: Modernity and Double Consciousness* (London, 1993); *We Have the Right to Exist: A Translation of Aboriginal Indigenous Thought. The First Book Ever Published From an Ahnishinahbæotjibway Perspective*, trans. Wub-E.-Ke-New (New York, 1995); Richard Kerridge, 'Introduction', Richard Kerridge and Neil Sammells, eds, *Writing the Environment: Ecocriticism and Literature* (London, 1998), pp. 1–11 (p. 6); Alison Kafer, *Feminist, Queer, Crip* (Bloomington, 2013), pp. 129–48; Kathryn Yusoff, *A Billion Black Anthropocenes or None* (Minneapolis, 2018).

[5]   Timothy Clark, *The Value of Ecocriticism* (Cambridge, 2019).

[6]   Helena Feder, 'Introduction: The Unbearable Closeness of Reading', Helena Feder, ed., *Close Reading the Anthropocene* (London, 2021), pp. 1–15 (p. 2).

[7]   Susan Lanzoni, *Empathy: A History* (New Haven, 2018). For differing critiques of 'empathy', see Daniela Caselli, 'Kindergarten Theory: Childhood, Affect, Critical Thought', *Feminist Theory* 11.3 (2010), pp. 241–54; Ruth Leys, '"The Turn to Affect": A Critique', *Critical Inquiry* 37 (2011), pp. 434–72.

[8]   Julian Henriques *et al.*, *Changing the Subject: Psychology, Social Regulation and*

These ideas operate in a great deal of teaching of activism, of approaches to literature, and of the operations and effects of ecocriticism specifically.[9] However, they are rarely reflected on as being themselves part of the reification of the systems they claim to challenge. For instance, despite the warning Feder gives about the dangers of 'all too easy' reification, most of her contributors in *Close Reading the Anthropocene* rely unquestioningly on representation.[10] Similarly, despite Feder citing the critiques by Gary Snyder and Kathryn Youssoff of a universalising 'we' in relation to environmental issues, her contributors rely on this same claim to an identifiable communality (in some cases, an explicitly American communality).[11] Likewise, Sidney I. Dobrin's *Blue Ecocriticism and the Oceanic Imperative* explicitly sets out to address 'critical questions about ocean and representations of ocean'.[12] Marek Oziewicz's introduction to his co-edited collection, *Fantasy and Myth in the Anthropocene*, entitled 'The Choice We Have in the Stories We Tell' warns that 'modern capitalism reproduces itself through "feed[ing] on and learn[ing] from resistance and critique"', and that, '[o]f course, not all humans have contributed to the Anthropocenic acceleration in the same way'.[13] Nevertheless, almost all of the book relies on both a communal idea of 'we' and on representation.[14] In classic neo-liberal manner, Oziewicz diagnoses that the 'urgencies of the Anthropocene [...] are primarily challenges to our story systems [, ...] the stories we have been telling ourselves about human exceptionalism [, ...] human entitlement [, ...] and human identity'.[15] Such an idea about story is liable to the criticism offered by Henriques and colleagues:

Subjectivity, 2nd edn (London, 1998), pp. ix, xiii.

[9]   On similar issues around teaching dis/ability activism, see Karín Lesnik-Oberstein, ed., *Rethinking Disability Theory and Practice: Challenging Essentialism* (Basingstoke, 2015).

[10]   Helena Feder, 'Introduction', Helena Feder, ed., *Close Reading the Anthropocene* (London, 2021), pp. 175–90 (p. 2). Only C. Parker Krieg raises anti-representational questions, 'From Scale to Antagonism: Reading the Human in Kurt Vonnegut's *Galápagos*', pp. 175–89.

[11]   The exception is Senayon Olaoluwa, 'Postcolonial Anthropocene and Narrative Archaeology in *Burma Boy*', Feder, ed., *Close Reading the Anthropocene*, pp. 93–102.

[12]   Sidney I. Dobrin, *Blue Ecocriticism and the Oceanic Imperative* (London, 2021), p. xi.

[13]   Citing Max Haiven, Marek Oziewicz, 'Introduction: The Choice We Have in the Stories We Tell', Marek Oziewicz, Brian Attebery, and Tereza Dědinová, eds, *Fantasy and Myth in the Anthropocene: Imagining Futures and Dreaming Hope in Literature and Media* (London, 2022), pp. 1–13 (pp. 5, 3).

[14]   *Ibid.*, p. 5.

[15]   *Ibid.*, p. 1. Diagnosing human exceptionalism in this way is an example of human exceptionalism (thanks to Natalie England for pointing this out).

The question of the subject's relation to discourse has been joined by the question of what is the relation of the speaking subject to the narrative that s/he produces. Not surprisingly, as long as the familiar dualisms dominate, the problems remain the same. For example, when narrative is used as an account of how someone [...] reconstructs the self through producing a new story for and about themselves, the subject is split into a creative narrator (whose creativity is unexplained, except as a reflection of newly available discourse) and the object of the narrative, the self who is a product of the story. Neither takes into account the historical production of people's lives and subjectivities, and neither considers the effects of practices and relations [...] nor unconscious processes, in constructing subjectivity.[16]

On representation, as Dana Phillips argues about the development of ecocriticism,

> I doubt whether the ecocritics' preferred counter to [the blasé attitude toward the natural world in literary studies] – a renewal of realism, at least where nature is concerned – is all that powerful a response, based as it is on some dubious ideas about the nature of representation and the representation of nature.[17]

In this chapter, I will argue that Henriques and colleagues' analysis of the problems of claims to story, and Phillips's diagnosis of the problems of representation, remain as relevant as ever. The political and ideological reasons for this mark the limits to what a great deal of environmental activism and teaching of ecocriticism is able or willing to reflect on, even in the face of what is constantly claimed to be the final, greatest, and most apocalyptic crisis ever encountered. Ecocriticism's current questions about signification draw on prior activist critical theory in feminist, African American, Aboriginal Indigenous, and animal studies. This chapter will use this to analyse the implications of the return in past decades (not just in ecocriticism, and not just in literary studies) to a reliance on representation, affect, effect, and impact (including in the neo-liberal university).[18] To do so, it will draw on the anti-representational critiques of Donna Haraway's early writings (including *Primate Visions*) and on the work of Jacques Derrida.[19] *Eco-*

---

[16]   Henriques *et al.*, *Changing the Subject*, pp. xiii–iv.

[17]   Dana Phillips, 'Ecocriticism, Literary Theory, and the Truth of Ecology', *New Literary History* 30.3 (Summer 1999), pp. 577–602 (p. 578). See also Dana Phillips, *The Truth of Ecology: Nature, Culture, and Literature in America* (Oxford, 2003).

[18]   Neil Cocks, *Higher Education Discourse and Deconstruction: Challenging the Case for Transparency and Objecthood* (Basingstoke, 2017).

[19]   Donna Haraway, *Primate Visions: Gender, Race and Nature in the World of Modern Science* (London, 1989). Recent ecocriticism tends to draw primarily on

Deconstruction: Derrida and Environmental Philosophy, edited by Matthias Fritsch and colleagues, proposes that

> Deconstruction [...] is well-placed to assume the task [to welcome anti-Cartesian re-thinking of the human-nature relation,] due to its long-standing critical engagement with this tradition from the vantage point of a nonhumanist philosophy of relational difference [and ...] from the fact that deconstruction targets logocentrism.[20]

Thus, this chapter demonstrates the consequences of reading *differently*, and what this might mean for literature, literary pedagogy, and activism. It does so by taking as a case-study an article which self-consciously engages closely with the issues of both reflection and representation: Stewart Cole's 'The Animal Novel as Biopolitical Critique: Henry Williamson's *Tarka the Otter*'.[21]
   Cole draws attention to the fact that one of the primary texts of modern nature and ecological writing, Rachel Carson's *Silent Spring* (and her earlier *Under the Sea-Wind*) were inspired by *Tarka the Otter*.[22] This is despite the common assumption that *Tarka* is a children's book, and therefore has 'received almost no scholarly attention'.[23] Cole sets out to challenge this situation:

> *Tarka*'s persistent classification as children's literature is rooted less in its specific textual qualities than in the anthropocentric assumption that humanity itself (or 'the human condition') is the only fit subject for serious literature. And yet even with the recent surge in interest among literary scholars in representations of animality and interrogations of the human/animal divide – an interest often motivated by a desire to subvert the anthropocentric founda-

---

Haraway's more recent writings, such as *Staying with the Trouble: Making Kin in the Chthulucene* (Durham, 2016), but the theoretical arguments of her earlier work are more in line with the critique here.

[20]   Matthias Fritsch, Philippe Lynes, and David Wood, eds, *Eco-Deconstruction: Derrida and Environmental Philosophy* (New York, 2018), p. 6.

[21]   Stewart Cole, 'The Animal Novel as Biopolitical Critique: Henry Williamson's *Tarka the Otter*', *ISLE: Interdisciplinary Studies in Literature and Environment* 26.3 (2019), pp. 540–69; Henry Williamson, *Tarka the Otter* (1927; London, 1995).

[22]   Rachel Carson, *Silent Spring* (1962; Harmondsworth, 2000); Rachel Carson, *Under the Sea-Wind* (1941; Harmondsworth, 2007).

[23]   Cole, 'The Animal Novel', p. 541. Sue Walsh argues that Steve Baker, *Picturing the Beast: Animals, Identity, and Representation* (Manchester, 1993), 'challenges the association of the animal with the trivial', but does not ask why both animal and child are seen as insignificant, 'Child/Animal: It's The "Real" Thing', Karín Lesnik-Oberstein, ed., Special Issue: Children in Literature, *The Yearbook of English Studies* 32 (2002), pp. 151–62 (p. 151). See also Karín Lesnik-Oberstein, 'Children's Literature and the Environment', Kerridge and Sammells, eds, *Writing the Environment*, pp. 208–18.

tions of both literary studies and the Western philosophical tradition more broadly – *Tarka* has languished unexamined, remaining unacknowledged [in] its status as not only a landmark piece of nature writing but also perhaps the earliest attempt in English literature to immerse readers in the sensory and emotional worlds of nonhuman animals.

But this essay is not simply a gesture of advocacy. While it is true that recent trends in scholarship have helped renew our reasons to read *Tarka the Otter*, I will go further to argue that in reading *Tarka*, we uniquely confront both the contradictions inherent in the anti-anthropocentric project of literary animal studies and the powerful reasons why, despite these contradictions, this project must be urgently pursued.[24]

The 'inherent contradictions', for Cole, turn upon the

various ways in which *Tarka the Otter* both serves as a foundational and indeed prescient example of how the insights of theoretical animal studies can be actualized in literary practice, while also standing as a cautionary embodiment of the difficulties of fully actualizing such insights in so resolutely human an art form as literature (and indeed in so resolutely human a medium as language) – difficulties that thinkers in animal studies have not yet fully addressed.[25]

While work by Derrida, Haraway, and Phillips might be said to counter the final claim, Cole's other point, that theoretical animal studies find it difficult to actualise their insights, is in tension with his own subsequent readings of *Tarka*. He professes to call 'into question the anthropocentrism inherent in the fictional enterprise, illuminating the biopolitical stakes of the human/animal distinction underpinning our every act of literary representation'.[26] However, what is not called into question by Cole is either anthropocentrism or literary representation: these concepts stand unchallenged. Anthropomorphism and anthropocentrism are ideas ubiquitously used in a great deal of ecocriticism, and in environmental studies more widely, but are rarely themselves considered as being rooted in an already known distinction: that between a known and knowable animal and a known and knowable human. Cole has pre-determined his argument before he starts, and in so doing demonstrates the critical parameters of *all* work founded upon 'representation'.

---

[24]   Cole, 'The Animal Novel', p. 542.
[25]   *Ibid.*
[26]   *Ibid.*, p. 543.

Qualifying the Animal and the Human

Such claims to knowledge about the human and the animal (even as nonhuman animal, a ubiquitous term in current ecocriticism) continue to pervade Cole's discussion, though he calls these claims into question in other ways. For instance, when he argues that 'in depicting the cast of animal characters in *Tarka*, Williamson neither anthropomorphises outright nor fully divests himself of an anthropomorphic lens'.[27] While the terms 'outright' and 'fully' qualify his position, they cannot remove its grounding in known distinctions and characteristics of the human and the animal. Indeed, Cole, in exploring the limits of his qualifications, produces ever more details of what these known distinctions and characteristics are. He speaks of the 'animal' and the 'inhuman' in 'Tarka's intimacy with his natural environment [, ...] the inhuman particularities of the otter's sensorium [, ...] the otters' language of *yinny-yikker*ings and *iss-iss-ic-yangs*'. However, says Cole, since this 'subject matter (i.e., an otter)' is described in the human 'medium' of English language, the two are 'utterly alien to one another'. [28] Cole's argument here twists to sustain the 'utterly alien' quality of 'its subject matter' and 'its medium', but in order to do so it has to overlook its own repeated 'its', which holds the two sides together. Furthermore, 'subject matter' and 'medium' hinge on representation being assumed to be an inevitable (even natural) mode of writing and reading, since Cole distinguishes between the two – even while discussing Williamson's claimed ability to bring them closely together.

One of the twists in Cole's argument is further revealed in how 'language' is put to work in his formulations. On the one hand, the otter has to be removed from language (it is described purely in terms of its 'sensorium'). However, on the other hand, Cole splits the '*yinny-yikker*ings and *iss-iss-ic-yangs*' (from 'the otter's language') typographically, between the italic '*yinny-yikker*' and the roman 'ings', in an effort to distinguish between what is said to be the otter's own language and the 'human' frame which holds it. Always carefully reflective, Cole admits that 'to portray an otter's agency in so inescapably anthropocentric a medium as human language involves taking translational leaps at every juncture'.[29] Yet this passage unproblematically knows the otter to have 'agency' prior to being portrayed, while 'language' (which Cole now thinks of as specifically 'human') is known to be only a 'medium' (not the otter or its agency). Moreover, precisely because 'human language' here is only a 'medium', it can both be deprecated as 'anthropo-

27   *Ibid.*
28   *Ibid.*
29   *Ibid.*

centric' (as if there could be an alternative, non-anthropocentric medium) and subject to 'translational leaps', which implies that there is something which is prior to such translation, for which translation is required.

Cole's reading continuously re-encounters the consequences of such claims, as when he speaks of how,

> Even here, though, the novel ends up both flouting and reasserting anthropocentrism. Take, for example, the novel's first occurrence of otter language: 'He was quite selfish over his prey when his mother went to see what he was doing, and cried, *Iss-iss-ic-yang*! an old weasel threat, which being interpreted means, Go away, or I will drink your blood!' [...] Notice here how the narrative once again takes recourse to the passive voice ('being interpreted') to de-emphasize the human provenance of the interpretive act, implying that the interpretation simply occurs rather than being explicitly translated by the narrative voice.[30]

First, there is the question of Cole's claim that this moment is 'the novel's first occurrence of otter language'. Cole appears to be referring to the italics of '*Iss-iss-ic-yang*!', since earlier in the novel it is claimed that 'a thin, wavy, snarling cry rose out of the water. It was the bitch's yinny-yikker, or threat'.[31] My point is not about when the 'first occurrence' was, but about what Cole thinks counts as 'otter language'. Italics can be read here as a kind of eruption of 'otter language' into the narrative, but the earlier 'yinny-yikker' is understood to be said by the narration, not the otter bitch. Second, that 'yinny-yikker', although in Roman font, is still said to be other, in rising as 'a thin, wavy, snarling cry', a 'threat' (featuring in the 'glossary of local words and phrases', in some editions of *Tarka*, as 'noisily aggressive').[32] I am not claiming that 'local words and phrases' (regardless of the font) could be a pure eruption into the text any more than 'otter language', but instead that all words are claimed as such by the narration, where the meanings are deferred continuously without being able to settle on any final origin for their representation. The fact that, according to Cole, the 'human provenance of the interpretive act' can be 'de-emphasized' by the 'narrative [...] recourse to the passive voice' relies on layers of separated 'subject matter' (origin) and 'medium' (representation or interpretation), in order to diagnose intentional repressions of what Cole claims to be able to read regardless.

---

[30]   *Ibid.*, p. 546
[31]   Williamson, *Tarka*, p. 9.
[32]   *Ibid.*, front matter and p. 271.

Cole's discussion gets more and more involved in these alternating *rapprochements* and separations, as he continues, for instance by providing an 'almost [...] random' example of the difficulty arising when the otter is framed by human language:

> Early in the novel the narrative voice tells us that: 'The dog ['dog is the word for a male otter'] turned east, and ran along the otter-path used by otters long before the weir was made for the grist mill below Leaning Willow Island' ... In this sentence, the cardinal direction 'east,' the historical perspective implicit in the statement that the otter-path was 'used by otters long before the weir was made,' and the place name 'Leaning Willow Island' all highlight the explicitly human frame of reference within which the otter's actions are depicted. Otters themselves don't turn 'east'; we cannot know how they conceive of directions other than as instinctual urges *that way* or *down that riverbank* or *towards that tree*.[33]

For Cole, the 'explicitly human frame of reference' here is not that 'the dog [...] turned', or 'ran along the otter-path', or moved towards 'the grist mill below'. It is also not about 'the otter's actions', which are known to be separate from what is 'depicted'. Similarly, while Cole says that 'we cannot know', 'we' are told that we do 'know' that otters 'conceive of directions other than as instinctual urges *that way* or *down that riverbank* or *towards that tree*'. Moreover, '*that way* or *down that riverbank* or *towards that tree*' are here apparently not to be considered to be an 'explicitly human frame of reference': italics are again put to work to uphold a separation between this frame and 'instinctual urges'.

Interestingly and typically, Cole expresses concerns about his own formulations, but his concerns are not mine: the separation he upholds between a knowable and known animal and an animal beyond his 'explicitly human frame of reference'. In a footnote, Cole speaks of how his phrase 'instinctual urges' is problematic, citing Philip Armstrong, in *What Animals Mean in the Fiction of Modernity*.[34] According to Cole, Armstrong highlights how the concept of instinct is often mobilised to subordinate the will of non-human animals to our own. Commenting on *Moby Dick*, after discussing nineteenth-century accounts of whale behaviour as entirely instinctual, Armstrong points out that 'The same concept of instinct, which denies the whale's lack of purposive or effective agency, will prove adaptable both to an emerging evolutionary natural history, and to a capitalist attitude that sees

---

33   Cole, 'The Animal Novel', pp. 543–4.
34   Cole, 'The Animal Novel', p. 564, fn. 5.

nature as a resource'.[35] Neither Armstrong nor Cole see a difficulty in claiming to know that their respective animal has 'will' and 'purposive or effective agency', and that this 'agency' (unlike 'instinct') will not prove to be adaptable to either 'an emerging evolutionary natural history' or to 'a capitalist attitude that sees nature as a resource'. 'Will' and 'agency' are, apparently, not subject to 'biopolitical' forces or 'capitalism' – they are known to be just the truth about the whale.[36]

Cole argues that *Tarka* 'urges us to extend our pervading models of agency and subjectivity beyond their customary anthropocentrism to include nonhuman animals', but differentiates his own position by stating that 'agency and subjectivity' are, after all, 'models' which are not yet 'extend[ed]' to the 'nonhuman animals'.[37] However, this claim is in line with previous twists in his article, for *who* then is the 'us' who he urges 'to extend our pervading models beyond their customary anthropocentrism'? And why are these 'models' desired as extensions to and inclusions of the 'nonhuman animals'? In other words, what are the 'biopolitics' of admiring the acknowledgement of the 'will' and 'agency' of Armstrong's whale, even though 'instinct' is seen to be a problem? [38]

Cole's discussion continues by tracking alternations between what is seen to be the retrievable real animal and the human language which constantly threatens to impinge on that animal, concluding finally that

> formally, [this] might be taken as the novel's central insight as an embodiment of the posthumanist thrust of theoretical animal studies: that only by shedding the anthropocentric 'I' can we learn what only our peripherality can teach us; otherwise, we condemn ourselves to separateness, to speciesism, to a misrecognition of our own animality – to fruitlessly spurring tracks in the mud. At the same time, however, any portrayal of our peripherality in the literary medium remains at best a linguistic trick; for the anthropocentrism epitomized in the

[35]   Philip Armstrong, *What Animals Mean in the Fiction of Modernity* (London, 2008), p. 114.
[36]   On the same claims to 'voice' and 'agency' in relation to childhood, see Karín Lesnik-Oberstein, 'Introduction: Voice, Agency and the Child', Karín Lesnik-Oberstein, ed., *Children in Culture, Revisited: Further Approaches to Childhood* (Basingstoke, 2011), pp. 1–18.
[37]   Cole, 'The Animal Novel', p. 544.
[38]   Cole does not reference his use of 'biopolitics'; mine is drawn from Michel Foucault, *The Birth of Biopolitics: Lectures at the Collège de France, 1978–1979*, ed. Michel Senellart, trans. Graham Burchell (2004; New York, 2010).

pronoun 'I' lurks everywhere in the language, bound to edge in from the frame no matter how objectivized the picture.[39]

Even though Cole concedes this inherent and inescapable paradox, however, further difficulties arise, which depend on and uphold representation as being beyond the 'biopolitical'. On the one hand, Cole diagnoses the paradox that, for 'the posthumanist thrust of theoretical animal studies', the anthropocentric 'I' may be what must be shed. On the other, the 'I' thus shed is camouflaged and 'lurk[ing] everywhere' in the language – including in the 'we' that 'can [...] learn'. Cole is critiquing this approach as failing to see that the shedding of the 'I' is 'at best a linguistic trick'. He speaks of the 'I' as 'anthropocentrism epitomized', and its non-epitomised substitutes also persist. For Cole, degrees of anthropocentrism are retained willy-nilly in the posthumanist arguments which claim to be in the service of what 'we can learn [and] only our peripherality can teach us', and what 'we' should not 'condemn ourselves' to. Here, the animal and human, consequently and inexorably, are kept by posthumanist animal studies in their separate and known places, as what has to be defeated is 'a misrecognition of our own animality'. Yet as Cole critiques these arguments, he upholds the known categories:

> In Williamson's case, his attempt to depict the mode of existence of a nonhuman animal while simultaneously confronting the difficulties of doing so in the human language of the literary medium continuously alerts us to the contingency of our own ontologies: on the one hand, anthropocentrism can prevent us from recognizing the commonalities with nonhuman beings that our shared animality has bequeathed us, while on the other hand, even our sincerest attempts to grasp and articulate the commonalities and alterities that bind and estrange human and nonhuman animals can readily be frustrated by our confinement within an inherently anthropomorphizing linguistic medium.[40]

Cole definitely knows that there are 'commonalities with nonhuman beings that our shared animality has bequeathed us', upholding both the sameness and the differences between the 'nonhuman beings' and the 'us', who are, by implication, 'human beings'.

In saying this, Cole also places himself as necessarily outside the 'anthropocentric' in *not* being 'prevent[ed] from recognizing the commonalities', nor being 'frustrated by our confinement within an inherently anthropomorphizing linguistic medium'. A further twist here is that Cole is, by implica-

---

[39] Cole, 'The Animal Novel', p. 552.
[40] *Ibid.*

tion, outside of that inherent 'medium' which 'anthropomorphizes', because he has to have a perspective on it in order to claim a knowledge of what it is. Both the anthropocentricism and the media are escaped then, even as Cole's discussion rails at the limitations they seem to impose. I do not argue that there is some other way in which anthropocentrism could or should be dodged, but that the terms of such arguments – *both* 'of the posthumanist thrust of theoretical animal studies' and of Cole himself – are already thoroughly and unavoidably pre-determined by their rootedness in representation as the unquestioned and unquestionably neutral and natural mode of reading and writing.

Language and Representation

What happens if reading proceeds on a different basis? What if this opened up questions of the 'biopolitical' when writing, reading, and teaching with activism in mind? Again, Cole's reading of language in *Tarka the Otter* is useful to think about these questions:

> Williamson seems to have at least intuited [...] the paradox of linguistically conveying agential animal action. His textualization of the otters' own 'language', then, seems both an attempt to mitigate this paradox by allowing the otters (and at points other animals) to speak in their own voices, while also implicitly undermining notions of human exceptionalism rooted in language use – one of the key premises upon which conceptions of a stark human/animal divide are founded.[41]

As before, Cole knows 'agential animal action' as such prior to Williamson 'linguistically conveying' it, keeping representation firmly in place. Cole also knows Williamson to textualise that which is not textual: not 'the otters' own "language"'. However, that not-quite 'language' is nevertheless without question the otters' own, and Cole recognises Williamson to be 'allowing the otters [...] to speak in their own voices'. 'Agency', 'action', and 'their own voices' are prior – even if they have to be allowed that speech by another. This other is, in Cole's argument, only recognised sometimes. For at least the first section of the novel, 'humans are notably absent from this section and most of the novel, and in fact the paragraphs surrounding this scene of naming reside mostly with Tarka's mother, as the third-person omniscient narration describes the care with which she cleans her newborn cubs and the

---

41   *Ibid.*, pp. 545–6.

emotions she feels at their birth'.[42] Cole treats this 'third-person omniscient narration' as not being human (only person), unless Cole here is writing only of human *characters* as absent, rather than of a narration which (if not claiming to be animal) is at least other to Tarka's mother when describing her. Human characters which are read to be 'absent' may be confirmed when Cole subsequently and repeatedly claims the presence of the human, after all:

> one wonders how a human author, in human language, with a human audience, could more effectively convey the individual particularity of animals (thus affording them the agency and subjectivity too often denied them in the Western philosophical tradition from Aristotle to Heidegger) than by having them named.[43]

Paradoxes-within-paradoxes recur here, as the 'agency' and 'subjectivity' (elsewhere in Cole's discussion known as unquestionably belonging to animals prior to any description or translation) are here afforded by 'a human author, in human language', in the service of being 'effectively' conveyed to 'a human audience'.

Furthermore, what is to be conveyed is the 'individual particularity of animals', where the category of animals is not disrupted by the 'individual particularity' that 'naming' is invoked to achieve. This invocation of an 'individuality', 'particularity', or (in the ubiquitous neo-liberal incarnation) 'diversity' cannot achieve its own ends because it upholds the category it is supposed to disrupt – another instance of the 'biopolitical'. Cole refers to Jacques Derrida's work on animality, to justify the importance of naming as a producer of 'particularity':

> a climactic passage of [... Derrida's *The Animal That Therefore I Am*] straightforwardly impugns the human tendency to group nonhuman animals together as a single category: "The agreement ... that allows one to speak blithely of the Animal in the general singular is perhaps one of the greatest, and most symptomatic idiocies of those who call themselves humans."[44]

---

[42]   *Ibid.*, p. 545.

[43]   *Ibid.*

[44]   Cole, 'The Animal Novel', p. 545, citing Jacques Derrida, 'The Animal that Therefore I Am (and More to Follow)', trans. David Wills, *Critical Inquiry* 28.2 (2002), pp. 369–418 (p. 409). Cole's liberal interpretation of Derrida is common: see, for instance, Kelly Oliver, 'Sexual Difference, Animal Difference: Derrida and Difference "Worthy of Its Name"', *Hypatia* 24.2 (2009), pp. 54–76.

But does Cole need to read Derrida as 'straightforwardly' impugning the 'human tendency' to make such a group? There is a paradox-within-paradox in Cole's reading of Derrida: Cole himself groups nonhuman animals together as a single category (that of nonhuman animals), the issue which concerns Derrida in the passage Cole cites. Cole uses David Wills's translation of Derrida, in which 'l'une des plus grandes *bêtises*' is rendered as 'perhaps one of the greatest, and most symptomatic idiocies'.[45] Derrida here is not arguing for individuality and variety as the neo-liberal solution to 'grouping together', but is instead working through how 'l'Animal' is of necessity (that is, inherently) in relation to the human, not a knowable limit between the two. *Bêtises*, in this sense, does not allow for a definite settling of whether this is the 'human' or the 'animal'. Indeed, from which perspective could this 'limit' be knowable? An alternative English translation of Derrida's words uses 'asinanities' instead of 'idiocies', which better follows through on the implications of '*bêtises*'.[46] As Derrida argues:

> It follows, itself; it follows itself. It could say 'I am,' 'I follow,' 'I follow myself,' 'I am (in following) myself' [...] If I am (following) this suite [*si je suis cette suite*], and everything in what I am about to say will lead back to the question of what 'to follow' or 'to pursue' means, as well as 'to be after', back to the question of what I do when 'I am' or 'I follow', when I say '*Je suis*', if I am (following) this suite then, I move from 'the ends of man', that is the confines of man, to 'the crossing of borders' between man and animal. Passing across borders or the ends of man I come or surrender to the animal, to the animal in itself, to the animal in me and the animal at unease with itself.[47]

This is why Derrida's piece is entitled *The Animal That Therefore I Am (More to Follow)* (*L'Animal Que Donc Je Suis (À Suivre)*).

Where many ecocritics, like Cole, enthusiastically pounce on what appears to be a clear focus on the 'animal', and what simply seems to be Derrida's passionate denouncement of the human control over, and abuse of, animals, what they lose is the 'That Therefore I Am (More to Follow)' part. Derrida's contemplation concerns 'when I say "I am"' and how this possibility of 'say[ing]' is a 'following', without origin or end. In other words, this is neither an I nor an animal nor a human (nor anything else) which can be the

---

[45] Jacques Derrida, 'L'Animal Que Donc Je Suis (À Suivre)', *L'Animal Autobiographique*, ed. Marie-Louise Mallet (Paris, 1999), pp. 251–301 (p. 291) [my italics].
[46] Jacques Derrida, *The Animal That Therefore I Am*, ed. Marie-Luise Mallet, trans. David Wills (New York, 2008), p. 41.
[47] Ibid., p. 3.

secure and secured prior object of representation (accurate or otherwise): an I always necessarily has to be announced *from elsewhere*.

Derrida's difficulty appears different to that of Cole, given Cole's conclusion that 'such naming subverts the human tendency to conceive of nonhuman animals in the general singular "the Animal," while at the same time re-enacting the originary Adamic gesture of subjection and domestication, [and] points to the inherent difficulty of effecting any authentically posthuman decentering in human language'.[48] Again, Cole knows such a 'human tendency' as prior, as also 'nonhuman animals' (who were not to be 'grouped together' but now are, as elsewhere in the article). Moreover, the inherent 'difficulty of effecting any authentically posthuman decentering' is attributed here to 'in human language', implying that authenticity can be recognised (and therefore potentially achieved) outside 'human language'.[49] Unlike Derrida, Cole (in what I am calling the biopolitics of representation) insists on not considering the implications of reading *from where* the claims about humans and animals are made: which is necessarily other to both, and therefore is neither in its perspective on them.

If we return to *Tarka* in relation to these questions: it is two thirds of the way through the text when an I is first mentioned, though Cole calls it 'anthropocentrism epitomized', a pronoun which 'lurks everywhere in the language, bound to edge in from the frame no matter how objectivized the picture'. This is quite different from Derrida's I, as in 'It could say "I am," "I follow," "I follow myself," "I am (in following) myself."' Cole's I is prior to that not in 'the picture' which is defended against such edging in by being 'objectivized', albeit never sufficiently. This implies that the 'picture' was not objective to begin with, as it has to be 'objectiv*ized*', so that the I apparently has had to be expelled and subsequently defended against. But how and why is I out of 'the picture' at any stage of *Tarka*? I am not arguing that the novel fails to resist Cole's encroaching and 'anthropocentric' I, but what it would mean to read *Tarka* as 'objectivized'? Is the desired achievement to have a 'picture' with no perspective on it? In other words, a 'picture' that is not a 'picture', just the otter (for instance), 'itself', not seen by anything or anybody but known to be somewhere? There is a disturbing irony in the wish to objectivise ever-increasingly. Resistance to, or prevention of, such a terrible irony must rely on the upholding of some absolute distinction between objecti*vising* and objecti*fying*, lest there is a fall into what, it is claimed, must be resisted at all costs: objectification.

48 Cole, 'The Animal Novel', p. 545.
49 Thanks to Ting Fang (Grace) Yeh for helping clarify this point.

Cole, as careful as ever, concedes that the 'anthropocentric' I after all 'lurks everywhere in the language, bound to edge in from the frame'.[50] Following Derrida's line of thought, how could that I be 'anthropocentric'? Take the first line from Anna Sewell's *Black Beauty: The Autobiography of a Horse*, which, like *Tarka*, has a prominent place in the history of animal rights activism: 'The first place that I can well remember was a large pleasant meadow with a pond of clear water in it'. [51] Is this I to be regarded as anthropocentric because, as Cole writes about *Tarka*, the passage is written by 'a human author, in human language, with a human audience'?[52] Is an I anthropocentric because the differences and separations between the animal and the human are known and stable? If so, then another tragic irony lurks: this can imply, for instance, that animals cannot have an I because they do not have self-consciousness. I am not claiming that I know that animals or humans *do* have self-consciousness, but instead asking how any such claims are made, and from where, and what the consequences may be. Nor am I arguing that I know the I of *Black Beauty* to be a horse, so undermining Cole's I as necessarily anthropocentric. To do so would only reverse Cole's claim, while relying on the same stable differences and separations between the animal and the human. This is what I take Derrida to be working through in 'The Animal that Therefore I Am (and More to Follow)': that any I is not itself (either animal or human), but instead is always claimed retrospectively, from elsewhere. In this sense, *Tarka the Otter* neither lacks an I nor includes an I which is 'bound to edge in from the frame'. It is neither an 'anthropocentric' nor an 'objectivized' picture. Instead, the perspective on Tarka from elsewhere cannot be stably defined as animal or human, any more than the characters in the text are stably defined as such, according to that perspective. I am not relying on Cole's 'its subject matter' and 'its medium'.[53] All such divisions and oppositions operate on the grounds of representation, and in doing so constitute the outer limits of what Cole's article (or any critical reading based on representation) can reflect on.

To conclude: does a different reading of *Tarka* emerge from this discussion? Instead of reading being in the service of finding and assessing representations (as available and accumulated knowledge), reading becomes a means

[50]   Cole, 'The Animal Novel', p. 552.
[51]   Anna Sewell, *Black Beauty: The Autobiography of a Horse* (New York, 1911), p. 1. Both books have been read as being for children and for a wider audience alert to social critiques. See, for instance, Hilda Kean, *Animal Rights: Political and Social Change in Britain Since 1800* (London, 1998), pp. 165–80.
[52]   Cole, 'The Animal Novel', p. 545.
[53]   *Ibid.*, p. 543.

of thinking through, or thinking with. Scott Slovic argues that ecocriticism is 'either the study of nature writing by way of *any* scholarly approach or, conversely, the scrutiny of ecological implications and human-nature relationships in *any* literary text, even texts that seem (at first glance) oblivious of the nonhuman world'.[54] I would widen Slovic's definition: does ecocriticism have to know that it is 'ecological implications and human-nature relationships' which should be subject to 'scrutiny'? And do the texts have to be 'literary'? Representation predetermines these ideas, inducing in much ecocriticism a recurrent anxiety about what is seen to be its necessary interdisciplinarity with ecology or science. Many ecocritics are caught up in the difficulties of what Dana Phillips points out: that ecological 'realities are not necessarily more obvious than literary values, and they may be – probably are – much less so most of the time'.[55] Geoff Bennington likewise argues that the idea of interdisciplinarity is determined by the politics of representation:

> Post-theory we all do very different things, but they're all the same, because they all proclaim difference. That [...] is the call more or less concealed and more or less encouraged by recent, post-theoretical appeals to difference as *value* [...] Interdisciplinarity has become a watchword for a soft historicist cultural idealism.[56]

In fact, as Phillips also argues, representation also prevents the reading of ecology or science itself for, as Donna Haraway famously writes:

> The history of science appears as a narrative about the history of technical and social means to produce the facts. The facts themselves are types of stories, of testimony to experience. But the provocation of experience requires an elaborate technology – including physical tools, an accessible tradition of interpretation, and specific social relations. Not just anything can emerge as a fact; not just anything can be seen or done, and so told. Scientific practice may be considered a kind of story-telling practice – a rule-governed, constrained, historically changing craft of narrating the history of nature [...] To treat a science as a narrative is not to be dismissive, quite the contrary.[57]

[54] Scott Slovic, *Going Away to Think: Engagement, Retreat, and Ecocritical Responsibility* (Reno and Las Vegas, 2008), p. 27.
[55] Phillips, 'Ecocriticism', p. 582.
[56] Geoff Bennington, 'Inter', Martin McQuillan *et al.*, eds, *Post-Theory: New Directions in Criticism* (Edinburgh, 1999), pp. 103–19 (p. 103).
[57] Haraway, *Primate Visions*, pp. 4–5. On neuroscience and literature in the light of these issues, see Karín Lesnik-Oberstein, 'The Object of Neuroscience and Literary Studies', *Textual Practice* 31.7 (2017), pp. 1315–31; on mathematics and literature, see Karín Lesnik-Oberstein, 'Reading Derrida on Mathematics', *Angelaki: Journal of*

Science for Haraway is not the neo-liberal, individualist stories of, for instance, Oziewicz, but instead is akin to the critiques of Henriques and colleagues, in being a way in which 'scientific practice may be considered'. Without representation there is nothing preventing reading, no limit to just the literary or the environmental. Nor do these categories retain their key role in affecting readers (as the advocacy that both ecocriticism and environmental activism often strives for). Instead, as I have proposed here by thinking with *Tarka the Otter* and Stewart Cole's 'The Animal Novel as Biopolitical Critique', pedagogy and activism are better served by reading as a process of critical thinking without a specific aim in mind than by focusing on supposedly *affecting representations*. That such reading does not tell us exactly what to do, or how to do it, is precisely the point. Instead, it opens up questions and complexities. A great deal of ecocriticism and environmental activism remains adamant that affective representation and communication are central to their project.[58] However, the certainty and mastery which is offered by such knowledges of representation carries the risk of collusion with that drive to mastery which produced the environmental crises in the first place.

---

the Theoretical Humanities 17.1 (2012), pp. 31–40.
[58]   For such claims about 'communication', see Scott Slovic, Swarnalatha Rangarajan, and Vidya Sarveswaran, eds, *Routledge Handbook of Ecocriticism and Environmental Communication* (London, 2019).

7

The View from the Field: Activist Ecocriticism and Land Workers' Voices

PIPPA MARLAND

Post-Brexit, the question of new legislation around farming practices in the UK has been, and continues to be, an area of heated debate. In both political and agricultural circles, the UK's departure from the European Union was initially hailed as an opportunity to break free from the outmoded Basic Payment Scheme of the Common Agricultural Policy: to devise new strategies to cease subsidising farmers for simply owning land, and expand existing initiatives to reward farmers for producing environmental benefits as well as food. 2022 saw major upheavals in British politics (including the appointment of two new Prime Ministers in quick succession), and the long-anticipated Environmental Land Management Scheme (ELMS) in England (a multitiered plan to 'pay farmers and land managers to enhance the natural environment alongside food production') became subject to further review.[1] Ranil Jayawardena (briefly Secretary of State for Environment, Food and Rural Affairs between 6 September and 25 October 2022) sought to 'set the record straight' in terms of the Government's ongoing commitment to nature-friendly farming, in a film produced for social media. However, both this and Jayawardena's speech at the 2022 Conservative Party Conference were met with scepticism by wildlife charities, the National Trust, regenerative farmers, and high-profile environmental campaigners, such as Chris Packham.[2] The

---

[1] https://defrafarming.blog.gov.uk/2022/08/11/environmental-land-management-a-forward-look. There are similar initiatives by the devolved nations, with the Scottish government currently consulting on a new Agriculture Bill.

[2] Ranil Jayawaredena MP, Twitter feed (27 Sept 2022), https://twitter.com/ranil/status/1574781513106968579; Ranil Jayawaredena MP, speech to the Conservative Party Conference (3 October 2022), https://www.ukpol.co.uk/ranil-jayawardena-2022-speech-to-conservative-party-conference. See responses from Chris Packham, Newsnight Twitter feed (4 October 2022), https://twitter.com/BBCNewsnight/status/1577421471487594497, and from regenerative farmers James Robinson and Jake Fiennes, Helen Horton, 'Former Environment Secretary Urges Successor Not to Drop Nature-friendly Farming Scheme', *Guardian* (3 October 2022), https://www.theguardian.com/environment/2022/oct/03/uk-gov-

appointment of Thérèse Coffey as Jayawardena's substitute has been greeted with 'some surprise – and hope – by [the] environment sector', but the final format of ELMS remains in question.[3]

In the midst of this upheaval and anxiety, it is easy to see how some farmers may feel that their livelihoods and farming practices are at the mercy of political expediency. Such debates are not limited to the political and agricultural spheres but exist in the context of radically divided public opinion on food production, in which, more often than not, farmers 'are taking a bashing', as James Rebanks puts it. 'You can't go on social media, turn on the TV or radio, or read a newspaper without someone telling you earnestly that farming is more or less the devil's work and should be done away with at the earliest opportunity'.[4] These cultural tensions have come to the fore with the publication of George Monbiot's *Regenesis: Feeding the World without Devouring the Planet* (2022). Thinking on a planetary scale, Monbiot states that 'Farming is the world's greatest cause of habitat destruction, the greatest cause of the global loss of wildlife, and the greatest cause of the global extinction crisis'.[5] In place of conventional livestock farming (including organic production), Monbiot advocates the consumption of laboratory-produced protein. 'This technology could release almost all the land currently needed to produce protein, whether it comes in the form of plants or animals', he argues, and concludes that 'Much of our food supply could be farmfree [sic]'.[6] Monbiot's views have contributed to a divide between farming and conservation which has been widening since the environmental and ecological impacts of post-1945 industrialised farming practices began to filter into the public consciousness, via works such as *Silent Spring* (1962) by the American scientist Rachel Carson and *The Theft of the Countryside* (1980) by the British campaigner Marion Shoard.[7] In the nature writing since then, farmers have been increasingly vilified, as, for example, in Michael McCarthy's *The Moth Snowstorm: Nature and Joy* (2015), in which a caricatured 'Farmer Giles'

ernment-urged-not-to-abandon-nature-recovery-farming-schemes.

3   Helen Horton, 'How Green Will New Environment Secretary Thérèse Coffey Be?' *Guardian* (26 October 2022), https://www.theguardian.com/politics/2022/oct/26/how-green-will-new-environment-secretary-therese-coffey-be.

4   James Rebanks, 'How to Save British Farming (and the Countryside)', *UnHerd* (3 September 2020), https://unherd.com/2020/09/how-to-save-british-farming-and-the-countryside.

5   George Monbiot, *Regenesis: Feeding the World Without Devouring the Planet* (London, 2022), p. 90.

6   Monbiot, *Regenesis*, p. 188.

7   Rachel Carson, *Silent Spring* (Boston, 1962); Marion Shoard, *The Theft of the Countryside* (London, 1980).

gleefully spreads agricultural poisons across the land.[8] Of course, farming *is* an integrally vexed subject, and the intensification of agriculture in the last seventy-five years has contributed massively to local species decline and global climate change.[9] But it is also clear that, *pace* Monbiot, there is no single clear 'green' perspective on how the situation should be ameliorated. A response to Monbiot's *Regenesis* from the Sustainable Food Trust advances a number of counterarguments to his critique of organic farming, citing a study by the Food, Farming and Countryside Commission which suggests that 'a nation-wide transition to agroecology, accompanied by changes to what we eat and an end to biofuels production, would enable the UK to reduce its agricultural emissions by 55–70%'.[10]

This context, however, leaves some stories untold: those by farmers themselves. The two academic projects which form the case studies for this chapter – 'Tipping Points: Cultural Responses to Wilding and Land Sharing in the North of England' and 'The Pen and the Plough: Modern British Nature Writing and Agriculture' – listen to such voices.

There are a number of reasons for their previous erasure. The well-documented post-war schism between conservationists and agriculturalists, writ large in the nature writing of this period, has contributed to a widespread cultural distrust of farming, a sense that the British countryside has been betrayed by those who were assumed to be its custodians.[11] Social class, geographical location, and an increasing divide between the urban and the rural too have played a role in the gradual silencing of agrarian narratives. Anna Jones has argued that there is a 'Great Disconnection' between urban and rural populations, and that 'many rural people feel invisible'.[12] Even-handedly, Jones sees both farmers and environmentalists as culpable in the recent 'hardening of a decades-long conflict between agriculture and conservation'. She speaks compassionately about the implications of rewilding crusades, like those of Monbiot, for rural populations: 'You may as

---

[8]   Michael McCarthy, *The Moth Snowstorm: Nature and Joy* (London, 2015), p. 93.

[9]   Pippa Marland, Davy McCracken, and Tess Somervell, '"Down on the Farm" – Introduction to the Special Issue on Agriculture and Environment', *Green Letters* 24.4 (2020), pp. 335–43.

[10]   Sustainable Food Trust, 'Considering *Regenesis*: A Perspective' (15 July 2022), https://sustainablefoodtrust.org/news-views/regenesis-response.

[11]   See, for example, Marion Shoard, *The Theft of the Countryside* (London, 1980); McCarthy, *Moth Snowstorm*; George Monbiot, *Feral: Rewilding the Land, Sea and Human Life*, (London, 2013).

[12]   Anna Jones, *Divide: The Relationship Crisis Between Town and Country* (London, 2022), pp. 30, 34.

well declare war on rural communities', she complains, 'and shout: Get rid of people's jobs! Get rid of people's homes! [...] Wipe out an entire culture!'[13]

Jones's reference to culture is telling. It suggests that the culture of farming folk and rural people more broadly is undervalued by a largely metropolitan society, and that, in effect, farmers lack 'cultural capital' (in Pierre Bourdieu's terms, the 'distinctive value' adhering to individuals and communities as a result of education, class, and the symbolic, material, and social benefits of wealth).[14] Agriculturalists apparently lack this perceived value to such an extent that their lifeways can be presented as expendable in the context of environmental debate. It is an undervaluing that is mirrored in economic terms in the pressure on farmers to deliver ever 'more and cheaper food'.[15] The assumed lack of cultural capital of any community is a sociological, and by extension, an economic issue.

In the case of farming, it is one which is reflected in intellectual and literary traditions, such as the weight given to pastoral themes over georgic accounts of farming in nature writing and rural literature. Terry Gifford details the pastoral's roots in classical antiquity, emerging as a form in which 'supposed shepherds spoke to each other, [...], about their work or their loves, with (mostly) idealised descriptions of their countryside'.[16] As the literary pastoral developed, it characteristically featured a trajectory of 'retreat and return', in which the writer left the city on a journey of exploration, and then '"returned" some insights relevant to the urban audience'.[17] This is a pattern still present in British nature writing, in works from, say, Edward Thomas's *In Pursuit of Spring* (1914) to Robert Macfarlane's *The Wild Places* (2007).[18] The literary pastoral is a complex trope taking different forms, and I am not suggesting that it does not have an important role to play in contemporary place-based writing. Indeed, in Deborah Lilley's view, new articulations of the pastoral are self-reflexive and flexible enough to respond creatively to the current environmental crisis.[19] Nevertheless, the pastoral form is frequently one in which the view of a leisured, urban-dwelling observer is privileged over the

13   *Ibid.*, pp. 205, 209.
14   Pierre Bourdieu, 'The Forms of Capital', J. G. Richardson, ed., *Handbook of Theory and Research for the Sociology of Education* (New York, 1986), pp. 241–58 (p. 245).
15   James Rebanks, *English Pastoral: An Inheritance* (London, 2020), p. 152.
16   Terry Gifford, *Pastoral* (Abingdon, 2020), p. 1.
17   *Ibid.*, pp. 1–2.
18   Edward Thomas, *In Pursuit of Spring* (London, 1914); Robert Macfarlane, *The Wild Places* (Cambridge, 2007).
19   Deborah Lilley, *The New Pastoral in Contemporary British Writing* (Abingdon, 2019), pp. 1–16.

view of the agricultural worker in the field. By contrast, the georgic, also with roots in classical antiquity, is integrally concerned with labour (often with farm work and animal husbandry), so rather than promoting an idealised image of rural life focuses on what Philipp Erchinger and colleagues describe as 'the struggle with recalcitrant matters and unforeseeable adversities [that] is an inescapable part of human life'.[20] This offers deep satisfactions – but, as David Fairer notes, georgic labour 'rarely yields rewards easily'.[21] While there have been eras in which agrarian themes have come to the fore in the literary canon, the dominance of the pastoral has exacerbated the lack of cultural visibility of stories which reflect upon the struggles and satisfactions of working the land to produce food.

This chapter is divided into four parts. It begins by arguing that academic research is fundamentally political, in the way it identifies a 'gap' in knowledge and attempts to address that gap, and that work in the environmental humanities in particular is inherently *activist*. Public engagement activities in 'green' cultural research represent their own form of environmentalist praxis. The chapter then reflects further on the erasure of farmers' voices from the nature writing of the late twentieth century, briefly exploring the dominance of the pastoral over the georgic, then tracing the emergence of a contemporary georgic revival in recent farming-themed memoirs. The third section of the essay discusses the public engagement strands of the two research projects (designed, at least in part, to amplify the voices of contemporary 'naturefriendly' or regenerative farmers), to explore some of the possible methodologies and impacts of activist ecocriticism, based on my own experience as Co-Investigator on 'Tipping Points' and Principal Investigator on 'The Pen and the Plough'.[22] The chapter concludes with examples of farmers' and land workers' writing produced in a series of workshops, and poses the ongoing question as to whether ecocriticism might actively intervene in promoting new cultural narratives of farming, thus helping to foster a 'new georgic' literary tradition, in which the 'view from the field' can be brought to the fore.

---

[20]   Philipp Erchinger, Sue Edney, and Pippa Marland, 'Eco-georgic: From Antiquity to the Anthropocene – An Introduction', *Ecozon@* 12.2 (2021), pp. 1–17 (p. 1).

[21]   David Fairer, '"Where Fuming Trees Refresh the Thirsty Air": The World of Eco-Georgic', *Studies in Eighteenth-Century Culture* 40 (2011), pp. 201–18 (p. 204).

[22]   It is important, however, to acknowledge the collaborative nature of the projects. For example, the activities of 'Tipping Points' were largely overseen by an artistic director, Suzie Cross, and involved researchers, artists, conservationists, community organisations, and farmers themselves, while 'The Pen and the Plough' has benefited greatly from the participation of The Nature Friendly Farming Network and the involvement of the writers Patrick Laurie and Emily Diamand, https://www.nffn. org.uk; https://gallowayfarm.wordpress.com/; http://www.emilydiamand.com.

Ecocriticism as Activist Research

At the outset of British ecocriticism, Jonathan Bate argued that 'Literary criticism has never been a pure discipline', and that from classical times onwards 'political and moral concerns have borne in upon the discussion of literature'.[23] Nevertheless, Bate felt that even within this broadly political context a new form of politics was required, one that moved away from 'the crude old model of Left and Right' to embrace a position in which the polarisation of 'red' and 'blue' might give way to a non-denominational 'green'.[24] His call came in response to divided critical opinions about William Wordsworth, whose early radicalism and increasing establishmentarianism in later life had led to conflicting readings of his work, including, in some, a sense that Wordsworth had betrayed his own political roots. In Bate's view, Wordsworth's real radicalism lay in his love for, and attentiveness to, the natural world, so he promoted a nature-oriented reading of the poet's work. However, Bate's later book, *The Song of the Earth*, was more cautious about the possibilities of poetry or environmental criticism to catalyse political change. 'Ecocriticism does have a contribution to make to green politics, as postcolonial and feminist reading contribute to race and gender politics', he writes, 'but its true importance may be more phenomenological than political'. In other words, Bate suggests that ecocritical scholars might best devote their study to revealing the ways in which poetry enacts a 'presencing' rather than representation of the natural world.[25]

Yet Bate's initial sense of the innately political nature of literary criticism can be justified by how ecocriticism can be politicised, intervening in environmental debates that exist beyond the academy. The foundational idea of academic research, that of attempting to address a lack in existing knowledge and understanding, is already a form of what Eleanora Belfiore calls 'intellectual activism'.[26] However, academics are often discouraged from regarding our work as such, Charles Hale argues. 'Despite the growing acknowledgment that all research is positioned and that our convictions do tend to seep in to inform our analytical frameworks, the emphasis in mainstream

---

[23]   Jonathan Bate, *Romantic Ecology: Wordsworth and the Environmental Tradition* (London, 1991), p. 1.

[24]   *Ibid.*, p. 3.

[25]   Bate, *The Song of the Earth* (London, 2000), pp. 75, 262.

[26]   Eleonora Belfiore, '"Impact", "Value" and "Bad Economics": Making sense of the Problem of Value in the Arts and Humanities', *Arts & Humanities in Higher Education* 14.1 (2015), pp. 95–110 (p. 96).

academia still is on keeping that seepage to a minimum'.[27] Hale, an anthropologist, thinks 'there is no necessary contradiction between active political commitment to resolving a problem, and rigorous scholarly research on that problem'.[28] He advocates what he calls 'activist research', which, he explains, 'endorses the contrasting tack of making our politics explicit and upfront, reflecting honestly and systematically on how they have shaped our understanding of the problem at hand, and putting them to the service of our analytical endeavor'.[29]

Ecocriticism and, more broadly, the environmental humanities, are fields in which active, upfront political commitment frequently drives research. As scholars, ecocrits are motivated by an awareness of growing environmental crisis, of climate breakdown, and mass extinctions. Such awareness underpins a desire both to critique narratives which have contributed to damaging cultural perceptions of nature and, at times, to identify more earth-friendly stories. Recent developments in ecocriticism have gone further, attempting to help shape new ways of understanding human/environmental relationships (for example, in the ontological shifts which inform material ecocriticism and biosemiotics).[30] While there has been a tendency to make naïve declarations about the efficacy of literature to bring about behavioural change, there is no doubt that the stories we tell ourselves as communities help to shape our interactions with the world. Hale (drawing on the work of the political scientist Donald Stokes) conceives of activist research as 'both theoretically driven and intended to be put to use', a formulation that fits well with most, if not all, ecocritical endeavours.[31]

Academic public engagement is even more clearly a form of activism, since it brings issues the research has addressed to public audiences, and extends this conversation, often via collaborations with community groups and non-Higher Education institutions. Such conversations benefit both the academy and the public, in that they involve the dissemination of academic findings, and, in a democratising process, simultaneously invite new ideas and perspectives into the debate. The National Co-ordinating Centre for Public Engagement articulates this idea of shared, collaborative outcomes:

---

[27]   Charles Hale, 'What is Activist Research?', *ITEMS: Social Science Research Council* 2.1–2 (2001), pp. 13–15 (p. 14).

[28]   *Ibid.*, p. 13.

[29]   *Ibid.*, p. 14.

[30]   See for example, Serenella Iovino and Serpil Oppermann, eds, *Material Ecocriticism*, (Bloomington, 2014) and Wendy Wheeler, *Expecting the Earth: Life, Culture, Biosemiotics* (London, 2016).

[31]   Hale, 'What is Activist Research', p. 14.

Public engagement describes the myriad of ways in which the activity and benefits of higher education and research can be shared with the public. Engagement is by definition a two-way process, involving interaction and listening, with the goal of generating mutual benefit.[32]

Public engagement is a key element in grants awarded by funding bodies such as the Arts and Humanities Research Council. UK Research and Innovation, the non-departmental public body which oversees research funding for academic institutions, states as one of its four main goals the aim to 'engage under-represented communities and places with research and innovation'.[33] This produces a productively grey area: engagement activities are designed to take their cue from research findings, but often take the form of interventions which are oriented towards democratising social and political decision-making processes, or amplifying those voices which may be suppressed or ignored in public discourse.

Both projects discussed here highlight questions about the reach of environmentally motivated public engagement, and the potential results of mutual interaction with culturally under-represented communities. 'Tipping Points' was funded by the Arts and Humanities Research Council (as a follow-on from the 'Land Lines: Modern British Nature Writing' project) and 'The Pen and the Plough' by the Leverhulme Trust.[34]

Each was underpinned by a conviction that it was important to help restore productive dialogue between farmers and environmentalists. Over 70% of the UK's land area is under agricultural use, and the methods and practices adopted by farmers in the coming years will have an enormous impact on meeting the country's Net Zero target and on attempts to restore

[32] National Co-ordinating Centre for Public Engagement, 'What is Public Engagement' (2020), https://www.publicengagement.ac.uk/about-engagement/what-public-engagement.
[33] UK Research and Innovation, 'Vision for Public Engagement' (2019), https://www.ukri.org/wp-content/uploads/2020/10/UKRI-1610202-Vision-for-public-engagement.pdf.
[34] 'Tipping Points' (no date), https://landlinesproject.wordpress.com/tipping-points-cultural-responses-to-wilding-and-land-sharing-in-the-north; 'The Pen and the Plough' (no date), https://thepenandtheplough.wordpress.com. While the project teams gratefully acknowledge the financial support of the Arts and Humanities Research Council (AHRC) and the Leverhulme Trust (for the author's Early Career Fellowship), we stress that the public engagement activities described in the essay were not commissioned by the funding bodies, and that the views underpinning those activities should not be interpreted as representing those of either the AHRC or Leverhulme Trust.

biodiversity, improve soil health, reduce pollution, and mitigate flooding.[35] The project teams pointed out how the unheard stories of rural life included those of members of the regenerative farming community, who had (some for many years) been seeking to implement nature-friendly practices, whether or not government legislation had required them to do so. Trying to forge links between the environmental humanities and farmers engaged in agro-ecological practices included fostering mutually respectful dialogue between farmers and conservationists about the future of farming, through a series of 'slow conversations' which took the debate away from the heat of social media. Finally, as predominantly literary scholars, the project teams wanted to explore the possibility of raising the profile of the georgic in contemporary literature, through foregrounding new written narratives of regenerative farming. Both projects provided funded life-writing workshops for farmers and agricultural labourers. Through these, researchers at the universities of Bristol and Leeds set out to amplify regenerative farming voices: helping to bring their stories to the attention of the public through the medium of film and online exhibitions, and to educate mostly urban audiences about the material and economic realities of contemporary farming.

The Erasure of Farming Voices: Pastoral Versus Georgic

There is a parallel between a decline in farming narratives in post-war nature writing and an increasingly explicit blame placed on farmers in this period. In the 1946 collection *Nature Through the Year*, descriptions of the seasons are interspersed with pages devoted to agricultural activities, as if the two were part of the same eternal cycle, nature and the farm almost synonymous.[36] The 1930s and 1940s saw an extraordinary flowering of agrarian literature, much of which is now identified as classic British nature writing. Even Stella Gibbons's brilliant satire on rural life, *Cold Comfort Farm* (1932), did little to dent the appeal of tales from farming life, including A. G. Street's *Farmer's Glory* (1932), Adrian Bell's *Men and the Fields* (1939), Fred Kitchen's *Brother to the Ox* (1939), John Stewart Collis's *While Following the Plough* (1946) and *Down to Earth* (1947) (reprinted in one volume as *The Worm Forgives the Plough*, 1973), and E. M. Barraud's

---

[35]   There are also concerns in the Conservative party about whether the government will continue to support the Net Zero Strategy, Helen Horton, 'Green Tories Fear Next Party Leader Could Ditch Net Zero Strategy', *Guardian* (10 July 2022), https://www.theguardian.com/politics/2022/jul/10/green-tories-fear-next-party-leader-could-ditch-net-zero-strategy.

[36]   *Nature Through the Year* (London, 1946).

accounts of her experiences in the Women's Land Army, *Set My Hand Upon the Plough* (1946) and *Tail Corn* (1948).[37]

While these works are not necessarily free from the idealising tendencies of pastoral, they were written by authors who were themselves engaged in labouring on the land, and, in the case of Kitchen, introduced a working-class voice into literary agrarian writing. At times, these writers explicitly challenged pastoral perspectives. Bell, for example, in *Corduroy*, a volume of his novelised memoirs of farming life, critiques Thomas Hardy's poem 'In Time of the "Breaking of Nations"', in which the poet conjures a vision of a farmer harrowing a field:

> Only a man harrowing clods
>   In a slow, silent walk
> With an old horse that stumbles and nods
>   Half asleep as they stalk.[38]

Having himself experienced harrowing, Bell finds fault with Hardy's representation: 'Why the belittlement of that word "only"? Had Hardy ever done any harrowing he would not have written a stanza suggesting that man and horse were half asleep'.[39] He concludes that 'Hardy, I saw, despite the legend of his rural understanding, had the non-ruralist's attitude'.[40]

Collis adds his voice to Bell's, in his account of working on the land during WW2, objecting to the phrase 'half asleep': 'From the road a number of agricultural jobs look remarkably quiet, serene, slow, and easy; but if you stand beside the man in question you may find that he is putting out all his strength, is moving quite fast, and is in anything but a serene state of mind'.[41] Barraud expresses a similar sense of frustration with the non-ruralist viewpoint when she writes of how 'Drilling looks easy, like so many farm jobs, when you stand comfortably on the road watching the work'.[42] Not only does the literary pastoral misrepresent the actual nature of the worker's

[37]   Stella Gibbons, *Cold Comfort Farm* (London, 1932); A. G. Street, *Farmer's Glory* (London, 1932), Adrian Bell, *Men and the Fields* (London, 1939); Fred Kitchen, *Brother to the Ox* (London, 1939); John Stewart Collis, *The Worm Forgives the Plough* (London, 1973); E. M. Barraud, *Set My Hand Upon the Plough* (Worcester, 1946) and *Tail Corn* (London, 1948).
[38]   Hardy, 'In Time of "The Breaking of Nations"', https://poetryarchive.org/poem/time-breaking-nations.
[39]   Adrian Bell, *Corduroy* (1930; London, 2011), p. 22.
[40]   *Ibid.*
[41]   Collis, *The Worm Forgives the Plough*, p. 26.
[42]   Barraud, *Tail Corn*, p. 25.

activity, the persistence of such pastoral tropes eclipses the viewpoint of the farm worker, rendering it culturally irrelevant.

The agricultural memoirs of the 1930s and 40s were among the last which could be read as nature writing. However, it was not simply the dominance of the pastoral which explains the decline in post-war, agrarian-themed, georgic literature. In a chapter in *Nature Through the Year* entitled 'The Farm', there are observations which can be read retrospectively as the death knell of British rural biodiversity, even as they celebrate 'advances' in the science of farming and changing practices of food production: 'Science [...] has made possible the growing of much earlier and later grasses' among other crops, to the extent that 'Nowadays the farmer is sowing and harvesting all the time'.[43] World War II has been identified as a hinge point in farming history, as marking 'the real agricultural revolution'.[44] Agricultural historians Paul Brassley and colleagues trace an (albeit geographically uneven) 'almost unimaginable change in English agriculture' in the second half of the twentieth century, as concerns about national food security led to a scaling up of British farming, accompanied by the removal of hedges and use of fertilisers, pesticides, and machinery which massively increased yields.[45] It was not long before the huge toll these practices were taking (on avian life, for example) became obvious, losses increasingly noted in literary works such as J. A. Baker's *The Peregrine*, in which the birds were seen dying 'on their backs, clutching insanely at the sky in their last convulsion, withered and burnt away by the filthy, insidious pollen of farm chemicals'.[46] Shoard was even more explicit in blaming farmers for the depleted biodiversity levels and reduced aesthetic appeal of the countryside:

> Although few people realise it, the English landscape is under sentence of death [...] The executioner is not the industrialist or the property speculator, whose activities have touched on the fringes of our countryside. Instead it is the figure traditionally viewed as the custodian of the rural scene – the farmer.[47]

Such changes to the rural scene, and growing dismay at the environmental impacts of agricultural practices, were accompanied by a corresponding decline in farming narratives. As the nature writing genre began to burgeon again in

---

[43]   *Nature Through the Year*, p. 73.
[44]   Paul Brassley, *et al.*, *The Real Agricultural Revolution: The Transformation of English Farming, 1939–1985* (Woodbridge, 2021).
[45]   *Ibid.*, p. 2.
[46]   J. A. Baker, *The Peregrine* (1967; London, 2015), p. 31.
[47]   Shoard, *The Theft*, p. 9.

the early twenty-first century, its writers were rarely involved in work on the land, but, rather, enacted the pastoral pattern of retreat to the rural followed by a return to the urban, in search of insights for a predominantly urban audience.

Recent years, though, have seen a resurgence of farm-themed literature by authors who are themselves farmers: Rebanks's bestselling memoir *The Shepherd's Life* (2015) and profoundly georgic sequel, *English Pastoral: An Inheritance* (2020), Patrick Laurie's *Native: Life in a Vanishing Landscape* (2020), Lynn Cassells and Sandra Baer's *Our Wild Farming Life: Adventures on a Scottish Highland Croft* (2022), Jake Fiennes's *Land Healer: How Farming Can Save Britain's Countryside* (2022), Lee Schofield's *Wild Fell: Fighting for Nature on a Lake District Hill Farm* (2022), and Sarah Langford's *Rooted: Stories of Life, Land and a Farming Revolution* (2022).[48] The books have one characteristic in common, beyond their shared theme of farming: they are all motivated by concern about the environment, and a desire to shape farming practices in ways that nurture the health of the land rather than damaging it. I have identified this burgeoning genre elsewhere as a 'new georgic', in which 'farming can be understood as involving not only the production of food but the production of nature itself'.[49]

The resurgence of farming literature has been accompanied by a renewed relationship between this work and nature writing; several of these titles have been nominated for, and on occasion won, prizes for nature writing.[50] In a sense, then, this phenomenon might be regarded as farming achieving a new degree of cultural capital. Nevertheless, in the context of political conflict with which this essay began, the nature-friendly orientation reflected in these farmers' works remains under threat, from both conservative (and Conservative) political interests (prioritising economic growth over environmental protection) and conservationists broadly identified with the left, such as Monbiot, who advocate for a massive reduction in farming *per se*. Meanwhile, the pastoral trope persists in contemporary discourse. As Jayawardena was proclaiming his environmentalist credentials in his speech

[48]   James Rebanks, *The Shepherd's Life* (London, 2015) and *English Pastoral: An Inheritance* (London, 2020); Patrick Laurie, *Native: Life in a Vanishing Landscape* (Edinburgh, 2020); Lynn Cassells and Sandra Baer, *Our Wild Farming Life: Adventures on a Scottish Highland Croft* (London, 2022); Jake Fiennes, *Land Healer: How Farming Can Save Britain's Countryside* (London, 2022); Lee Schofield, *Wild Fell: Fighting for Nature on a Lake District Hill Farm* (London, 2022); Sarah Langford, *Rooted: Stories of Life, Land and a Farming Revolution* (London, 2022).

[49]   Pippa Marland, 'Rewilding, Wilding and the New Georgic in Contemporary Nature Writing', *Green Letters* 24.4 (2020), pp. 421–36 (p. 423).

[50]   Rebanks's *English Pastoral* (London, 2020) won the James Cropper Wainwright prize for nature writing in 2021.

to the Conservative Party conference, he did so by activating the language of pastoral: 'And, in this brief, at DEFRA, I will work day and night to preserve our green and pleasant land. Our rural landscapes – the clouded hills, the mountains green – are precious to all of us'.[51]

Jayawardena is of course summoning William Blake's 'And did those feet in ancient time' (popularly known as 'Jerusalem') to his aid, with the allusive 'green and pleasant land', 'clouded hills', and 'mountains green'.[52] There is a double irony, given Blake's own satirical intent in the poem, which has been interpreted as a comment on the 'blighted state of England with its "dark satanic mills" of morality, authority and mental enslavement'.[53] But Jayawardena is also echoing Blake's adoption of a pastoral mode in its ancient association with shepherds and sheep, conjuring to mind Blake's evocation of the 'lamb of God' walking those 'clouded hills' and 'mountains green'. While these landscape features may possibly call to mind the upland sheep farms of the British Isles, they are a long way from the realities of the lambing parlour or the sheep dip, and they are certainly not the scene of hard georgic labour; the view from the field is displaced by the idealisation of a 'green and pleasant land'. The anecdote suggests that while the literature of farming may once again be taking its place on the shelves of nature writing, its messages are not yet being fully heard.

'Tipping Points' and 'The Pen and the Plough': Making Slow Conversations and Writing from the Land

Hale offers a tripartite model of activist research, of the sort which under-pinned the research projects. It

> a) helps us better to understand the root causes of inequality, oppression, violence and related conditions of human suffering; b) is carried out, at each phase from conception through dissemination, in direct cooperation with an organized collective of people who themselves are subject to these conditions; c) is used, together with the people in question, to formulate strategies for transforming these conditions and to achieve the power necessary to make these strategies effective.[54]

---

[51]   Jayawardena MP, speech to the Conservative Party Conference.
[52]   William Blake 'And did those feet', *The Selected Poems of William Blake*, ed. Bruce Woodcock (London, 2000), pp. 319–20.
[53]   *Ibid.*, p. 317.
[54]   Hale, 'What is Activist Research?', p. 13.

There are many different kinds of farmers and farming, and some farmer-landowners are members of an extraordinarily privileged elite. However, within the farming community, there are also many farmers who feel a sense of politically exacerbated vulnerability. In broader terms, farming is a profession notoriously susceptible to isolation, financial stress, and mental health issues. The 2021 Royal Benevolent Agricultural Society's 'Big Farming Survey' of the health and well-being of the farming community in England and Wales discovered that 36% of farmers are 'possibly or probably depressed'.[55] When I mentioned this in an interview with Welsh hill farmer and member of the Nature Friendly Farming Network, Hywel Morgan, he replied:

> And the other percentage don't say nothing, but they are, probably. I think it's huge, isn't it? I drive a feed lorry a couple of days a week and you get to talk to farmers, get to know them and get to talk to them, and you sense it. Some farmers even tell me how depressed they are, how they're struggling.[56]

While questions about the well-being of farmers were beyond the projects' remit, we were keen to understand, as Hale suggests, the root causes of the politically and socially challenging position in which some contemporary farmers find themselves, and to cooperate and collaborate with the farming community to help their stories come to light. Equally, we shared the grief and anxiety of those who work in the fields of conservation and the environmental arts at the nature-depleted state of the UK. We did not necessarily take a stand on regenerative farming *per se*, but thought about how the different groups might find strategies to work together in pursuit of a common goal of environmental regeneration.

A crucial part of this was to bring these groups of people together, to try to find common ground in a mutually respectful dialogue. To this end we began a series of 'slow conversations', either online or in face-to-face small group interviews (when COVID-19 lockdown restrictions permitted).[57] The first iteration of the conversation was an innovative online dialogue between

---

[55]   Royal Agricultural Benevolent Institution, 'The Big Farming Survey' (October 2021), https://rabi.org.uk/big-farming-survey.

[56]   Pippa Marland, 'An Interview with Nature-friendly Farmer Hywel Morgan (10 March 2022), https://thepenandtheplough.wordpress.com/2022/05/17/an-interview-with-nature-friendly-farmer-hywel-morgan-pippa-marland.

[57]   The term 'slow conversation' was devised by Emily Diamand in her work with one of the project partners, Northern Heartlands, and in collaborative discussion with Barbara Bray, Amy-Jane Beer, and researchers at the Universities of Bristol and Leeds, 'Love and Soil' (10 May 2021), https://www.youtube.com/watch?v=U7Jl_FJBQHY&t=2s.

farmers, conservationists, artists, writers, and academics, who were able by means of a privately accessed website to read and respond (through textual replies or audiovisual media) to the thoughts about nature and the environment posted by other members of this hybrid community. The conversation took place over a period of around six weeks, allowing its exchanges of views to be thoughtful and unhurried.

With the permission of the contributors, the dialogues were then edited and condensed into a publicly available film: 'Love and Soil'.[58] A second film, 'Nuclear Legacies: Nuclear Energy and Farming Landscapes in Cumbria', was created by Dr Lucy Rowland in collaboration with the artists Somewhere-nowhere. This features an interview with Lake District farmer Will Rawling, who talks frankly about the challenges of farming near to the Sellafield nuclear waste management site, as well as the impacts of the 1986 Chernobyl nuclear disaster.[59] The third film in the 'slow conversation' trilogy is 'Newland: New Vision for a Wilder Future', made by 'Tipping Points' artistic director Suzie Cross and her colleague Dave Lynch.[60] A study in slowness, it uses drone footage and the words of a father and son farming team, Andrew and Ted Hughes, as they talk us through the landscape of their farm, which they are gradually restoring for biodiversity and soil health.

The final strand of our work with farmers was a series of life-writing workshops for farmers and land-based workers. The participants included tenant farmers, stock men and women, and farmers working their own land, several of whom are actively engaged in regenerative farming. The first set of workshops was organised as a collaboration between the 'Tipping Points' and 'The Pen and the Plough' projects, but the model was then taken up by the Landscape Decisions programme, who put on a second round of workshops. There are exhibitions of the resulting work on the various project websites.[61]

---

[58] 'Love and Soil' (10 May 2021), https://www.youtube.com/watch?v=U7Jl_FJBQHY&t=2s. Responses to the film were positive, such as that by the classicist and ecocritic Katharine Earnshaw: 'This slow conversation has led to a powerful meditation on farming, the environment, and what an inclusive, communicative future might require', Katharine Earnshaw, Twitter feed (10 May 2021), https://twitter.com/Earnshaw_K/status/1391825106494689283.

[59] Land Lines, 'Nuclear Legacies: Nuclear Energy and Farming Landscapes in Cumbria and Invisible Poem' (16 June 2021), https://www.youtube.com/watch?v=WFW5nSL6nhE

[60] Land Lines, 'Newland: New Vision for a Wilder Future' (21 June 2021), https://www.youtube.com/watch?v=O-trb4dhnKs&feature=emb_imp_woyt. The film won the Arts and Humanities Research Council Research in Film Awards, Best Climate Emergency category (2021).

[61] The two exhibitions of writing are available at https://thepenandtheplough.

Workshop leaders, best-selling farmer-writer Patrick Laurie (author of *Native*) and Emily Diamand (award-winning author and rural communities expert), introduced the online land workers' writing exhibition:

> Farmers and land workers are frequently mentioned in nature writing, but they often feature as part of the scenery; they're ambiguous figures at work in the background. It's no surprise that these people should seem marginal in a country where less than one percent of the population is involved in producing food, but it can mean that farming voices are unusually hard to hear. This issue is compounded by the fact that agriculture is under tremendous pressure to follow new angles in the light of climate change and biodiversity collapse. It's easy to characterise farmers as "the bad guys", and while some innovative farm businesses are leading the charge to make farming more sustainable, many are anxious and confused by fast and unprecedented changes which threaten to destroy the landscapes we all love.
>
> Farming voices are no more valuable or authoritative than those from any other quarter, but they do have an undeniably unique sense of place and experience which deserves to be explored. At its best, it feels less like a sense of ownership or mastery, and more like a complex grasp on belonging; a deep immersion in the landscape which can feel like a dialogue between people and places.[62]

The resulting examples from the workshops give a powerful sense of what it means to farm in our time. They encompass a sense of embodied involvement, moments of anxiety, of traditions changing by necessity, and of viewpoints located firmly in the barn, the farmyard, and the field. While the pieces are not directly concerned with regenerative practices, they bring the reader closer to the day-to-day experiences of farming, from painstakingly rebuilding dry stone walls to the heartbreak of crop failures, to dealing with a difficult lambing or calving. As such, the narratives speak more to the strug-

---

wordpress.com/2021/06/01/pen-and-plough-writing-workshops-exhibition and https://landscapedecisions.org/2022/01/07/written-in-the-land-reflections-and -exhibition. The excerpts from farmers' and land workers' writing are taken from the online exhibitions of their work, where they were published with the participants' kind permission and informed consent. The quotations from the anonymised feedback are similarly used with permission.

[62] Patrick Laurie and Emily Diamand, 'Pen and Plough Writing Workshops Exhibition' (no date), https://thepenandtheplough.wordpress.com/2021/06/01/ pen-and-plough-writing-workshops-exhibition. Public responses to the exhibition were strongly positive, such as that on the 'Pen and Plough' website: 'immensely interesting, thought-provoking and meaningful. These are all excellent writers, and I hope they continue despite the draw of actual farming life. We need these perspectives'.

gles and setbacks that characterise the georgic mode than to the idealised rural lives of the pastoral.

The first two extracts evoke a sense of the economic precarity of farming. In the first, Jennifer Macdonald, who with her husband runs an eighty-acre social enterprise farm on the Isle of Arran, describes the financial 'gamble' that their work often entails:

> The dark months of winter having stolen almost all of our ability to produce a stable income, the expenses of living still greedily continue and, just when we are about to run out of cashflow completely, the most expensive time of the year arrives. This is often accompanied by a late frost that steals the first three weeks of earnings, or a late housing notification for bird flu, doubling our bedding budget for the year. These spring surprises happen every year, so we scrabble together more bankroll to keep the bookies at bay. These early year stresses flare up our adrenal glands before the fun of the year even begins. Before we battle the chaos of the Scottish weather, negotiate the constantly evolving consumer palette and try our best to survive the unavoidable dangers that keep all self-employed people terrified; possible illness or injury. Which is ridiculous really, as in this industry there is no sick pay or days off – the animals we care for need to be fed irrespective of our personal circumstances.

In the second piece, tenant farmer's daughter and land rights activist Kirsty Tait reminds us that many of the UK's farmers do not own the land they work. Because of this, family traditions going back generations are vulnerable to land sales and building developments:

> We do not possess our farms as property but, as a family, we have been lucky to be possessed by them for almost a century. This land has given us much more than we have given it. We stand on the shoulders of many farmers who have worked this soil before us. Once heathland, burned to provide agricultural land, a soil sample taken dates agricultural activity to AD 585–700. My mum and brother now stand as perhaps the last tenant farmers of this land. Designated for development, its economic value soaring, this age-old soil and labour will be buried over. The land will take on a new identity and my family will need to embark on another journey: choosing their way in, or choosing their way out, undecided as yet.

As well as economic precarity, there is the hard physical graft of farming life, and its associated stresses, family tensions, and material detritus. Second generation farmer Adam Crowe contrasts these challenges with the meditative conversation with his ancestors that the practice of drystone walling enables:

Today I am walling alone. I had to get away from Dad, the cowshit, the lonely nitrile gloves and feed bags and bits of string strewn around the yard. The skipload of rusty wire, the barking dog, the e-mails, the fading carpets of the too-quiet house. And put stone on top of stone until things are in order.

I hear the cuckoo as I stoop, my back to the valley, and lift a stone into the gap. The stone is a lump of shale that comes apart when I pick it up, sharp flakes falling away from the rift. [...]

The wall is a conversation. The words put in my mouth by my forebears form differently on my tongue, so that when I speak it is in a subtly different dialect. Our talk has always yielded a lot of space. With so many jobs to do, with such strange weather, some things we leave off halfway, to pick up another day. This is what succession means: choosing the next stone and building one course higher. Some are too heavy for my long back, some fall apart in my hands. Some wobble and won't sit still, and some clonk into place as though they were made to fit just there.

Father and son dynamics also feature in Welsh beef and arable farmer Will Evans' poignant account of building a fence with his father, who is growing older, both of them labouring in icy weather:

The old man and I have worked together for so long now that it mostly happens by instinct. We know how one another operates and it usually goes well enough now we've both mellowed with age, although there's still the occasional flare up and harsh words but that's fathers and sons for you.

We arrive at the open field on the wide flood plain that's so wildly unprotected from any shelter and the west wind is screaming down from the mountains of the Berwyn Range full of spite and swirling sleet and drowns out anything we may or may not say anyway.

We quickly unload what we need to make a start. The old man isn't as strong as he once was; those arms that lifted countless thousands of bales of straw from newly harvested fields to stackyard and threw hundred weight bags onto broad shoulders to go up sandstone granary steps year after year are beginning to fail now. We both know it, so I do the heavy lifting as discreetly as I can.

But in the midst of this economically, physically and emotionally testing work, there are moments of deep joy and satisfaction too. Galloway farmer Helen Ryman describes gathering in her blackface ewes for a health check before they lamb:

I stand centre in the back pen amongst a swell of fleeces, pushed and tested by the ebb and flow of strong angry bodies. Long stapled, coarse wool billows in the wind. Black faces glint iridescent blue, while pristine white caps the eyes and settles around a square muzzle. The sheep are in good nick. Just in case I was in any doubt, their vigour is confirmed by jet black heels flying past me at eye level.

I whisper to Emma: "Walk up", and she responds gladly, with a light-footed cat like gait paired with a heavy dogged glare towards the twin carrying ewes. Clicking and clattering punctuates the air. Horns clash with others horns and rasp against the diamond-flecked stonewalls. The sheep bubble about – jostling, turning – then funnel into a long wooden-built narrow race, its sides polished to a high sheen by decades of greasy fleeces following this same path.

Stockman, shepherd, and livestock manager Kevin Ford describes the relief of being able to assist a ewe with a difficult lambing and the sense of the miraculous that still comes with a successful birth:

Once kneeling against her lower back, a protective arm length glove covered in gel is placed on the upper part of the lamb's leg that's showing, gently sliding between mother and lamb. [...] The other leg found backwards against the side of the lamb, easy to rectify, closing eyes and picture what you feel. Hand moved to chest of lamb, gentle pressure backwards, at the same time get middle finger behind knee joint, bring forward so leg begins to bend, with lower part of leg cupped between fingers, gentle push upwards and draw the leg forward, until it's presented against head like the other one. Now both legs are out and nose offered forward, a little gel around the neck of the lamb and inside the ewe as she contracts, gentle pressure pulling both legs of the lamb. Within seconds, a new life enters the world. A piece of straw up the nose of the lamb to make it sneeze; the first breath of new life, a new story to be told. Placing the lamb in front of the ewe, she starts to clean her new arrival, mother–baby bond connected in smell and sound, nature's true miracle, never to be broken.

All these pieces show a strong sense of struggle and hard-won satisfaction, one which resonates with the georgic tradition.

Participants themselves reflected on the feeling of self-worth and professional validation which the workshops encouraged, and the possibility, at least, of a long overdue sense of cultural capital. One wrote of 'What a wonderful way to bring people together and create a sense of worth for those rural voices who are so often vilified or unheard'. Another stressed the way in which the course helped farmer-writers gain confidence in telling their stories: 'As a rule a lot of farmers lack confidence when it comes to activities in academia and writing so having a course specifically geared to support their needs with understanding tutors is a fantastic opportunity to help farmers get their important stories out into the public'. There was also a perception that getting these vital narratives into the public domain might counter popular misconceptions: 'a lot of us in rural and agricultural communities have an immensely deep connection to the land that we work, and want to put that into words but often haven't had the formal education required to know how to do it, so the potential value of courses like this is huge'.

Conclusion

Public engagement is closely linked with impact in academic circles: researchers are encouraged to ask 'what has your work changed?' While this sense of potential real-world effects aligns the idea of engagement with activism, as Belfiore notes, it is notoriously hard to demonstrate this with Arts and Humanities-oriented activities.

What were the project team hoping for, beyond the central aim of amplifying farmers' voices? A range of desired outcomes included enhancing public awareness of an under-represented sector, boosting nature-friendly farmers' sense of self-worth and achievement (and thereby perhaps encouraging more farmers to follow suit in implementing agro-ecological methods), and generating a more informed level of public support for farmers who are trying to work with nature as well as producing food. What we have seen is a web of individually small but possibly incremental gains, evidenced by the viewing figures for the films and the writing exhibitions, the feedback from participants, and an award given to the 'Newland' film.[63] As researchers, we are aware that some voices have not been heard, from those of farmers involved in intensive farming to those of itinerant farm workers from other European countries (though, as a result of Brexit and the pandemic, there are now fewer of these).[64] Nevertheless, we have contributed to a range of different ways of envisaging better environmental futures, and have achieved our aspiration to 'make conversation' across the silos of conservation and farming as well as intervening in the literary account of the rural and agrarian world and adding to a groundswell of interest in regenerative farming and the work of farmer-writers. In the longer term, our engagement activities might assist in promoting new cultural narratives of farming, helping to foster a 'new georgic' tradition in which the view from the field can be brought to the fore, and tipping the literary scales more towards earthy, hands-on accounts of a relationship with place than to the distant, pastoral view.

[63] By December 2022, 'Love and Soil' had been viewed over 700 times, and both 'Newland' and the Pen and Plough writing workshop exhibition over 1000 times each.
[64] On post-Brexit migrant labour levels, see Paul Milbourn and Helen Coulson, 'Migrant Labour in the UK's Post-Brexit Agri-food System: Ambiguities, Contradictions and Precarities', *Journal of Rural Studies* 86 (2001), pp. 430–9.

8

Nature Walking:
Marching Against Privilege

DOMINIC HEAD

The problem of privilege and exclusion hinders the ethical credentials (and range) of new nature writing. This issue is being addressed with increasing urgency, by publishing houses as well as by ecocritics, and it receives direct treatment in several contemporary books about walking in nature. A sub-genre is thus emerging which represents a new chapter in a long tradition of established literary connections between walking and wonder and enlightenment, as well as vagrancy. Yet the element of privilege in this tradition persists, a fact pointedly highlighted in Kathleen Jamie's observation about 'the association of literature, remoteness, wildness and spiritually uplifted men', in her review of Robert Macfarlane's *The Wild Places*.[1] The most obvious consequence of such privilege is white dominance. In the introduction to a prominent recent collection of nature writing oriented towards the Anthropocene, editor Tim Dee laments his failure 'to find anything other than white contributors'.[2] But there is an equally long and commonplace experience of finding rejuvenation and repair through retreat, and an established practice of walking as protest: both of these resources inform and reinvigorate the contemporary literature of nature walking. The *politicised* literature of nature walking in the British archipelago is often deemed to begin with Wordsworth, who 'linked walking with nature, poetry, poverty and vagrancy in a wholly new and compelling way', as Rebecca Solnit puts it.[3] This essay is concerned with this Romantic legacy, and how Wordsworth's particular constellation of ideas (walking, nature, writing, and social justice, understood as an indissoluble nexus) informs the contemporary literature of nature walking, written in the context of climate change, and fashioned

---

[1]   Kathleen Jamie, 'A Lone Enraptured Male', *London Review of Books* 30.5 (6 March 2008), pp. 25–7 (p. 26).
[2]   Tim Dee, ed., *Ground Work: Writings on Places and People* (London: Jonathan Cape, 2018), p. 14.
[3]   Rebecca Solnit, *Wanderlust: A History of Walking* (2001; London, 2014), p. 105.

by mutating forms of interconnected impoverishment. The defining textual effects and narrative features of this literary mode are my particular focus, but I want to keep its familiar topical concerns in view, the better to demonstrate how content infuses the form of this subgenre of nature writing.

Walking in nature as a form of protest is associated most strongly, perhaps, with the mass trespass on Kinder Scout in the Peak District in 1932, a 'protest for a greater right of access to the moors'.[4] As Nick Hayes points out, the significance of the trespass itself was symbolic rather than material in effecting change;[5] and this points to the configuration that concerns me, in which narrative spawns imaginings or re-imaginings of access to the countryside, which might in turn have a bearing on political praxis. In Solnit's reading, the Kinder Scout trespass marks a crucial staging post in this literature: she shows how Wordsworth's nature walking relied upon, and subverted, the eighteenth-century cultural vogue for building gardens in which to walk, and she remarks upon this 'great irony–or poetic justice–of the history of rural walking; that a taste that began in aristocratic gardens should end up as an assault on private property as an absolute right and privilege'.[6] But this already opens up a possible contradiction in the origins of the written political nature walk, rooted in the impulse to walk for pleasure, while nevertheless seeking to evoke the necessary walking of subsistence work (as in 'The Ruined Cottage', where a walker's chance encounter with an old man unleashes a tale of suffering about the lives of those who are forced to walk).[7] In this sense, the Wordsworthian disposition to infuse walking with moral rectitude, but from a position of choice rather than one of necessity, involves an imitation of impoverished lives even while it honours them. This is an important disjunction because it pinpoints the essence of the literary

[4]   The protest eventually achieved its aims in 1953 when '5,624 acres of land belonging to the Duke of Devonshire were signed over to the Peak District National Park', Nick Hayes, *The Book of Trespass: Crossing the Lines That Divide Us* (2020; London, 2021), pp. 3, 21.
[5]   Greater causal factors, Hayes suggests, were the introduction to Parliament of the 'first open access act' by James Bryce, the establishing of the first rambling clubs in northern England by G. H. B. Ward, the persistent lobbying conducted by 'politically minded activists across the country', the work of Octavia Hill 'who set up the National Trust', and the National Parks and Access to the Countryside Act (1949), *The Book of Trespass*, p. 21.
[6]   Solnit, *Wanderlust*, p. 167.
[7]   As Solnit succinctly puts it, 'everyone in the story is in some kind of pedestrian motion: the strolling narrator, the nomadic Pedlar, the husband enlisted and gone to a distant land, the heartbroken wife wearing a path into the grass by pacing back and forth, watching the road for his return', *Ibid.*, pp. 112–13.

friction in this genre of writing: its self-reflexiveness confirms its distance from its moral point of focus, a distance that its procedures serve to heighten rather than diminish.

The history of walking helps to put this contradiction in context, and to explain its importance for contemporary writing. For Joseph Amato, the key change in human walking accelerated through the twentieth century, and was essentially a consequence of modernity, as 'walking went from occupying the center of human life to assuming a much-diminished place in it'. This shift 'from the realm of necessity to that of leisure and choice' certainly resonates with social change and increasing urbanisation in England. And the shift is consolidated irreversibly by the invention of the motor car.[8] Yet the shift from necessity to choice also reinforces the imaginative and literary potential of walking, which, as a consequence of its 'diminished and relegated condition', then 'assumes a powerful symbolic role as a means of protest and develops an enhanced potential to evoke alternative worlds and experiences'.[9] The Wordsworthian disjuncture, in which leisure walking complicates the moral position of reflecting on walking for necessity, is thus overlaid by a paradox that leads into the contemporary moment, when walking assumes a powerful symbolic role *precisely because* its practical importance recedes. Yet that diminishing role might also be seen as an erosion of the imaginative potential of walking. In Solnit's view, the fading of 'walking as a cultural activity' brings with it a dilution of 'an ancient and profound relationship between body, world, and imagination'. To convey this sense of cultural loss, she deploys the ecologist's term 'indicator species' to identify a species that reveals the health of an ecosystem. 'Walking', she suggests, 'is an indicator species for various kinds of freedoms and pleasures: free time, free and alluring space, and unhindered bodies'.[10] The new symbolic potential of walking, which Solnit is keen to promote, is thus precarious, capable of losing its potency, both granted and eroded by its diminished role in contemporary societies. Yet realising this also highlights the great importance of nature walking literature now, a mode of writing that addresses the freedoms that Solnit lists, but which are under stress in the era of ecological crisis: free time, free and alluring space, unhindered bodies. At the same time, this importance is galvanised by a self-conscious embrace of the contradictions and paradoxes I have observed,

[8]   Joseph A. Amato, *On Foot: A History of Walking* (New York, 2004), pp. 16, 229. Amato comments that 'perhaps more than any single invention, the car has made the walker feel like a trespasser on the earth', p. 253.

[9]   *Ibid.*, p. 18.

[10]   Solnit, *Wanderlust*, p. 250.

most notably the tension between creative contemplation and the abjection of impoverishment, which requires complex forms of rendering.

This essay seeks to identify the central literary effects and textual features of this subgenre, in which such contradictions and paradoxes find arresting configurations. I refer to three strands in the genre. First, there are books about the healing properties of walking, books in which nature walking helps overcome impoverishment and suffering: Raynor Winn's *The Salt Path* (2018) and Katharine Norbury's *The Fish Ladder* (2015). Winn's book overlaps with the second strand, comprising books in which the tradition of the vagrant is in dialogue with homelessness. Neil Ansell's *Deer Island* (2013), *The Last Wilderness* (2018), and *The Circling Sky* (2021) are startling reinventions of the literature of the solitary wanderer, in which nature observation and ideas of eviction and homelessness are brought together in mutually informing patterns. The third and final strand concerns how walking literature has framed questions of ethnicity and unequal access to the outdoors. Jini Reddy's *Wanderland* (2020) and Anita Sethi's *I Belong Here* (2021) are at the forefront of this new wave in Britain, refracting the 'repair' of nature walking through the lenses of exclusion and racism, thereby extending the intellectual territory established in the play *Black Men Walking* (2018) by Testament.

Walking and Healing

Katharine Norbury's *The Fish Ladder*, presented as 'a series of walks or journeys' on the 'theme' of 'following watercourses from the sea to the source', is also a journey of healing, in which the author, who was raised by adoptive parents and has suffered a recent miscarriage when the narrative begins, confronts questions surrounding her own 'source'.[11] One of the book's most powerful scenes describes a night/early morning walk to the lighthouse at Spurn Point at the Humber Estuary. In this case she is walking *away* from the source, a pattern that is then inverted in her daytime walks towards different river sources, and towards healing. The night walk establishes a low point of acute vulnerability when her path to the lighthouse is blocked by a man behaving erratically and throwing rocks into the sea (p. 23). Fear forces her from her path and into the dunes, and the frustration at being thwarted is also anger at the gender inequality that obstructs women walking: 'I knew that, if I was a man, and I was ten years younger, I probably wouldn't care. I was irritated that

[11]   Katharine Norbury, *The Fish Ladder: A Journey Upstream* (London, 2015), pp. 4, 3. Subsequent references to all primary works give page numbers in parentheses in the main text.

my long blonde hair and slight frame rendered me vulnerable, unexpected' (p. 26).[12] Norbury makes this moment of danger emblematic of her vulnerability in a broad sense. We are reminded of her fear of 'the madman at Spurn Point' (p. 170) in the book's most affecting sequence, in which Norbury gives an account of her adoptive father's illness and death from cancer, and her own breakdown and subsequent recovery stimulated by cycling country lanes (pp. 175–83). Solitary rural journeying is thus linked both to her vulnerability and rehabilitation, and it is this combination that makes walking the key to her self-discovery, in which trauma and fulfilment are contiguous.

This emphasis on literal walking sits interestingly with the book's more self-conscious literary dimensions, and specifically its intertextual relationship with two novels by Neil M. Gunn, *Highland River* (1937) and *The Well at the World's End* (1951). The intertextual relationship with the latter illustrates well the points I wish to make about the ways in which physical walking is mediated in literature. Norbury uses Gunn's book quite explicitly to frame the quest of her book, so that her search for the 'source' is made to mirror the search of Gunn's protagonist, Peter Munro, 'for the well at the world's end' (*Fish Ladder*, p. 11). In fact, she is in search of the actual physical well that appears at the beginning of Gunn's novel, a well with water so clear that it seems to be empty.[13] This, it seems, is the well she and her daughter Evie eventually find (following directions from Neil Gunn's nephew) at the end of the book. They drink a benedictory draught and drive home, keeping just ahead of a brooding storm, counting the rainbows (p. 282). Such an ambivalent mood is representative of new nature writing, where affirmation is usually qualified by a looming climatic threat. Here, the ambivalence has partly to do with the manufactured aspect of the benediction, apparently associated with finding a specific well, with resonant literary associations, but which is really about the effort which generates the love and care she shares with those closest to her. The specific 'source' is thus a metaphor for the 'wellspring' of hard-won human connections Norbury enjoys, and which she reminds us of in these closing paragraphs, emphasising the importance of her adoptive mother (Evie's 'granny'), of her partner and Evie, and of the half-brother she has found on her journeying (p. 282).[14] This echoes

---

[12]   This is a clear illustration of Solnit's account of how women's engagement in solitary walking is hampered by social pressures and by the fear of physical assault, *Wanderlust*, pp. 232–46.

[13]   Neil M. Gunn, *The Well at the World's End* (1951; Edinburgh, 2008), p. 5; *Highland River* (Edinburgh, 1937).

[14]   The 'fish ladder' itself – a structure which permits the migration of fish around obstacles, but also the migration upstream of salmon returning to their spawning

the quest of Munro in Gunn's *Well at the World's End*, which ends with Munro's conviction that the source of his 'ultimate vision' is to be found in the person of his wife, not in an 'immortal well' or a particular place.[15] Norbury's summary of Gunn's book catches perfectly its elusive mysticism and the way that 'truth hovers at the corner' of Munro's vision, without being fully glimpsed (p. 11). Yet its mythical wavering between life and death seems to achieve a resolution of sorts and concludes with his recognition of a beauty beyond that which he sees in 'the mortal eye' of his wife, but which he nevertheless reaches through her.[16] This apparent conclusion of the quest, in a revelation afforded through a living relationship, is what chimes most obviously with *The Fish Ladder*. Norbury's quest thus emulates Munro's, but the two books ostensibly move in opposite directions, Gunn's book starting with the specific well and its clear water, before embarking on a nebulous (and ultimately circuitous) pilgrimage, while Norbury's culminates in the location, she believes, of the well that Munro departs from. It is a paradoxical gesture on Norbury's part: she emulates the indeterminate mood of Gunn's text, and yet makes a sort of shrine out of its specific point of departure.

Walking and Homelessness

There is an element of necessity in Norbury's walking quest for healing self-definition, even if that project is consciously defined and chosen at the outset. This problematic equation, in which the literary-historical choice to walk might be said to compromise the writer's engagement with the suffering imposed on a walker/vagrant, almost disappears in Raynor Winn's *The Salt Path*, a moving account of the author's 630-mile walk along the South West Coast Path with her ailing husband, who has been diagnosed with a terminal illness. The walking project is foisted upon them: they are forced into the expediency of constant movement and wild camping after they lose their home, with nowhere else to go. The motif of homelessness is what lends the book its special poignancy, and distinguishes it from run-of-the mill books in the same genre, because most books about walking – and especially those about long-distance walks, or outdoor endurance – are project books, written by writers deciding to take on a challenge that will make good copy.[17] At a

---

grounds–is another analogy for Norbury's quest for sustaining familial 'sources'.

[15] Gunn, *The Well at the World's End*, p. 330.

[16] *Ibid.*, p. 333.

[17] There are exceptions, of course. For example, John Francis's account of twenty-two years of walking, seventeen of them conducted under a vow of silence, is a book

telling moment in *The Salt Path*, Winn contrasts her experience with that recorded by Phoebe Smith in *Extreme Sleeps*, a book about 'wild camping at every extremity of Britain'. Smith's difficult night on a ledge at England's 'most southerly point' ends, Winn suggests, with 'a quick walk up the coast and back into the car, off to the next extreme rocky outcrop'. Winn has a momentary wish for such luxury, the knowledge that the task of endurance can be brought to an end at any time, but concludes 'that wasn't our path; it was hers'.[18] And this passage ends with a genuine revelation which stems from Winn's enforced path: she realises, as summer is coming to its end, that 'something in me was changing season too'. She has come to a point of acceptance about the couple's homelessness and impoverishment, and finds she is no longer 'clenching in anxiety at the life we'd been unable to hold on to', but now living in 'a softer season of acceptance' (p. 184):

> I was a part of the whole. I didn't need to own a patch of land to make that so. I could stand in the wind and I *was* the wind, the rain, the sea; it was all me, and I was nothing within it. The core of me wasn't lost. Translucent, elusive, but there and growing stronger with every headland (p. 185).

Winn begins here by expressing her new feeling in the language of full immersion in the nonhuman, a familiar trope in nature writing, and one that is invariably revealed as an impossible desire.[19] But the statement that 'the core of me wasn't lost' signals a withdrawal of the impossible claim of integration with nature ('it was all me') but without relinquishing the desire for connection. The progressive acquisition of strength as the experience of outdoor life continues ('stronger with every headland') is the discovery of a new sense of self interacting with the nonhuman, rather than some sort of mergence. The notional historical transition in the activity of walking, from necessity to choice, is pointedly challenged by Winn's experience of obligatory walking. And this also has an important literary significance, in that the solitary writer evokes vagrancy and its circumstances, not through the kind of imitative walking which might be said to unsettle the moral high ground of Wordsworthian empathy, but by living through and enduring the circumstances of vagrancy. In this way, Winn's book distinguishes itself from

---

in which the walking is more significant than the book-making, *Planet Walker* (2005; Washington, 2008).

[18]   Raynor Winn, *The Salt Path* (London, 2018), p. 184; Phoebe Smith, *Extreme Sleeps: Adventures of a Wild Camper* (Chichester, 2013).

[19]   For an example of a nature writing classic in which the impossible desire for total immersion in the nonhuman is a recurring theme see Annie Dillard, *Pilgrim at Tinker Creek* (1974; London, 1976).

project walking literature: this is also the implication of the book's comic strand, in which Winn's husband ('Moth') is continually mistaken for Simon Armitage, who is out and about giving poetry readings on the South West Coast Path, gathering material for his own book.[20] Raynor and Moth do not know who Armitage is, but they enjoy some occasional hospitality in the homes of the poet's fans as a consequence of this mistaken identity.[21]

The abjection of Raynor and Moth reaches its lowest point towards the end of their journey, when, exhausted with illness and food poisoning, they are trying to catch some sleep on Weymouth beach. They are recognised as homeless by two other homeless men, who offer them hospitality and take them to their secluded woodland encampment out of town, home to a fluid population engaged in shift work of one kind or another, 'part-time, insecure jobs, low wages, seasonal living that made it difficult to secure a rented home' (p. 236). This glimpse into the lives of the working homeless, a hidden underclass of contemporary England, is truly affecting because the walking writer, who has almost walked herself to a standstill, is more abject than they are, and willingly accepts their generosity. John is the man who recognises Raynor and Moth's true plight, a farm worker who lost his tied cottage when his employer's farm was sold, and who cannot afford 'an expensive rural rent' (pp. 235–6). The wood that forms their home is under threat: 'the purists want to return it to indigenous heath', he says, but his defence of the status quo is based on a contrasting and informed appreciation of the existing fauna – the buzzards, foxes, badgers, woodcock, sloe worms and adders – and he articulates a sense of at-oneness with this wild environment: 'where will the buzzards go? It's their home. It's our home' (p. 237). Once more, this is a telling inversion of the Wordsworthian encounter with vagrancy, the position of the walking writer/poet whittled down to static dependence, while the 'vagrant', defiantly independent, offers the commentary and the assistance. In Plymouth, when Raynor and Moth sleep amongst the homeless, narrowly avoiding being embroiled in a fight, the position of the wandering writer is finally emptied of any advantage (pp. 254–7). It is this final abjection that makes her concluding pleas about homelessness affecting, as she invites us to extend the empathy we have invested in the personal story to engage with the plight of the legions of the homeless, and in such a way that we will

---

[20]   Simon Armitage, *Walking Away: Further Travels with a Troubadour on the South West Coast Path* (London, 2015).

[21]   Winn later clarified the confusion: 'Moth looks nothing like Simon Armitage', but was mistaken for him by people living along the path, who were anticipating the arrival of a man, 'middle-aged, with a rucksack, heading west', *Landlines* (London, 2022), p. 223.

dismiss the stereotype of homelessness (that is, that the homeless constitute a small minority led astray by self-destructive addiction): 'if they–*we*–all stood together, men, women, children, we would look very different to one man alone in a shop doorway' (p. 260).

The power of *The Salt Path*, then, comes from the vulnerability of the experience depicted. On a formal level, as I have indicated, this power and immediacy short-circuits the paradox of choice and necessity in the genre of nature walking, so that vagrancy is part of the writing persona, not separate to it. Neil Ansell's work likewise keeps the paradox in the frame, in texts that still manage to evoke the precarity of homelessness. In *Deer Island*, Ansell intersperses accounts of a series of walking trips to the Isle of Jura with his memories of working with homeless people in London in the 1980s, a juxtaposition that invites us to reflect on the relationship between wild walking and homelessness. An obvious reading of this narrative structure is that the wilderness offers some respite for Ansell in a three-year phase of his life working with the homeless and becoming mentally exhausted, 'worn out from making friends with people and then having to watch them die'.[22] The phase of charity work is succeeded in the later 1980s by a period when Ansell lives in a squat. The traumatic urban squalor is relieved by the occasional bright moment of camaraderie and resistance, but genuine relief comes in the interspersed episodes on Jura, which seem to represent escape and repair. However, the book also blurs the opposition, making us question the extent to which we view Jura/deer island as an antidote to oppressive London.[23]

One way in which Ansell closes the gap between urban deprivation and wild splendour is by implicitly comparing different forms of shelter. Exploring a series of what were once sea caves on the west coast of Jura, which now provide protection for the prolific red deer, Ansell comes across two skeletons of otter cubs and imagines their plight after their mother had died or abandoned them (pp. 105–6). This empathy for the fauna on Jura parallels the sympathy expressed earlier for the hardened drinkers he encounters in a derelict house, with a host named Casey, a Belfast Catholic who wears 'a chunky crucifix', and who makes him 'feel welcome' in his induction 'into the world of the homeless', even though Casey is grieving for his partner, who had died two weeks earlier (pp. 17–8). After Casey dies, Ansell is entrusted

---

[22]   Neil Ansell, *Deer Island* (Toller Fratrum, 2013), p. 31. Ansell worked as a volunteer for the Simon Community, which is run on the principle that volunteers and homeless people live together.

[23]   Ansell suggests that 'the name Jura comes from the old Norse and means deer island' (p. 42). For other explanations, see 'Jura – Island of Deer or The Cursed Isle?' (2009), https://isleofjura.scot/jura-island-of-deer-or-the-cursed-isle.

with his treasured stainless-steel Catholic crucifix, 'an ugly thing' (p. 89), that becomes the symbolic totem that will connect the two environments. Ansell hitches back to Jura, finds 'a beautiful spot on a rocky promontory facing out to sea', and dismantles the seaward side of a cairn, burying the cross inside and carefully rebuilding the structure. Questioning his own motivation, Ansell comes 'to realise that what I was really being asked to keep safe was a memory, not a physical object' (p. 113). The importance of the gesture is established in a moment of prolepsis in the book's opening section, when Ansell describes the mysterious burial of an object, 'a little piece of myself [...] a fragment of who I am' in 'a favourite place' (pp. 9, 10). Without fully explaining what he is doing at this point in the narrative, he says that he has chosen 'an ancient cairn', possibly 'built in memory of the long-ago dead' or 'simply [...] accumulated [...] by passing walkers, rock by rock', to secrete something, concluding that sometimes a 'symbolic gesture is all that we have to give' (pp. 10–11). The introduction of this 'talisman' of deprivation into 'the wildest of wild places' (p. 54) stakes a claim for the homeless amongst the island's walkers. Jura, a place associated with privilege, as well as artistic withdrawal and creativity, is thus refigured.[24] In a broader view, Ansell knows that the ecological crisis is intimately connected with social inequality, the displacement of people, and homelessness; the cairn containing Casey's crucifix is a symbol of this context.

In *The Last Wilderness* Ansell's geographical focus shifts to the Rough Bounds of Lochaber, Na Garbh Chriochan in Scottish Gaelic. The treatment of 'wilderness' depends on the perceived remoteness of the region, and especially of Knoydart; but Ansell also alerts us to Knoydart's 'long history of settlement by crofters, of emigration, of forced clearances', which the description of 'wilderness' misrepresents.[25] The book is constructed as five separate journeys to the Rough Bounds within the space of a year, another reinvention of the nature walking genre, for this new investigation of 'life as a solitary wanderer' (p. 4) brings eviction and homelessness into dialogue with nature observation, as Ansell amasses evidence of human population to undermine perceptions of the apparent remoteness of the Rough Bounds. Concerning Rhu Arisaig, one of the peninsulas that make up this landscape, he writes of its southern shores as 'completely depopulated' rather than 'uninhabited'. A former community of 'perhaps fifty crofts', was displaced

---

[24]   Madeleine Bunting writes of the 'periodic influxes of the powerful, wealthy and glamorous, in search of space and privacy', *Love of Country: A Hebridean Journey* (London, 2016), p. 40. Jura was where George Orwell wrote *Nineteen Eighty-Four* (London, 1949).

[25]   Neil Ansell, *The Last Wilderness: A Journey into Silence* (London, 2018), p. 3.

by sheep farming (pp. 171–2). A 'Neolithic relic' on 'the south side of the peninsula' shows 'there were people here five thousand years ago' (p. 172). Further north, on the Knoydart peninsula, there may once have been 'over a thousand crofters' before 'one of the most notorious instances of the Highland clearances'. The small population that 'has slowly begun to build up again' comprises a community of people who have 'consciously chosen to isolate themselves from the world' (p. 214), and to live in–and remind us of–this site of historical oppression.

When Ansell arrives at the northern slopes of Loch Hourn, he finally discovers something like genuine wilderness, a location 'too remote for human exploitation' (p. 228). And yet Ansell is actually engaged in a re-evaluation of the quest for pristine wilderness, which he conducts, tellingly, by re-examining his penchant for nature walking. From his five-year sojourn in Wales, earlier in his life, 'what stands out most', he writes, 'is my long solitary walks in the hills, the long weeks when every night was spent sitting alone in front of a log fire, in silence, seeing no one'.[26] In another pointed juxtaposition, however, he reminds himself of the 'many years living and working among rough sleepers, and among drug users and street drinkers, the dispossessed'. The turn to remote nature through solitary walking remains connected, then, to the writer's empathy, fostered in the urban realm, but from which he retreats as 'a matter of self-sufficiency' (pp. 56–7). And the preservation of this empathy is not just a matter of self-protection through retreat: the solitary nature wanderer's vocation requires a form of basic existence that approximates the state of homelessness. The pursuit of the wild is also, in Ansell's work, a way of embracing precarity, and, through a chain of association, discovering affinity with the dispossessed and the homeless. The apparent opposition between states and places which Ansell presents us with – the solitary wilderness walker's pursuit of remoteness, set against the social vision – is really a way of presenting aspects of a single predicament.

Walking and Exclusivity

In *The Circling Sky* Ansell records a series of walks in the New Forest, and offers interconnected reflections on belonging, exclusion, dispossession, and the act of walking itself. Central to the book is the plight of the Nevi Wesh Romany people, known to historians as the New Forest Gypsies. Ansell records that 'Gypsies had lived in the forest for centuries, moving on every

---

[26]   Ansell, *Last Wilderness*, p. 56. See also Neil Ansell, *Deep Country: Five Years in the Welsh Hills* (London, 2011).

day or two', but suffered increasing persecution and intolerance through the twentieth century, when they were forced into compounds, until the last residents were 'forcibly evicted' in 1963.[27] Thus, 'the five-hundred year history of the Gypsies of the New Forest was brought to a violent end' (p. 232).[28] Ansell makes us see the appalling treatment of the Romany Nevi Wesh through contemporary lenses of intolerance and exclusion. He laments today's unequal access to, and usage of, public land, citing a figure that just 'one per cent of visitors to our national parks' come 'from minority communities' (p. 64). He is sensible of how economic factors cut across questions of ethnicity, but ethnicity is at the heart of his concern. He understands that England is a country where 'wealth and the access to land that it brings are largely handed down through the generations'; such inequality makes the idea of *belonging* problematic, and Ansell understands how people 'may quite reasonably wonder whether they will ever be made to feel welcome in places where no one looks like them, in what has the appearance of white space' (p. 65). He feels the New Forest 'may be a little less exclusive than most' given its proximity to large urban centres (p. 65), but the general point still applies. And the fate of the Romany Nevi Wesh resonates with the problem of unequal access today.

The importance of walking to Ansell's theme in this text hinges on his personal history, as someone who was born in the New Forest. This history lends authority to the reflections prompted by his excursions into this terrain, which tend towards the topics of belonging and exclusion. Localism in its more pernicious manifestations is the root problem of exclusivity, Ansell shows. The beneficent localism that 'can make us fight for our corner and preserve it for future generations' is a step away from 'believing that you can only really belong in a place if you have deep roots there' (p. 196). Walking in the New Forest, the place he identifies with most strongly, encapsulates the dilemma for Ansell: he finds it 'intriguing to imagine that I may be following in the footsteps of my ancestors, but must remind myself that this gives no special relationship with this place, and no intrinsic insight; I must earn that by myself, one step at a time' (p. 197). Ansell divests himself of any personal claim in another intellectual paradox: the authority to reflect on questions of belonging, traversing through this space, is bestowed by personal knowledge and historical association; but this authority is consciously relinquished, even though the text depends on it. The slate is wiped clean, and a renewed

[27]   Neil Ansell, *The Circling Sky: On Nature and Belonging in an Ancient Forest* (London, 2021), p. 228.
[28]   See also 'New Forest Gypsies' (undated), https://newforestguide.uk/history/new-forest-gypsies.

personal walking effort must be embarked upon in a perpetual process of renewal in the engagement with place. And it is walking, ultimately, that militates against the desire to put down roots:

> It is an occasional fantasy of mine that one day, after a lifetime of roaming, I will finally reach a spot where I think: This is it, this is perfect, there is no need for me ever to move again. The fear is that what had seemed perfect one day might seem wanting the next [...] I can never have everything that I want, all in one place, all in one time, and so I suspect that I am destined to keep on wandering (p. 114).

Walking, in this articulation of the aspirations it embodies, brings with it the desire to find and possess a place, but it must also disappoint that desire if the imperatives of walking continue to be met, since 'the point of a walk is not to reach the end, but to reach the middle' (p. 114). The paradox of walking puts the walker in the company of the migrant, of the homeless, of the Romany, and of Ansell in the New Forest perceiving 'that this land is everybody's and nobody's' (p. 333).

Two notable contributions to nature walking literature in Britain investigate the hostility of racism in the countryside, the experience of confronting 'the appearance of white space' as Ansell puts it: *Wanderland* by Jini Reddy (a Londoner) and *I Belong Here* by Anita Sethi (a Mancunian). Each of these writers makes a distinctive contribution to the genre, and each one asserts her right to wander in rural England. Reddy approaches the question of racism more tangentially than Sethi. *Wanderland* articulates her annoyance at the 'generalisation' that 'people whose skin colour is not white [...] never connect with nature'. At this point in the text she presents herself as 'just a human enjoying the sea, like any other', something she's been doing 'for a long, long time' like other writers of colour, 'whose voices are never heard'.[29] This is an interesting and paradoxical moment: Reddy wants to resist being categorised on the basis of her ethnicity – she wants to be 'just a human' – and yet, in the same passage, she laments the racial bias of nature publishing, and the voices that have been silenced as a consequence. This moment is representative of *Wanderland,* a book that engages with racism without quite tackling it head-on. Reddy's ambivalent attitude to nature taxonomy is a case in point. Her feeling that it is not in her DNA to become a taxonomist (pp. 119–20) seems to echo the concern of other nature writers about Carolus Linnaeus and

[29]   Jini Reddy, *Wanderland: A Search for Magic in the Landscape* (London, 2020), p. 109.

the colonial origin of natural history.[30] Yet she side-steps this double bind, and expresses some enthusiasm for taxonomy (p. 119); later, when she finds herself unable to name plants, she feels her 'ignorance keenly', and wants to 'make amends' (p. 138).

Wanderland eschews, then, some of the obvious themes of racial exclusivity in nature writing. Reddy's focus, rather, is on addressing racism by reconfiguring established elements of walking literature. The theme of the labyrinth, for example, might be said to order her quest, which is articulated as an extension of her 'outsider-ness' as someone who is 'British by birth, Indian by descent, Canadian by upbringing with parents born in South Africa' (p. 14). Her desire to bring this sense of personal exclusion to bear on a quest for 'the wild unseen' (p. 15) moves her away from the tangible reality of racism and towards an intangible mysticism, that might be unleashed by 'the oracle-like powers of the labyrinth' (p. 35). Rebecca Solnit's discussion of labyrinths, and their importance to ideas about walking, is relevant here, especially her characterisation of the discipline required to follow a labyrinthine path: 'sometimes you have to turn your back on your goal to get there, sometimes you're farthest away when you're closest, sometimes the only way is the long one'. Solnit records that, for her, 'it was breathtaking to realise that in the labyrinth, metaphors and meanings could be conveyed spatially'.[31] This strikes me as a profound observation, and it is certainly one that helps us understand the peculiar power of walking literature more readily. Reddy evokes something of the near–far paradox of the labyrinth, and she also invokes the idea of pilgrimage, but only insofar as it fits the idea of her quasi-spiritual goal (p. 36), where 'the inner journey is as important as the outer' (p. 132).[32] Yet this embedding in literary and cultural tradition is also a way of masking Reddy's subtle radicalism: she unleashes the destabilising qualities intrinsic to these forms in such a way as to challenge the certainties of place and identity that engender racism. Her 'outsider-ness' is made to displace any such certainty. Such a mood emerges when she is walking in Snowdonia, in her response to the notional appeal of feeling rooted in 'the Welsh mythic landscape'. She asks: 'which specific culture am I meant to

---

[30] See, for example, Jamaica Kincaid, *My Garden Book* (New York, 1999), pp. 165–6.

[31] Solnit, *Wanderlust*, pp. 69, 70.

[32] The precise significance of Reddy's allusions to labyrinth and pilgrimage is elusive, which makes her purpose distinct from Solnit's summation of the labyrinth, which, unlike a maze, has only one route and so offers 'an inflexible route to salvation' (the kind of certitude Reddy avoids). For Solnit, a labyrinth might be said to comprise a compressed pilgrimage, especially in a church setting (contra Reddy's approach to the maze), Solnit, *Wanderlust*, pp. 71, 70.

identify with?', implying that the question is unanswerable for those 'from a multicultural background' (p. 248). Non-identification in this instance is simultaneously a sign of exclusion *and* a rebuke to those who mythologise their sense of belonging.

Sethi's *I Belong Here* embodies a more explicit response to racism. This is conducted through a Pennine journey, the significance of which lies in its extended response to a race-hate crime. Defiantly, Sethi asserts her right to belong, invoking the Kinder Scout Mass Trespass in her reworking of protest walking.[33] It is a literary tradition that her book serves to complement but also adjust, and, to that end, she makes several references to her affinity with other walking writers.[34] Such allusiveness is itself a feature of the walking genre, as it is in much nature writing. And yet, working against the emphasis on textuality, another familiar effect in nature writing is to blur the distinction between metaphorical and literal signification, to make the personal experience of the writer seem to be embedded in an actual place or landscape.[35] This effect is evident in key moments where Sethi uses literal and metaphorical wordplay to link external landscapes with internal histories. In one important passage, in which she expresses the internalised trauma of racist abuse, she reflects on how psychological scars can be healed through immersion in nature, and associates this with her reflections on scars in rock formations. But she reminds us that a 'scar' is a wound that hasn't healed so that wounds and body markings become self-defining, but also a way of linking landscape and body (pp. 203–7). This is a complex form of self-projection, where signs of racist trauma might be mirrored, symbolically, in the landscape that is also sought out as a means of repair.

This paradox is the essence of Sethi's journey itself, an assertion of rights that also exposes her to fresh instances of racism and exclusion (p. 275). The consequence of this method is to prioritise questions of exclusion and trauma so that the landscape can seem to become a sounding-board for the personal journey. Sethi's reflection on 'faults' in the limestone pavement at Malham

[33]   Anita Sethi, *I Belong Here: A Journey Along the Backbone of England* (London, 2021), p. 14. Kinder Scout is a common touchstone in walking literature (as the texts examined in this essay indicate), which can make the appeal to it seem *de rigueur*. However, such an impression should not dilute the significance of this key moment in the history and literature of walking in Britain.

[34]   Sethi expresses the 'strong companionship' she feels for Raynor Winn, Robert Macfarlane, Edward Thomas, and George Borrow (p. 70).

[35]   A famous example is Peter Matthiessen's quest for the snow leopard in the Himalayas, which is really a quest for the ultimate perception of Zen Buddhism: the austere and difficult terrain of the leopard's habitat mirrors the challenge of the inner journey, *The Snow Leopard* (1978; London, 1998).

Cove is a good example of this procedure, as she foregrounds an analogy between the grykes of Malham Cove, 'seemingly barren and yet teeming with life' (p. 150), and the 'fault-lines' in society. She places stress on victimhood, and makes any sense of marvelling at the wild an occasion for us to rethink 'fault-lines' by association with her experience of standing up to race hatred, which also means allowing yourself to reveal your vulnerabilities, a necessary precursor to personal regeneration (p. 148).

Wanderland and *I Belong Here* are radical re-orientations of the literature of nature walking. They recalibrate the tropes and conventions of nature writing where these are felt to be exclusive, especially when each writer is distracted from any sense of temporary immersion in the nonhuman by the need to respond to hostility, or justify their simple *presence* in the landscape when confronted by racism, whether explicit or casual. Each book is a statement of the need for inclusivity, and the urgency of this requirement speaks to the need to expand the responsiveness of generic convention – to embrace explicitly the experience of people of colour – as much as it does to the ignorant racism that is shown to be abroad in rural England.

Black Men Walking and the Racist Inversion of Vagrancy

Before drawing together these reflections on generic limitation and formal reinvention, it may be useful to expand the discussion by considering a different literary form – drama – through the play *Black Men Walking*, written by Testament (Andy Brooks) and directed by Dawn Walton.[36] This important landmark in Black British walking literature, inspired by the Sheffield Black Men's Walking Group, depicts a walk in the Peak District undertaken by three members of the group, each one facing a personal crisis. The key character in the play, however, is Ayeesha, a young female rapper who saves them when the weather turns foul. But this 'salvation' is more than literal: she redeems the play's theme of asserting black identity in the landscape by giving a contemporary significance to the resonance of the hidden black history of Yorkshire. Testament uses a chorus of 'Ancestors' to point this out ('We walked England before the English [...] We have always been here!', pp. 2–3)

---

[36]   The play seems to have been collaboratively written: in interview, Dawn Walton explains that she and Testament 'sat in a room and threw paper at each other' until the play 'formed itself over about 18 months'. See Pippa Marland and Anna Stenning, '*Black Men Walking*: An Interview with Dawn Walton and Testament', David Borthwick, Pippa Marland, and Anna Stenning, eds, *Walking, Landscape and Environment* (London, 2020), pp. 100–12 (p. 102).

and to reinforce the claim that the character Thomas wishes to assert through the group's excursions: 'We are Yorkshire. We are Britain' (p. 72).

The play explores the extent to which the British rural environment is hospitable to Black people. A mantra of the walking group, as depicted in the play, is that the members are 'creating a safe space' (p. 14). Consequently, Walton argues that the importance of a rural setting to the group is that it is 'a safe space' with 'no interruptions from other forces, other than Nature itself'.[37] But this notional escape from the 'micro-aggressions' of casual racism is really wishful thinking, as the characters' off-stage encounter with a policeman suggests: he warns them about the weather, but they sense his suspicions about them, the racial profiling that conditions his perception of them (pp. 22, 24–6). The depressing fact that Walton and Testament are confronting is the persistent 'expectation that you don't have Black people in the countryside'.[38] In this sense, walking in the play is political, drawing on the resonance of protest walking, and this makes the Peak District a pointedly chosen setting: Testament cites the Kinder Scout trespass as a key instance of 'walking as a political act', of 'asserting the right to be here'. But he makes much more of the act of walking than this, and points out how it 'functions on multiple levels': it is 'a communal experience'; it is a 'meditative pursuit', where 'connect[ion] with the landscape' is facilitated by 'sinking into one's own consciousness'; it is a way of making the past resurface, as Thomas does through his visions of the 'Ancestors'. In this sense, 'the blurring of temporal lines' is an act of physical assertion, 'something he walks through'.[39] Walton also emphasises the importance of the act of walking, beyond its physical and mental health benefits: it is also about 'reclaiming a whole history [...] taking that epic journey through time'.[40] In this way, the play makes walking – and nature/rural walking in particular – central to a revisionist Black British history: the Sheffield walkers who inspired the play are Yorkshiremen who walk 'their land [...] to claim it'.[41]

The formal conundrum considered at the beginning of this essay was what I called the Wordsworthian disjunction, a textual fault line which emerges from the effort of the wandering writer to empathise with the life of the vagrant. Without truly inhabiting that plight, the writer might be said to be imitating it, and the resultant gap between moral intent and contradictory action produces an aesthetic frisson in walking literature. This reflexiveness

[37]   Marland and Stenning, '*Black Men Walking*', p. 103.
[38]   *Ibid.*, p. 105.
[39]   *Ibid.*, p. 109.
[40]   *Ibid.*, p. 105.
[41]   *Ibid.*, p. 106.

reminds us of the writer's limits, while it also intensifies our sense of the vagrant's plight. Yet we might also feel such texts are cultivating empathy for a situation they cannot truly capture, a specific form of *mise en abyme*. As I have moved through successive topics, this formal disjunction has been inverted in different ways, most notably, perhaps, in Winn's *The Salt Path* where the writer becomes the true vagrant, relying on the kindness of the homeless at the depths of her abjection. The element of necessity in Norbury's walking quest for healing self-definition produces a similar inversion, displacing her book's literary self-consciousness. In Ansell's work, the pursuit of the wild is also a way of embracing precarity, uncovering the context the writer shares with the dispossessed and the homeless; again, the formal disjunction between writer and vagrant is diminished. In the final three texts, the importance of this formal issue recedes in a revealing way. The main male characters in *Black Men Walking* are middle class, walking from choice, yet they are caught between the sense of creating a safe place through walking in nature, and being made to feel out of place in the English countryside. In the same way, racist hostility taints the walking journeys of Jini Reddy and Anita Sethi, two professional writers of colour. In all three texts, the walkers occupy the contemporary equivalent of the wandering poet's position, yet are interpellated as outsiders, treated with the same suspicion as the quintessential vagrant. In such texts the Wordsworthian disjunction is an unavailable aesthetic luxury, and the walkers are forced to occupy a different site of expression. The experience of racism allows them to reveal the contemporary irrelevance of this generic feature for people of colour, and to begin to forge new formal devices that retrieve the black walker's position from the social margins. Such effects are suggested by Testament's reinvention of the dramatic chorus, by Reddy's dismantling of the mysticism surrounding heritage and belonging, and by Sethi's appropriation for her personal story of the scars in the landscape. These are all reconfigured literary fault lines, which challenge, through walking, the ways in which black identity is effaced from the landscape.

9

To Be a Witness in the World

AMANDA THOMSON

Late Summer

Some of the grasses at this time of year, heading into August, have grown to almost waist height, and there's one spot where we see the purple dots of melancholy thistles amongst the green and yellows and hay-coloured grasses. The early harebells are already flowering purple and thick dewdrops hang from their stems. In these Scots pinewoods of Abernethy, the blaeberries are already ripening and there are patches of the forest where the bushes are laden, and when you walk through, the cuffs and shins of your trousers are stained purple. We're trying to think about what the weather was like last year in what felt like a bumper year for blaeberries, but we're not quite sure what the differences are between one year and the next, or why one year has a better crop than the last, though I am sure there are those we could ask. Our neighbour walked past with intent the other day, scooper in hand, and perhaps she'll drop by later with a jar of jam for us. It's the time of year for creeping lady's tresses to push their way up, their slender stems a brighter green that seems to better fit to springtime, and they peek so delicately up through the heather and blaeberries they're easy to miss, and often I miss noticing them till their flowers are already fading.

Autumn

The year's moved on again and now the blaeberries are past their best, their leaves have turned yellow and are mottled with browns and blacks, and the heather's turning from its varying shades of purple to the mauves of its dried-out husks. The yellow rattle has turned to the papery shells that give it its name. Someone reminded me the other day that the term in old Scots language for yellow rattle is the gowk's shilling, gowk being a Scots word for cuckoo, and if you shake their stems you'll surely see why both names are appropriate. How quickly the season has turned, and it's into autumn.

The air feels different. Has its nip. The sun has lost some of its warmth, sits lower, rises later, and casts longer shadows that reach out into the day. The bracken's turning to rust, and the birches that sit amongst the pines are more easily identified from afar by their yellow tinged countenance. There've been rumours of the first skeins of geese, though I've still to see any, but any day now, I hope.

Poa

The other week I walked with my partner and a friend as we carried out a botanical survey as part of the National Plant Monitoring Scheme. It's a longitudinal survey, done mostly by volunteers, and established to monitor the habitats where our wild plants are growing and changes that might be occurring, using them as indicators to show the state of the UK's natural environment.[1] Our friend, a botanist before she retired, pointed to grasses and sedges and rushes, and systematically gave them names like purple moor grass, sweet vernal grass, curvy hair grass, Yorkshire fog, and poa. They meld and blend and, without attention, all look the same to me. They come together to form communities that we'll call meadows and grasslands and verges, and you'll have to look, really look, to understand the differences between each of the species. Sometimes the eye is not enough and you have to use a handheld loupe to really see the details that make something what it is. She uses unfamiliar terms that I now don't remember, and points to the tiny husks of micro-moth pupae that nestles within a rush's inflorescence. Context is important for identification too. The time of year, the other plants that are around and in amongst them, how wet or dry the earth is in which they grow. Sometimes though, we need to remember that plants can be out of context and place too – some whose seeds have landed someplace unexpected and somehow managed to survive. Maybe that's where some of the excitement lies – in birding too – those unexpected discoveries.

In the space between the last time we surveyed this site in early summer, when we mapped the squares, and when we returned, the land has changed, and some plants have appeared, some disappeared, and what was easy to walk through in May has become a tangle of branches and thickening, lengthened stems, and what we thought would be easy to find again isn't so easy. We wonder in the space between the then and now if we've missed some plants completely. And anyway, I'm quite often distracted to what's up and around us too. A pair of jays that flew over; speckled wood butterflies flitting in and

---

[1]   National Plant Monitoring Scheme, 'Welcome', https://www.npms.org.uk.

out of the shade amongst the birches and bracken, buzzards crying so high
and far away we can barely see them and when I look up I see two of them
tangling, and I notice the clouds are cumulus, with high cirrus above moving
faster, to the west. In one survey square we startled a meadow pipit from its
nest that was hidden in a hollow of heather.

Our survey site is a kilometre square on a hillside shared with sheep, close
to a grouse moor, and essentially nondescript. We've selected five squares to
survey within it, and we're given specific guidance to the sizes and habitats
it should include. There's nothing special about it at all, and that, perhaps
is its point. We've decided on, then marked out plots that we'll count for
what plants are inside them. Once our details are submitted, they will be
aggregated with the other kilometre squares similarly monitored, creating
a nationwide survey. So if a noteworthy plant sits an inch outside what we
have designated to be our plot, it goes unrecorded, though it may fall inside
someone else's, and thus be recorded elsewhere. Not all of us have to live in,
or see, or experience the remarkable, and there's a shout out to be had for
the remarkable that can be found in the quotidian. And I think of the birds
and beasties that fly over or are found within that go unrecorded, and how
we hold the memories of the day, the walking, the weather, the crunch of
dry heather underfoot, the conversations we shared, and, if we choose, we
might write about them, and use these moments as starting points that will
take us to someplace else. How, when the meadow pipit flew off, I looked in
to where it had come from and saw three tiny pearls of brown eggs, how we
finished surveying that square quickly and tried to do some of it from afar,
so the pipit would come back to the nest and resume its vigil, and suddenly
we were talking about vulnerability in a way we hadn't before on that day.

These Small Encounters

Louisa Gairn writes that 'In Scotland, contemporary poetry, and lyricism
more generally, constitute an ecological 'line of defence', providing a space
in which reader and author can examine their relationship to the world
around them', and I like that acknowledgement of the need for that line,
that space.[2] Work that starts with an 'I' (and not all of it does or has to)
can start with the smallest observation and experience, and in writing it, the
experience, or something akin to it becomes acknowledged and, often, if we
are lucky, has a shared resonance. We are in and of the natural world, and
when we go 'into' it, we take our lives, experiences, our headspaces too. We

[2]   Louisa Gairn, *Ecology and Modern Scottish Literature* (Edinburgh, 2008), p. 156.

don't leave the us of it behind, and it's important to be invited into others' spaces too. In writers such as Robin Wall Kimmerer, Jessica J. Lee, Terry Tempest Williams, and closer to (my) home, Kathleen Jamie, we see how place, creative non-fiction, family history and lived experience interweave to create deeply personal stories that emanate out, touching water, rocks, birds, trees, earth, and everything in between, and chimes or challenges, in different ways, with our own experiences, or what we have known, or not known, before. In *Arts of Living on a Damaged Planet*, Anna L. Tsing and her colleagues write that 'Creative writing invites us to imagine the world differently, to listen beyond newspaper headlines to hear those quiet stories about the Anthropocene whispered in small encounters', and I like that invitation, for when I think of these small encounters, it's how everyday moments of meeting and connection can resonate out and out and out.[3] And there will be something in what we choose to notice, to observe, to bring to attention, though what that *thing* is might not be apparent immediately. Nor might what we originally thought the important element in what we are writing about be what's seen to be important to other people, sitting, as it will, in the entanglement of everything else that comes with it.

Mary Oliver writes, 'One tree is like another, but not too much', and I wonder what would happen if we were to write about every tree, what we might see, how we might learn something different.[4] We might consider the varying nooks and crannies and nuances of each trunk and what beasties, fungi and lichens each might contain, or how the leaves of the mature birches that live next to a granny pine rustle differently in a breeze, or let more or less light onto the forest floor. In the Scots pinewoods of Abernethy I can see places in the forest where, perhaps, a heavy snow one year has caused all the top branches of young trees to bend, and there's a curve of trunk at the same height high up in several of the trees in a particular spot. Or perhaps the tender tops of some saplings were browsed by a herd of deer passing through, or damaged in some other way and the main trunk of a tree has split into two. And perhaps such things happened years or decades ago, but the evidence remains.

[3]   Anna L. Tsing *et al.*, *Arts of Living on a Damaged Planet: Ghosts and Monsters of the Anthropocene* (Minneapolis, 2017), pp. M8–9.
[4]   Mary Oliver, 'Upstream', *Upstream: Selected Essays* (London, 2019), https://www.penguinrandomhouse.ca/books/318638/upstream-by-mary-oliver/978159 4206702/excerpt.

The Colours of Yellow

I spend much of my own time amongst the Scots pines, but in her book of essays, *Small Bodies of Water*, Nina Mingya Powles talks about another tree, the kōwhai.[5] 'This is where I begin', she writes, 'with a kōwhai tree in a garden in suburban London during an April heatwave. I don't know how to continue; the sight was too much for me, too unreal'. But then she does continue, and begins by taking us back to her earliest memories of these trees, so entwined with her New Zealand upbringing: 'They shed their gold on the street corners and in the front gardens where I grew up. The exact colour of the bell-shaped petals, dark yellow like melted butter, is for me deeply entwined with memories of my parent's house by the sea and the sunlit garden behind it'. She talks about the tree's scent, how it moves in a breeze, and how this tree, with other plants and birds, sits as one of her 'markers of home'. And then, using this tree as a marker, she weaves in and out of places known and newly found; the history of how the kōwhai tree came to be in London, a history entwined with colonialism and violence and economic botany; heatwaves and Sylvia Plath; the colour yellow itself; a rumination of seasons, language(s), pollen, planting and growth. It's a beautiful essay, showing how one object, one plant, can reveal our entangledness in the world, and shows the different directions that we might go on.

The In-betweens

Creative writing – creative non-fiction and the essay form – came to me in the midst of doing a practice-based doctorate. My Ph.D was in Interdisciplinary Arts Practice, and was based around the forests of the north of Scotland, more particularly the Scots pinewoods of Abernethy and the Forestry Commission forests of Morayshire. Abernethy, in particular, is the forest that grabbed my attention, and where I have been making artwork about and writing about ever since. I've come to know this place over time. I can't remember the first time I visited – though I know it was my much younger self, when I'd have come to see the ospreys. I've been here more regularly since the early 2000s when I used to visit and sometimes house-sit for friends who'd go away for three, four weeks every summer. My doctoral fieldwork was based on encountering the place and seeing it through other people's eyes and expertise, so I walked Abernethy with foresters and ecologists and volunteered with the RSPB, learning to see it in different ways. Now, it's where I live.

---

[5]   Nina Mingya Powles, *Small Bodies of Water* (Edinburgh, 2021).

I was drawn to creative writing to find the in-between space between academic encounter and art-making. By writing into a form that was new to me I was able to create a way of conveying the complex histories of place – a way of taking into account the multiple layers of stories, the thens to nows, the heres to theres, the smalls to larges – that each place contains. My doctorate, on how we might come to conceptualise place, pulled on geography, anthropology, ecology and history, but I couldn't help but find that the style of academic writing, while trying to explore and explain words like 'affect', was deadening that which it sought to explain. At the same time, the art which I was making – etchings, filmworks, soundworks, artist books – while working on several levels, wasn't quite working in terms of expressing the complexities of the stories that these woods contained, or the feelings, of wonder, joy, peace, uncanniness, that they engendered in me. How do we deal with the need for words for some of the time, and the importance of space, and the need for wordlessness at others? These woods, these places are living, breathing and ever changing, always 'becoming' and holding so many (more) questions within them still. It's a place that, in its ecology and nature, I've used in my book *Belonging* to tie together strands of thinking about place and language, family history, racism, discrimination, and the Anthropocene, to consider ideas of home and what might make us feel that we do, or don't belong.[6]

What do we as writers and readers, thinkers and artists (and ecologists and critics and scientists) need to help us breath into this life, this world? What gives us the space to reflect and consider, to see what we have, or what we have lost? How we might pay attention, but at the same time, give space for us to insert the realities of *our* lives, our knowledge and experience, and to see things anew, or at a slant? And how we might give space for other people's experiences too, and what they might bring to us?

In *Sightlines*, published in 2012, Kathleen Jamie writes beautifully of a visit to a gannetry, and her words remind me so much of the feeling of a trip I took to the Isle of May, off the east coast of Scotland, which took us around the Bass Rock, one of the biggest gannetries in the world. 'Half a mile ahead', she writes, 'a column of birds turned bright and white in the summer air. They were visible as a loose plume as we walked over the island towards them, and doubtless visible for miles out to sea. It was exciting, like a fun fair'.[7] Yet this experience, the joy, the idea of a colony being 'like a fun fair' takes on a whole new resonance with what we know of how bird flu has affected our colonies

6   See Kathleen Yusoff, *A Billion Black Anthropocenes or None* (Minneapolis, 2019); Amanda Thomson, B*elonging: Natural Histories of Place, Identity and Home* (Edinburgh, 2022).
7   Kathleen Jamie, *Sightlines* (London, 2012), p. 36.

in this last year.[8] In Jamie's 2022 essay in the *London Review of Books*, 'Stay alive, stay alive', her attempt to make sense of the bird flu that has devastated our colonies takes on all the more poignancy after she has captured the joy, excitement, camaraderie and delight of that earlier day. She writes now, 'They're hanging dead from the cliffs. They're floating dead on the water, a wreck of feathers. They're dead on the beaches, all down the coast'.[9] The tenor, the atmosphere of a visit to this same place has changed completely. Jamie shows the importance of how understanding how something once was helps us make sense of what it has become. Such writing not only marks such changes, but does it beautifully, poetically and in a way that records not just detail and fact, but the very human, emotional, devastating consequences of it. Consequence and connection, interrelatedness, and ideas of vulnerability spill back and forth between the beyond-human natural world and ourselves and are integral to Jamie's writing and how it works and functions.

To Notice and To Know

I walk through the Scots pinewoods of the forest of Abernethy once more, knowing that the capercaillie population is in a conservation red zone, at crisis point. A young red squirrel leaps from the branch of one tree and onto another, knocking and scattering pine needles as it does so. It skelters down the trunk and off and away, so close I hear the scratch of its claws. I walk through thick minglings of heather and blaeberries, and know that the blaeberries are important for the young of the capercaillies that live in these pinewoods, and that the heather can sometimes overwhelm the blaeberries. The RSPB have started to use robocutters to chop back the undergrowth in some places within the reserve. These machines mimic the actions of the (now extinct) aurochs that, in ancient times, roamed in habitats such as this and would have chomped back the understory to a version which might have better suited the caper, and, with the other animals also extinct from this place now – lynx, wolves, even bears – would have created a very different ecology within it. In these woods, the sun's rays shimmer through at just the right angle to highlight the purple of the heather. If we think more about heather, in early spring and autumn the upland moorlands can sometimes glow in a different way when our heather-thick grouse moors are burned to promote the young growth which, while creating food sources for the grouse,

8   *Nature's Home: The RSPB Magazine* (Autumn/Winter 2022).
9   Kathleen Jamie, 'Stay alive! Stay alive!', *London Review of Books* 44.16 (18 August 2022), https://www.lrb.co.uk/the-paper/v44/n16/kathleen-jamie/diary.

affects and limits other species as well as damaging peatlands and their capacity for carbon capture. And from there, we might also fall into questions of land ownership, entitlement and access, and what constitutes 'sport'.

I know that while these Scots pines are the descendants of the original pinewoods that covered much of Scotland after the last ice age, many of the trees here now have been planted and stand straight and are of uniform height and age, and we might use them to wonder what 'natural' means. In *Belonging*, I've pondered the implications and connections of these woods to empire with the turn to timber production that took place in the eighteenth century, when amongst their other uses, their trunks were turned into ship's masts, and I wonder where around the world they went, and for what purpose. We can start off with an 'I' and small, seemingly insignificant observations or speculative moments of noticing and attention and context, that together move into something else, allowing for connections, visible and invisible. We can use where we are now, and our own careful observations and knowledge, to go both back and forward, and out into our world, and beyond. I wonder where these woods will take me next.

Index

Abbas, Ackbar 29
Abernethy pinewoods 165–72
ableism 74
abolitionist poetry, storm imagery in
    51–7
activism
    academic public engagement
        133–4, 139, 146
    Platform group 61, 62
    see also environmentalism
Adala ('American Eclogue') 54–5
Adam Bede (Eliot) 7, 16
'After the Hurricane'
    (Hutchinson) 59–60
Agamben, Giorgio 25
agency, of nonhuman animals 117–18
agriculture
    automation of 75
    'Big Farming Survey' 140
    and Brexit 127
    Common Agricultural Policy 66
    and conservation 128, 135, 136,
        140–1
    drystone walling 143–4
    economic precarity of 143
    environmental impact/role of 25,
        57, 128, 129, 134–5, 137
    fence-building 144
    Monbiot's critique of 128, 129
    physical work of 143–4
    post-World War II 137
    Precision Livestock Farming 75
    regenerative farming 135
    sheep farming 144–5
    see also farmers/land workers; farming
        narratives

'agrilogistics' 13–14, 100
agroecology 129
Ahuja, Neel 31–2, 39–40
air pollution 21
Albert Dock, Liverpool 61
Algeria 64
allegory, and Anthropocene 65
alterity
    of plants 81
    in science fiction 71, 72
Amato, Joseph 149
'American Eclogue' (Mulligan) 52,
    53, 54–5
Anglo-Saxons 96, 97
'The Animal Novel as Biopolitical
    Critique...' *see* Cole, Stewart
animal studies 114
    see also critical animal studies;
        Human-Animal studies
animalisation of others 74, 88
animality, Derrida 121–3, 124
Ansell, Neil 150, 155–7, 164
Anthropocene
    and allegory 65
    and climate change 58–9
    ghosts of 66–7
    and literary criticism 51
    and plantation system 50
    and representation 110, 111
    as science fiction 72 n.5
    shock of 58
anthropocentrism 114, 115–16,
    118–19
    and the narrative 'I' 123–4
anthropomorphism 114, 115, 119–20
anti-pastoral tradition 9–10